TRAVELS IN GEORGIAN DEVON

The Illustrated Journals of the Reverend John Swete, 1789-1800

VOLUME FOUR

Edited with an Introduction by
Todd Gray BA, PhD, FRHistS

General Editor
Margery Rowe BA, DAA

DEVON BOOKS

First published in Great Britain by Devon Books, 2000

Copyright © 2000: The Swete Diaries and images Devon County Council
(Devon Record Office) and Devon Gardens Trust
Copyright © 2000 Todd Gray: Introduction

ISBN 1 85522 755 X

Cataloguing in Publication Data
CIP record for this title is available from the British Library

DEVON BOOKS
OFFICIAL PUBLISHER TO DEVON COUNTY COUNCIL

In association with

HALSGROVE
PUBLISHING, MEDIA AND DISTRIBUTION
Halsgrove House
Lower Moor Way
Tiverton
Devon EX16 6SS
www.halsgrove.com

Tel: 01884 243242
Fax: 01884 243325

Printed in Singapore by UIC Printing Pte Ltd

CONTENTS

The Picturesque Sketches of Devon

FOREWORD

The completion of the four volumes of *Travels in Georgian Devon* represents a publishing landmark in the co-operation between Devon County Council and Halsgrove through its joint imprint, Devon Books. Through this venture almost two hundred books have been published, many of which would not otherwise have been made available to the general public.

However, the publication *Travels in Georgian Devon* is of particular importance in the history of Devon Books for it embodies the aims and principles of that imprint established at its creation in 1984: that is, to bring together the expertise and the co-operation of interested parties in the creation of publications based on material held by Devon County Council. Those organisations and individuals who have contributed to this prestigious project can now share the pleasure of seeing the series complete.

The tireless professionalism of Todd Gray and Margery Rowe is fundamental to the success of this project, as has been the support and enthusiasm of the Devon Gardens Trust and its membership. The Devon Record Office, which holds the original Swete diaries, and its staff, and the members of the Devon Books Editorial Board, both past and present, are due particular recognition.

It is unlikely that John Swete had any notion that his illustrated journals would become one of the most treasured items of Devon's literary heritage. But there is little doubt that he would be greatly pleased to see it finally in print over two hundred years later.

Fred J. Symons
Chairman,
Devon County Council

INTRODUCTION

This last volume of the Reverend Swete's tour of Picturesque Devon comprises his final five surviving journals. In these there are six journeys: the first is a continuation of his tour of south-west Devon in 1796, the second is a short visit the following year to Fordland not far from Swete's home in Kenton, the third and fourth are tours to Dartmoor made in 1795 and 1797, the fifth is a short description of the Exe estuary and the final journey is one he made in 1800 through East Devon. Most of the tours were undertaken with only the company of a sole manservant but Swete did travel with a friend on Dartmoor and with his family in West Devon. Nearly all of it was done on horseback but there was some travel by boat from Noss Mayo to Puslinch and along the river Exe.

By the time of his last tour Swete had been recording the picturesque nature of Devon for some eleven years and was then aged nearly fifty. The style of writing had changed over the years: in many ways he had become a more interesting writer and expressed interests in a wider range of subjects. Why he chose to stop at that point is unexplained. Perhaps he had become bored with writing his journals or it may have been that he had seen all in Devon that interested him. He chose to describe Powderham, at great length, in his last journal. This was a place with which he was extremely familiar and it is interesting that he waited for some ten years to pass before giving it his full attention. Certainly there were few places in Devon that he had not yet seen. It may be that there were further journals which have not survived. One of the three journals known to have been destroyed and which would have been included in this volume had it survived was his nineteenth journal, in which there was a description of the city of Exeter in 1797, but there is no indication of any further works.

In these last volumes the Reverend Swete returned to the key national figures in garden design and in the picturesque debate. He wrote of Humphry Repton, Richard Payne Knight, Lancelot 'Capability' Brown, William Mason, Uvedale Price and William Gilpin, particularly in relation to the grounds at Powderham Castle. He quoted extensively from the writings of many of them. When describing his own attempts to depict the mouth of the river Exe at Dawlish Warren Swete wrote:

> Little more however can be effected on a confined scale (if the Scene to be delineated should happen as in the present case to be extensive and of wide compass) than a mere simple display of the disposition and locality of objects: of these the Sight may be gratified even in their complication, variety or indistinctness, and in the reality there may be Beauty which the stroke of the Pencil may either be unable or unfit to express. There cannot be doubt but that there may be found innumerable Scenes in Nature to delight the Eye besides those which may be copied as Pictures: and indeed, one of the keenest and most intelligent Observers of Picturesque Scenery (Mr Gilpin) has (as it is observed) often regretted that few are capable of being so represented without considerable licence and Alteration…

But it was when describing the grounds at Powderham that Swete wrote in more particular terms.

> *I have hinted that small circular plantations of firs, instead of contributing to the embellishment of grounds, most sensibly detract from their beauty and their consequence. In this (if I err not) I deliver the sentiments of those whose Taste in Landscape Gardening appears to be the criterion of truth; and by which the Fashion of the day, has regulated all its improvements.*

Several pages later Swete was still debating the merits of the landscape at Powderham, how it fitted into theories of design and taste.

As will be seen in the pages below, Swete wrote quite extensively of his own opinions on fine taste in landscaping particularly in relation to the work of Brown, Knight and Repton. He also maintained his discourse on which ways the landscape was Gothic, beautiful, romantic, sublime or of course, picturesque. Not surprisingly, Druids also remained an interest as did lime kilns and quarries, sonnets continued to be composed, Latin and Greek were used throughout his text, Swete maintained his sniping at Polwhele's history of Devon, most notably regarding the improvements at Powderham and at Nutwell, and he remained as forthright in his opinions as in earlier volumes. Moretonhampstead, for instance, was dismissed as being 'in general mean and dirty' and Silverton had 'nothing to detain me'.

But he also wrote of more curious topics than perhaps was common in his first few journals. Swete noted a family had lived at the Mew Stone, a landslide at Newton Ferrers, of an Alpine bridge at Fordland, questioned the correctness of placing Chinese pagodas within the British landscape, pondered whether it was the quality of the water or the humid atmosphere which was responsible for the low level of intelligence in Cornwood, repeatedly noted potato gardens in unusual places across Devon, a bullfight on Dartmoor, dismissed the men attending Tavistock's fair by noting they were only interested in wrestling and drinking, was intrigued by an oyster found in an Ashburton inn with two mice trapped inside, described a one-eyed and one-handed ferryman at Starcross, the history of a corpse found on Dawlish Warren is given as well as an account of the rabbits there, judged the tastefulness (or lack of it) of the planned canal at Powderham, an ancient stone coffin converted to serve as a flower planter, greyhounds and geese guarding a country house and describing a red-brick cube of a house.

Curiously, when Swete travelled across Dartmoor he was interested more in the improvements then being undertaken than in the picturesque nature of the moorland. He wrote at length on the nature of Dartmoor, in particular of the minerals, plants and wildlife. Swete compared the writings of Robert Fraser (*General View of the County of Devon*) and William Marshall (*The Rural Economy of the West of England*) with his own observations. Such topics as the building of Prince Hall, the endeavours with drainage and water courses, and the potential merits of canals on the moor occupied his attention. He was also interested in the introduction of Scottish cattle, the cutting of peat and the use of manure. Although these are valid subjects for any traveller to observe, it is interesting that he took so little interest in comparative areas in other parts of the county.

The Sketch Books

A number of his initial watercolours have survived. From these Swete later on, generally during the colder winter months while in the comfort of his own home, painted the watercolours which appear in his journals. Among those which have survived are Blackinstone Rock which he copied faithfully into the journal. There are also the initial watercolour of Moretonhampstead church, the cliffs at Dawlish, the quarry at Powderham, three views of Nutwell Court, the village of Lympstone, Grange, Cullompton church tower, Holcombe Rogus and the chapel at Columbjohn. Slight differences can be seen in all six of these watercolours against the final versions.

(DRO, 564M/F13/131)

View entitled 'Blackstone Rock', dated 1797
(Z19/2/21/no #)

(DRO, 564M/F13/135)

View entitled 'Moretonhampstead Church', dated 1797
(Z19/2/21/no #)

(DRO, 564M/F15/115)

View entitled 'Passage thro' the Cliffs at the Warren', no date given
(Z19/2/21/no #)

(DRO, 564M/F16/65)

View entitled 'Powderham Castle', no date given (Z19/2/21 no #)

(DRO, 564M/F16/69)

View entitled 'Powderham Church and Nutwell', no date given (Z19/2/21 no #)

(DRO, 564M/F16/84)

View entitled 'Nutwell – East View', no date given (Z19/2/21/5)

View entitled 'Nutwell',
no date given
(Z19/2/21/4)

View entitled 'Lympstone',
no date given
(Z19/2/21/no #)

View entitled 'Grange. Seat
of Francis Rose Drewe Esq',
no date given
(Z19/2/21/no #)

(DRO, 564M/F17/73)

View entitled 'Columb-ton',
no date given
(Z19/2/21/10)

(DRO, 564M/F17/113)

View entitled 'Holcombe Court.
Seat of Peter Bluett Esq.',
no date given
(Z19/2/21/16)

(DRO, 564M/F17/175)

View entitled 'Chapel to
Cullomb John', no date given
(Z19/2/21/no #)

Oxton after the Reverend Swete

Oxton passed to John Beaumont Swete following his father's death in 1821. The property passed from the Swete family only twenty-seven years later to Major General Edward Mortlake Studd and Oxton continued to be owned by his family until about 1915. It was during the first world war that Joshua John Neale acquired Oxton but ten years later it was sold to Richard Granville Hare, the fourth Earl of Listowell. Not long afterwards the property was sold again, and housed Bletchington House School, an all-girl private school, during the second world war and through to the mid 1950s. Oxton then became a vacant building and was converted to flats in the 1960s.

It is from the Neale family papers that a collection of more than one hundred photographs of Oxton has turned up. Among the surviving images are views of Swete's ruined arch (since destroyed), the terrace steps, the rose garden, kitchen garden with Mr Celly, head gardener, the Shed and the Gazebo.

The ruined arch

The terraced steps

The rose garden

The kitchen garden

Mr Celly, head gardener

The vegetable garden

The rebuilt shed

Conclusion

It took the Reverend Swete eleven years to complete 'The Picturesque Sketches of Devon'. In these we have a unique view of Devon, and parts of the surrounding counties, a generation before the coming of the railway and mass transport. Even if the current taste is not for discussing the merits of the English landscape in terms of it being more romantic or sublime rather than picturesque, or even gothic, Swete's depiction of Devon in the closing years of the eighteenth century is invaluable. Moreover, many of the places he described and painted remain remarkably unchanged.

Oxton today

Swete seldom admitted to travelling with a servant or at least that he was not travelling alone. In his last journal there is a mention of 'Old John', his otherwise silent companion. It would be fascinating to have had his version of the travels: what did he think of his employer's search for the picturesque? In many ways the reader is like this faithful manservant, dependent upon Swete for arranging the tour but more critically so for the observations made in image and word. At least the Old John could make up his own mind independently. And yet, we subsequent generations owe a debt to an individual who could not have imagined that two centuries later his personal water-colours and descriptions of Picturesque Devon would be owned and viewed by countless strangers.

ACKNOWLEDGEMENTS

Thee Reverend Swete's journals have taken two hundred years to publish and many individuals, including members of the Swete family, librarians and archivists, have over those years contributed to their preservation and, lately, to their publication. Those who helped in this volume include Mr Jack Neale who very kindly has allowed the reproduction of the photographs of Oxton from the early twentieth century, John Faircloth who untangled the more recent history of Oxton, Professor David Braund who translated the Reverend Swete's Greek and Mrs Margery Rowe who through her work as General Editor has given unstinting support and encouragement in seeing this project through. It should also be seen as one of the key achievements of the Devon Gardens Trust. The series would not have happened without the impetus from the Trust in 1993 and active support through the following seven years. Permission to publish the main illustrations and text has been given by the Devon Record Office and for photographs by the Neale family.

NOTES ON EDITING

This edition has had three main phases. The volumes were transcribed in 1994 as a project of the Devon Gardens Trust, the transcriptions were subsequently scrutinized by the staff at the Devon Record Office and then compared with the originals, corrected and annotated by the Editor and General Editor. Spelling, capitalization and punctuation have normally been left as in the original journals, all Greek words have been translated and noted within square brackets, and gaps where words are missing, including through damage sustained in the second world war, are indicated within square brackets.

JOURNAL FIFTEEN

Devon Record Office, 564M/F13

Journal Fifteen continues the Reverend Swete's tour in 1796 from Journal Fourteen through Yealmpton to Puslinch, Wembury, Newton Ferrers, Saltram, Cann quarry, Newnham mills, Cornwood, Ivybridge, Ashburton and return to Oxton on 3 October. On 14 August 1797 he left Oxton and made a short visit to Fordland and visited Kenn, Alphington and Ide. The journal also contains an account of a visit to Dartmoor made in 1795 in which Swete visited Bridford Bridge, Moretonhampstead, Fingle bridge, Chagford and Postbridge.

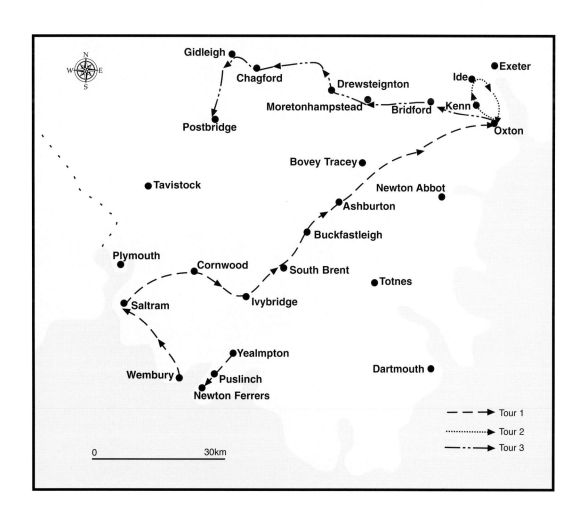

PICTURESQUE SKETCHES
OF DEVON

John Swete
Oxton House
May 13. 1797

Emerging into day from the dark recesses of the Cavern, I proceeded to reconnoitre the remaining parts of the Quarry, which in this Eastern point (from the circumstance of its not having been worked) was more luxuriantly overgrown with brushwood and Weeds. After a short wandering in this little picturesque Wilderness, by a returning path We came to an old Kiln, which had also been in disuse since the trade had been removed to a more productive part of the Rock; this had begun to assume some of the traits of a Ruin; the line of coping had become irregular and the ivy had made no inconsiderable incroachment. The Quarry was well distinguished in the background and the whole scenery harmonized so well together, as to form a pleasing and even romantic Landscape. The opposite Sketch [*below*] comprizes these Objects; and that which follows offers a retrospective View of the first Lime-Kiln, and the Weir contiguous to it on which I have already expatiated.

Our Walk now led us through a meadow towards the Church of Yealmpton, which from whatever point it was beheld, appeared a venerable Edifice; its Architecture however seem'd to be altogether Gothic – I could perceive in its

View entitled 'Yealmpton Old Kiln', dated 1797
(DRO, 564M/F13/3)

exterior aspect no vestige of the Style that was predominant when it was erected – the Saxon Arch had given place to the pointed one of a later period; and the only one that approach'd to a circular turn, was embodied, as it were in an ancient wall, overspread with ivy, and filled up with common Masonry; We are told by records that Ethelwold, a Saxon King had his chief Palace at this place and that in its Church Lipsius his Lieutenant was interr'd; – these records may have deliverd a just account; but Time has destroyed every atom of the Kings palace and the Lieutenants Monument that might have tended to its confirmation. The only Relic of Antiquity now to be discover'd is a large stone in the Churchyard on which the word Topeus [in pencil] is to be distinguished; what it means is yet a mystery; Antiquaries own themselves at a stand, and the only conjecture which I know to have been produced; is that which is hazarded by Mr. Gough in his Edition of Camden Brittannia where the supposition is, that it possibly might be the appellation of some Chieftain in days of Yore, who had derived his name, or had conferr'd the honour on the River which runs by the Priory of Plympton Mary which as I have before noticed, is called at present the Torey. On the Supposition that this ingenious hypothesis be the real fact, the whole that has been acquired is, that the Inscription commemorates the Name of a Man; but as to any thing further, who He might have been, when He might have lived, or of what nation He might have ranked, whether , Armenian, Greek, Roman, Saxon, Dane or Norman, We are as much in the dark as we were before.

Having past the Church and a pleasant cottage occupied by Capt. Clements of the Navy, We turn'd down a lane to the right, which quickly brought us to the River Yealm, over whose stream an old bridge of two arches that were in a state of decay, having been taken down, a new one with a single Arch of considerable span was erecting at the expence of the County. In this lane, on a green contiguous to the bridge, and in every hedgerow in the environs of the Village there was such a profusion of tall and Stately Elms that at a very little distance, the low pastures and inclosures were concealed from the sight and

the richly-meadowed Valley seem'd to be little otherwise than a magnificent Wood – the abundance indeed and the size of these noble trees may be partly inferred from their reputed worth, for it was asserted to me, (and from the appearance I gave it credit) that in this Manor of Yealmpton Mr. Bastard was possess'd of not less than ten thousand pounds worth of timber, which was almost wholly Elm; As the New bridge had destroyed whatever traits of the Picturesque the Spot had been enriched with during the continuance of the Old one, which (when in its dilapidated State, must have been considerable. We past by the skirts of some Cottages, following the course of the River on its opposite bank, till we came into some rich and beautiful meadows.

From them I took the Sketch, of the Stream and the Church with their rural and pleasing accompanyments; In the channel, there were a number of large stones, which broke the water, and gave a cheerfulness to the Scene, and but a little below, was a most enormous Mass, a fragment from the Marble rock, which lay in the midst, and was covered with brushwood. The view that follows, was taken from the pathway in the field above the Weir;

The Scenery is exceedingly picturesque, and in the back-ground, where it takes in the bold face of the Quarry, has a cast of the Romantic.

From the low inclosures, we now began an ascent to higher grounds, which I found in a rude state of Nature; on the summit, where the surface was not

overgrown with furse and briars, the rugged crags of the Rock appeared – this Wildness however contributed to heighten the beauty of the several parts of the landscape, which were commanded by the Eminence,ministering a fore-ground which was productive of admirable effect, by its high contrast with the distant points of Yealmpton Church on the East, and Puslinch and the Aestuary of the Yealm on the West, rich in its surrounding scenery of Woods and pastures and mellowed by remoteness.

On the bold point of a promontory, having the Quarry in view immediately before it Mr. Yonge (for we were now on his demesne) had made an inclosure, and having clear'd the ground of some of its crags, had thrown part into pota-toes, and converted the rest into a Nursery: Here also, beneath the thick covert of a fine oak He had placed a seat – which, as a refuge from the heat of the day, and as an intermission from fatigue, we were delighted for a while to occupy.

From Hence, over other prominent crags, whose interstilial hollows of Earth were thick planted with firs, and through a close thicket, we work'd our mazy way into the more open and cultured grounds thro' which we at length effected our return to Puslinch. I introduce the opposite View of Payne's, as (tho' taken from the other side of the Stream, on the elevated ground above the Quarry) it conveys somewhat of the view we enjoyed from the Promontory and gives a good idea of the situation of Puslinch with the beautiful reach of the River Yealm.

The contiguity of this charming Water to the House opened to us the prospect of an excursion for the morrow; in which our kind Host, though that morrow was usher'd in with a louring sky resolved to gratify us, and accord-ingly gave orders for his boat to be got ready and all its requisite equipment.

On our arrival however at the shore we found it to be low water, and were therefore under the necessity of walking on a pebly, or muddy strand for a full mile and half; this, to the Ladies in particular, was a circumstance that detracted in some measure from the pleasureableness of the scheme. At length however we gained the boat and passing with some difficulty over shoal ground, by degrees found ourselves in deep water; this was at present on account of the recess of tide confined to a narrow channel; the Scenery however of the banks was enliven'd by Horses and Carts, which were using every exertion to convey away sand for manure into the contiguous fields and by Persons, who were collecting Oysters, of which there were abundance.

The Hill on the left rose high and was covered with coppice: on the oppo-site shore the grounds, gently ascending were in a state of culture. On them, was a farm House lately built, in an exceeding pleasant spot by Mr. Lane, whose Seat of Coffleet lay at an inconsiderable distance from an adjoining creek which ran northward into the Country.

The Hill at the Mouth of this Creek was richly wooded. There commenced the demesne of Wembury, the Ruinous House of which opened to our view, gradually as we made our circuit of the Headland.

In proportion as the several beauties of the spot became exposed, so increased our admiration: though our expectations had been raised high, yet we found, that description had fallen short of the reality; Such magnificent and picturesque woods, are rarely to be met with any where; what an height-ening of Effect to discover them spreading themselves over the steep sides of Hills otherwise barren, and hanging as it were, over the waters which flowed from the Ocean.

On the first opening of the House and grounds I took an hasty sketch which I was enabled to do, by lying on our oars and which I have delineated in the preceding page; That which follows I have copied from one of Paynes, which as being taken at a less remote distance is infinitely more picturesque; from them a tolerably correct conception of the site of Wembury House, and the local beauties that spread themselves out before it, may be gathered; on them therefore I shall forbear further to expatiate: but adverting to its former state shall cursorily detail a few relative particulars, descriptive of its splendor and magnificence about a century ago.

Wembury was originally a Cell appertaining to the Priory of Plympton: at the dissolution it was purchased by a Mr. Rider whose grandson sold it to Sir John Hele. This Gentleman, descended from that antient and prolific Family, which I have in the course of these Volumes had occasion frequently to notice, was Eminent in the law during the reigns of Elizabeth and James, and had the honor of Knighthood conferr'd upon him by the latter at the time of his

View entitled 'Puslinch from Yealmpton Hill', dated 1797 (DRO, 564M/F13/17)

View entitled 'Coffleet: Seat of Lane Esq.', no date given (DRO, 564M/F13/21)

View entitled 'Wembury',
dated 1797
(DRO, 564M/F13/25)

Coronation. Retiring from the bustle of London, and his Profession, in the occupation of which He had honorably acquired a large fortune to the amount of £100-000. He returned to his native County, and wishing to fix his residence amongst his Kindred, He purchased Wembury where as Risdon expresses himself "Of an old Dorter, He made a magnificent House, equalling if not excelling all other in these Western Parts for uniform Building – a sightly Seat for shew – for receipt Spacious; for cost sumptuous; for site salubrious; near the Sea, upon an advanced ground, having a delightful prospect, both to Sea and Land;

But omitting divers other commodities there You may behold a large and profitable Pond strong walled, and gated, which at every flood openeth itself, when the Tide storeth it with Sea fish, for the provision of the House; and the Ebb shutteth the gate again; Prince, also, in his life of Sir John Hele, observes that the expenditure on this House was at least 20,000; that it was in all respects a complete and sumptuous Mansion; and in the equipment of it, among other circumstances, describes a rich and curious chimney piece which was set up in the Dining room and cost no less a sum than £500 – containing the representation of two Armies, drawn up in Battalia, all in polished Marble, done after the life with such exactness that nothing can exceed it: the very nails in the Horses shoes are not omitted".

After a generation or two, Wembury becoming the possession of an Heiress, who was married to Sir Edward Hungerford. it was sold to the Duke of Albemarle, whose Son disposed of it to Mr. Pollexphen, a Merchant and Brother to the Lord Chief Justice of the Name. On his decease, the Property devolved on the three coheiresses, Miss Chudleighs who sold it to Mr. Molesworth – Whose Daughter by marriage brought it to Lord Camden. The House having been unoccupied for a considerable period, became out of repair; and after the sale of the lead and furniture, it soon made hasty strides to desolation. – it has long been a Ruin, and tho' as such it heightens the picturesque effect; yet at the same time, While a comparison is made between its present ruinous state, and its former day of splendor and prosperity, the mind cannot fail of being affected by Sensations of regret.

After a long admiration of a scenery, with which the Eye could hardly be satiated, we pursued our course, which from the opposition of a returning tide, and a contracted channel, demanded greater exertions than had been hitherto used. The rocky barriers now rose high, thrusting themselves forwards on both sides of the Aestuary in bold Promontories; so as to cause a frequent repetition of Windings, a circumstance, that (superadded to the waters being pent within narrower bounds) gave far greater force and impetuosity to the flowing tide; than when it had been combated by our Oars in the more expanded sheet before Wembury.

After a short space, another Creek began to open upon Us on the opposite quarter Eastward. This insinuated itself a good way into the Country; and washed the lower Village of Newton Ferrers, of which we saw some buildings and a Quay on the left; to this there was another inlet at right angles directly opposite, where there was a Village also, called Noss. Belonging to this soon after we past a cottage, where a Ferry Boat was kept; of this Picturesque Lane I took an hasty sketch. The Boat accommodates only foot passengers, and is kept for the convenience chiefly of the Inhabitants of Newton Ferrers and Noss who, being landed at Wembury have only to traverse a narrow neck of land, either to Hoo, or Oarstone, where, again taking boat, they gain a short and ready conveyance to Plymouth, cutting off by this means more than half of the distance, which by the circuitous road of Plympton, would have amounted to a dozen miles.

Having left this little headland behind Us, in proportion as we receded from it, we (by a retrospective view,) beheld the tower of the Church of Newton rise gradually above the prominent hill which formed the eastern side of the Creek; the object was of the most pleasing cast, and attracted to itself nearly the whole of our notice, till we had past a ruinous Lime-Kiln, when by another mountainous projection on the right, it was at once excluded from our sight. This Eminence, rounded on its summit, having an intermixture of brake and greensward, at a considerable elevation from the water, after a rapid declivity, broke abruptly into a perpendicular though craggy surface. From the

View entitled 'Noss Ferry', no date given
(DRO, 564M/F13/31)

View entitled 'Wembury Church', dated 1797 (DRO, 564M/F13/35)

Woodlands at Wembury House, where had been the Park, the Hill, becoming wild and infertile, had been appropriated to a Warren – from thence it gradually declined towards the S.West, and just before its termination, gave its rock to be a sure foundation for the Parish Church of Wembury; Seldom will there be met with a Scenery so romantic and singular as the one we had before Us, when we had ran beyond the Promontory on which the Church was situated and had an opening into a Creek, which commencing at its base extended itself northward into the Country.

All in front, feeling the incessant influence of the spray, was barren, and naked, not a tree, and hardly a bush to be seen; at the visible extremity however of the Creek, where by an opposing Hill the channel was diverted by a quick turning to the West, a low Wood cloathing the lower and projecting part of the Eminence, made its appearance; and with the additional features of cultivation exhibited by inclosures on its uplands, gave a degree of softness to this remoter part of the Prospect, and a contrast to the rude Scene of rocks and Cliffs which we had immediately before Us.

The Country, as may be supposed from its local disadvantages, the nearer we made our approaches to the open sea, appeared very unproductive. The lands here and there were inclosed but as they were for the most part of considerable elevation, and exposed to every blast from the Ocean, so the general growth seem'd to be stunted, and the grass and furse crept as it were on the surface of the ground instead of rising from it. Of this ridge, which stretched itself onward to the North and constituted the boundary of Plymouth Sound at the mouth of the Tamar on the Eastern side, those heights, called Stoddon (which In a former Volume, I have noticed, for their delightfull prospects) were a part.

Rising from the Creek of Wembury, in proportion to their Ascent – the more bold and abrupt the Cliffs appeared: I have never before observed so unequal and rugged a face as they were – the Stratum was of a coarse Schist, shelving in general diagonally from its porosity, interstices, and horizontal ledges, a variety of marine and other plants had vegetated on it; and by their intermixture with mosses and lichens a beautiful diversification of tints had taken place, so as to render their aspect very gay and picturesque. In the deeper recesses also there were caverns of considerable magnitude, two of which I have exhibited in the opposite sketch, which to the wildness of the Scenery

superadded a Romantic cast: not unfrequent in front of these Cliffs a long ledge of Schist extended itself having originally constituted part of a more prominent Stratum: and which , (while the looser and more friable body, acted upon by the saline spray has been dispersed) has continued firm and indissoluble, notwithstanding all the buffetings of the Waves which incessantly beat upon it.

On the plane of one of these ledges, a mass of slate was pointed out to me, as singular in its figure – it was called "the tombstone" and indeed it was an exact representation of one of those heavy Monumental blocks which are commonly met with in Churchyards.

We now parted from the land, and getting into the open sea, steered our course towards the Mewstone, which was a small Island of Rock, at about two miles distance from the nearest Headland, and situate almost at the mouth of the Tamar. As we made our approach towards it, Plymouth Sound opened to our view and we saw several Ships of War riding at anchor. We had now so far neared the Island, as easily to discrinate Objects. We perceived on the Eastern side, where the Rock had a slope towards the Sea, the remains of a rude Cottage, and vestiges of what had been a garden – that such a wild spot, of so small a compass, as in a storm from any quarter to be in a manner deluged, should have had an Inhabitant, excited my admiration; and to my enquiries, I learnt that a Man and his family had been permitted to fix themselves on the rock and to cultivate those parts, where there was Earth to be found; the crop had been Potatoes, and on this the Family had subsisted, with the additional fare of what was left from Entertainments, here often enjoyed in fine Weather by Parties of Pleasure from Plymouth and the adjacent Country.

The Island at this time, was desolate and uninhabited: for the Crusoe had been promoted to another Isle of superior fertility which lay more Westward in the vicinity of Loo in Cornwall. The face of this Rock was perpendicular on every other aspect but that of the East, and on the S.West rose to a considerable height – it was about the middle of the last century, the Property of Sir Shilston Calmady, whose Daughter was the Wife of William the Son of Sir

Nicholas Martyn – and was the Grand Mother of my Grandmother. She (by name Elizabeth) long survived her Husband, and dying at Oxton, lies buried in the Martyn Aisle in the Parish Church of Kenton. On an horizontal stone, whereon with an inscription the Calmady Arms are engraved, the date of her Death is 1695. It would have been a gratification to me to have landed on the Mewstone: but as a ripple on the Water had occasioned a qualmishness in one of the Ladies, we were under the necessity of hastening our return. The tide now rolling on with impetuosity, carried us back at a rapid rate insomuch that the Boat made all the way that we could wish without calling in the aid of our Oars. In swift succession every Object that had before attracted our notice met our view, and was lost to the sight; one headland came quick on another, and shut out all retrospective Scenery. The Churches of Wembury and Newton; The Ferry of Noss, and the adjoining Creek, were seen but for a few minutes; nor, till we had arrived opposite Wembury House was our gaze at any individual object ought but transient – there we came into a wider expanse of Water, and a straiter channel – the whole bed from Shore to Shore was now occupied by the flood, and the wide sheet of luminous Water thus finely spread out, not only gave a striking change to the surrounding landscape but greatly heightened its effect. By means of the tide We now escaped the inconveniences which attended Us in Our Morning Walk; and wafted thus up the River towards Puslinch, we had the additional pleasure, of surveying the whole of the rich and woodland tract, whose lower parts we had traversed, and of having constantly in our View, the Elmy groves in the environs of the House.

We had now time to look around Us, and as we found much to admire, so there was somewhat to disapprove. We saw Warehouses, and Barns, decorated with Monastic, or Castellated Architecture: We saw them drest in Gothic guize though it was impossible to entertain an idea that they were other than Warehouses and Barns.

The Taste is certainly vitiated that would crest a modern House with battlements, or paint an Abbey Window on the gable end of a Barn or stable; ...to the spot the Building should ever be appropriate. We should not have a Castle in a meadow, nor a Monastery on a hill – nor in this Country should there be introduced a Style of Architecture which never prevailed in it. Edifices of foreign mode have at times been ushered into our Gardens and pleasure grounds, but when we behold Chinese Pagoda's embosomed in our groves of Oak albeit they may be sanctioned by the "Cynosure of British taste" *"risum teneamus*? On this subject Mason has the following lines:–

> *"And much I praise thy choice (the Stranger cryd)*
> *Such chaste Selection shames the common mode*
> *Which mingling structures of far distant times,*
> *Far distant regions, here perchance erects*
> *A Fane to freedom where Her Brutus stands*
> *In act to strike the Tyrant – there, a Tent*
> *With Crescent crown'd, with Scymetars adorned,*
> *Mete for some Bajazet; northward we turn*
> *And to a pigmy Pyramid pretends*
> *We tread the realms of Pharoah, quickly thence*
> *Our Southern step presents us heaps of Stone*
> *Rang'd in a Druid Circle"*

Thus has the Poet attempted by the force of Ridicule to explode the heterogeneous miscellanies of Buildings which by the Sir Visto's of the present times have been drawn together from remote parts of the Earth; and by a comic Painting of the puerile chaos, to render it contemptible. The last Image brings to my recollection the discordance which had violated the natural Beauties of an Island on the Derwentwater Lake: close by a fort spruced up with modern battlements, and whitewashed; in imitation of the British Circles, which are yet to be found on the summits of the Heaths in the neighborhood, was spread out a Druid temple, consisting of a number of huge stones standing erect and circular!! Objects so incongruous, and ill suited to the place, were perhaps never before brought together and in consequence of these and other absurdities, an Island that was equal, or superior to any that studded this beautifull Lake, was absolutely violated, and deformed.

Having past on our left a Creek which insinuates itself into the Lawns of Kitley, and with the Yealm Water incloses the Woody Headland, which here terminates in a point – we floated by a Slate Quarry belonging to Mr. Bastard, which was of a dark blueish purple and of an inferior quality – before us rose the high Elmy groves of Puslinch, which deprived Us of the pleasure of seeing the Mansion, but compensated for the loss, by their own magnificent and picturesque appearance.

The following day, being Sunday, we went to the Parish Church of Newton Ferrers, which lay Southward about two miles from Puslinch, and of which Mr. Yonge was the Patron and Rector. We had at first a steep ascent thro a Wood, at the back of Mr. Yonges House, and when we had gained the eminence, and past on to a Miles distance, had a View of Membland, once the habitation of the Family of Hillersdon, (of which, Andrew was Sheriff in the reign of Henry 6th) but now the Property and place of Residence of Peter Perring Esq, a Gentleman of Modbury, who having acquired a considerable fortune in the East Indies, on his return to Devon purchased this fine Estate of Mr. Bulteel. It stands high, on an open hill, at but a little distance from a range of Cliffs which rise to a vast height perpendicular from the Sea. Between it, and the road in a low Combe there appeared a large Wood of Oaks, which more particularly attracted my notice, as there was scarcely a tree to be seen on the heights around Memland; – Soon after, by means of an opening to the West, We were gratified with a fine View of the Ruin of Wembury, and its Noble Woods. On the entrance into the Village of Newton, which in its adjunct of Ferrers, has transmitted to Posterity the Name of its antient Lords, We past by the Parsonage House, a large irregular stone Building in the Style of Architecture of the last Century, contiguous also to the Church was an Antient Edifice, which had formerly been a Seat of a branch of the Prideaux family. The Church itself was spacious, and well seated possessing nothing however that was curious, or savoring of Antiquity.

After Evening Service, Whilst the Rector was Christening a Child, I stroll'd through the Churchyard and down the steep declivity of a field to the Creek, which I have before noticed, as running up from the Yealm, and separating from each other, the two Villages of Newton and Noss. On both sides of the Water, the banks rose high and steep, so as in some parts, almost to overhang a few of the fishermens Cottages, which were ranged in a line below them, so intermingled with Orchards and hedgerows of Elms, as to wear an appearance exceedingly picturesque. Happier would it have been for the Inhabitants of one of these Cottages, placed somewhat higher up the Creek, had the situation been less beautiful and more safe; for, by the Newspapers a few Months after this my visit a melancholy accident was announced to the Public; that on a "Sunday Night about 11 o clock, a Cottage, in which slept an industrious Widow, and her two Children, was overwhelmed by a sudden bursting of a very large field and orchard on a hill above the Cottage, in Memland lane: So instantaneous was the Separation of the ground, and so large was the Mass, that the Shock and the catastrophe appeared to have been but as One – the Cottage and the Barn contiguous were crushed to atoms, and the Poor Woman and her Children were demolished at the same moment – their bodies were afterwards, by the perseverance of the Neighbours, extricated from the cumbrous ruin of Earth, Elm, and Apple trees, which lay in a confused heap upon them. The Cause of this eruption may be imputed to the bursting of a Spring, which had for some time insensibly permeated the strata below the surface – when these were saturated, it forced itself a passage through the superincumbent mass, and carried away by the weight and violence of the

View entitled 'Saltram',
dated 1797
(DRO, 564M/F13/53)

body of Waters, all that hanging part of the hill which lay between it and the Creek: the chasm effected by the sliding away of the ground was considerable and the conjecture of its having been occasion'd by a pent up body of Waters, receives confirmation from the continued issuing of a stream from the Hollow.

As I moved on the little pathway, winding between Cottages and gardens, upon the low Cliff, I had a most charming prospect of the Creek, filled with the tide, on whose flowing bosom a variety of boats, and small craft with sails were floating, by the winding of the channel occasioned by intruding headlands, the continuity of the Water was cut off, so that, to my view its appearance was as that of a beautifull Lake. The opposite shore rose bold from the water, and extended its acclivities to an elevated height, the whole of which were either Woodlands, or inclosures intermingled with Cottages and Orchards: a more pleasing and picturesque Scenery cannot well be conceived! When I came to where the Road leading from the Church terminated in the Strand, I found the Houses more closed and frequent, so as to form another Village – and across the Water, opened the little cove of Noss with its farms and fishermen's Cots scatter'd on its shore or among its upland inclosures in the same style of rural beauty; the intermediate space is about a quarter of a mile in width; and when the tide is in, a ferry boat plies, and especially on Sundays to convey the Inhabitants of Noss to their Parish Church of Newton Ferrers; at low water the communication is effected by means of large stones which are placed at easy distances across the Mud.

On Monday, accompanied by our hospitable Friends, we departed from Puslinch on our return to Swilly. We took our way through Kitley and leaving Plympton on our right, by narrow lanes we traversed the Hills and thus shortened the distance to Saltram. I had a View of Lord Boringdons beautiful Villa from the eminence above it towards the East which not only commanded the circumjacent lawns and woods but took in the more distant Scenery of Plymouth, part of the Sound, Mount Edgecumbe and the Cornish Hills: this Prospect was a great extent, and as in the nearer points it was highly picturesque, so in the more remote ones it was finely diversified.

Arriving at the Lodge we past down the road, and at the bottom of the Park, leaving the House on the left, we turned towards the right, entering a hollow overhung with woods, which cast around a dark and solemn shade. Within this recess, I was told, the body of a young Woman had been lately found murder'd by some inhuman Ruffian, who had seduced her from her friends at Plymouth to this spot, where He had perpetrated the bloody deed. The detail given of this atrocious act, threw a "browner horror o'er the scene" and involuntarily induced us to accelerate our pace that we might emerge from the gloom of the Woods, now rendered terrific, by an association with this melancholy Event.

Our road now ran over the sod, raised athwart a valley of Marsh by the late Lord Boringdon; by which means the tide had been precluded from passing further upwards, and in consequence a vast tract of almost unprofitable ground had been reclaimed and converted into rich meadow. At the end of this Dam we past through another Lodge into the Plymouth road, which; having crost, we pursued our way on the Eastern banks of the Plym. We were now encompast with picturesque Scenery – the River and its circumjacent woods were in the most pleasing style of rural Landscape. The old House of Leigham made its appearance on the opposite side among some well–disposed grounds, and struck me as being a more eligible spot than that on which new Leigham had been built. After about a mile we reached Plym bridge; and again crossing the public road, ascended an eminence through wild Woods, which gave us a catch of Cann Quarry; to this We soon after came, and found it to be an object, well worth the deviation we had made from the direct course to Swilly.

The opening of the Quarry was romantic, and of the first magnificence; the depth was very considerable, and the height of the perpendicular face at the extremity at least an hundred feet. immense indeed was the excavation! the labour probably of more than a century – the whole stratum of Country was Schist, and this of the purest sort, was considered as the best slate in these parts – the colouring of the rock was extremely diversified, undergoing sudden changes from its natural blue to the varying tints of purple, yellow and the richer ochrous one; nor were the accompanyments less attractive – to the scenery of brushwood and stunted trees, were added the

View entitled 'Cann Quarry', no date given
(DRO, 564M/F13/57)

View entitled 'Plympton Mary Church', dated 1797
(DRO, 564M/F13/61)

mechanical apparatus appertaining to a Quarry – and the cheerful effect produced by the movement of carts and slides, and Workmen at their several labours.

Over two Weirs, that were fortunately nearly dry, we were enabled to pass from this noble Quarry of Lord Boringdons to the opposite side of the River – by the repair which these Weirs were undergoing we had an opportunity of returning by a different track but were deprived of the fine effect, which would have been given to the surrounding scenery of old Woods, by the tumbling of the Waters of these high mounds: the several beauties of this Enchanting spot should be inspected at leisure, and in exploring it, a thousand new ones would I doubt not successively occur, which could not be known to us in this our transient visit. Forcing our way through a thicket, we past another slate Quarry, the property of a Mr. Tolcher, and following the course of the River, regained the road we had before quitted at Plym bridge... from thence we followed the track I had already pursued by new Leigham, and gained Swilly about dinner time. Here and at Tamerton we had a re-enjoyment of the company of our excellent Friends, and experienced the most hospitable attentions, till Thursday morning, when we departed from the latter place, and having past by Whitley, a seat of Miss Gennis, ornamented by Woods and having a most commanding view of a reach of the Tamar and a most beautiful country: the Lady was about nineteen, an Heiress with a fortune of near £20 000. At Nackers Hole, turned from the Tavistoke road, left Widey on the right, and afterwards the two Leighams on the left – the Valley through which the road ran tho' narrow was rural, and at times was rendered Picturesque by the appearance of an old deserted Slate Quarry, and Woods on the skirting hills; at the extremity of this Valley I again reached the banks of the Plym at a short distance from Saltram Lodge, and by these frequent reviews obtained a pretty accurate knowledge of nearly the whole of this River, which in all the varieties of picturesque and romantic Scenery will perhaps be rivalled by few in the kingdom. Turning to the West at Plympton Mary bridge I again quitted the turnpike road, and pursuing my course in a northern direction had a view of the Church and bridge, which though nearly similar to one I had already delineated, I could not resist the pleasure of taking and reintroducing in the foregoing page.

The Road having been formed on the level contiguous to the River, ran in a line parallel to it, till I reached the little Village of Colebrook – by a bridge I then crost the rapid stream, turning quick to the right; from that time I lost sight of the River, untill I forded it opposite to Newnham Mills, which lay at a miles distance Northwards. The Scenery I had lately past through had been pleasing being richly stored with rural beauties. Here, however there was a profusion of picturesque images, with accompanyments that might be termed Romantic, for such surely may be considered, a cluster of Grist Mills, one building rising above another, fixed upon an high ledge hewn from an ascending steep – down which a stream, as a wild torrent precipitated itself, rushing from the thick covert of a cresting Wood and turning wheel after Wheel in a most singular and striking manner; the Style of the Mill House had also in it a good deal of the Antique. There was an Arch or two in the front of the lower Building, which had a circular turn, and spoke it to be an erection of no modern date; At the first view I had not a doubt but that it had been an appendage to the Mansion of the Family of the Strouds, which I understood was in the vicinity; A Mill, in antient times was rarely met with but in the neighborhood of an Abbey, a Castle, or some considerable place; the Park, the Warren, Dovehouse, fish ponds, Mill, generally were found together. They were all absolutely necessary to the œcononomy of a Great Man, who had not only to consult for his State from the means of his own establishment, but to make provision also for a vast troop of Dependants. His income therefore consisted not in money received as Rents (for there were but few Retail Markets for him to expend it in the purchase of the necessary supplies for his Kitchin) but in Corn and Cattle, and in the produce of the vast Farm He held in hand. His own Sheep and Bullocks were therefore fatten'd on his own ground, and were prepared for his table by his own Butcher. He had his Deer, his fish, his game in plenty around his Mansion. And the Miller who ground

View entitled 'Nuneham Mills',
dated 1797
(DRO,564M / F13 / 65)

View entitled 'Nuneham Mills',
dated 1797
(DRO, 564M/F13/67)

his Corn, the produce of his fields, at his own Mill, was no less (than those who provided for him the luxuries above mentioned) his Menial Servant. From these considerations and the Architectural cast of the Mill house I had reason to conclude that some part of this Building might be coaeval with the Antient Mansion of the Strouds. . that however I concluded not to be in existence, for as I entered the Park Gate which was contiguous to the bridge of rustic planks delineated in the preceding sketches, I perceived on an eminence, which rose gradually from the opposite bank of the River a Modern Structure, which I understood to be Newnham House, the Seat of Mr. Stroud. Offices and Walls on each side and behind it, detracted a good deal from the beauty and consequence which the Edifice might otherwise have possessed. These however

View entitled ' Nuneham Mills',
dated 1797
(DRO, 564M/F13/69)

View entitled 'Nuneham, Seat of Stroud Esq.', dated 1797 (DRO, 564M/F13/73)

were Objects, only visible, when the Eye was directed towards the House from the lower grounds, or on the approach. The View from the Windows, and indeed from every part of the Lawn must necessarily be of the highest beauty. The Valley that extended itself on the Western quarter, which consisted of the Park, diversified with knolls of greensward, embosomed in Woods of the finest growth, lay spread out at a distance in which almost every object was discriminated, and to this, may be superadded the frequent catches of the Wild River, that ran rapid through the thicket in the bottom, and in a still evening wafted up its murmurs to the House.

Just within the Park gate stood a fine Spanish Chestnut, wide spreading its luxuriant branches and the Woods, cloathing the Hills on the left swept onwards to the head of the Valley in rich magnificence. I saw of these and the River enough to convince me, that (had the time allowed) any toil in further exploring them would have been abundantly compensated;

Reluctantly therefore quitting a Scenery so very Picturesque I returned by the Mill to the Public road on which I had rode, but a short way, when from a rising of a Hill, I had a prospect of an old Mansion in a bottom on the left – its appearance was exceedingly antique – of the architecture which subsisted two or three centuries past. In a guess that I made as to this Edifice being Old Nuneham, I found, (from the information gained from a Laborer) that I was right. This was the antient though not the Original place of Residence of the Strouds – Stroud or Strode the spot from whence they derived their Surname, and where they flourished in the time of Henry 3rd being situated in the neighboring parish of Ermington. About the period of the fourth Henry this seat of Newnham, was acquired by the marriage of Melior the Daughter of Wm. Solman Esq, with John Strode the sixth Descendant of Adam who attended Edward the 1st into Scotland, having been with other Gentlemen of the County, summon'd by the Kings Herald, to assist him in that Expedition. In consequence of the accession of this Property Newnham became the abode of the Strodes and in this Mansion, (the Remains of which even now were respectable) this Family dwelt for several Centuries.

View entitled 'Nuneham Old House', dated 1797 (DRO, 564M/F13/77)

The Pile of Buildings was large, and apparently constructed at different periods – it was now inhabited (and had been for a considerable time) by a Farmer who rented part of the Demesne, and much of it, seem'd in a state of dilapidation.

Having, from within a gate of the Courtyard taken hastily the foregoing Sketch, I proceeded toward Cornwood, and in my way past by the Seat of Mr. Woolcombe, and soon after an handsome one erecting by a Gentleman of the name of Rosedew who had acquired a considerable Fortune by farming the Post Horse Duties under Government of the Western Counties; at no great distance from thence also I came to two seats of Mr. Treby Treby, and Mr. Pode, lying on each side of the road, nearly opposite to one another. There was

View entitled 'Alms Houses, Cornwood', dated 1797 (DRO, 564M/F13/81)

nothing in either of these places to detain me so that I continued my ride, till having descended a hill, overhung on the left by a wood, at the bottom I came to a stream near some Cottages, over which had been erected a bridge for the accommodation of foot Passengers. The Scene was exceedingly picturesque, the Waters rushing beneath the rustic bridge (which had been raised in the most simple, and artless style,) were productive of a cheerfull effect, and the 'tout ensemble' was too pleasing not to arrest my attention, and exercise my pencil; The Cottages I found, were Almshouses, and occupied by penury and Idiotism; of this last cast I was afterwards informed there were Several in the Parish – can this circumstance be attributed to the humidity of the atmosphere on these high lands, or to any peculiarity in the Waters? Mr. Coxe in his description of the Vallais seems to be of an opinion that the disease of the Goiters and Idiotism (both so prevalent in that country) may be derived from the same cause – and he deems it no ill grounded conjecture that the same causes which affect the body, should also affect the mind; or in other words "that the same Waters which create obstructions and Goiters, should also occasion mental imbecillity and disarrangement." That the Goiters originate in the use of Waters impregnated with "tuf" (the tophus of Linnaeus,) which is an incrustation similar to what is found in a spring at Matlock, he seems to have brought good arguments to substantiate; not so, I think, that mental Vacuity is derived from the same cause – however this may be among the Vallais, yet to the Inhabitants of Cornwood: if we start a conjecture, that the humidity of the air, or calcarious Waters (if they are so) may in any degree be productive of Idiotism, I fancy, I may assert that they do not bring, the bodily malady of Goiters. – In regards to the observation made on the Climature of this Parish, I believe I may be warranted in saying that it is more than common damp and wet – its direct exposure to the South West winds, and the Elevated summits of Stalldown, and the other hills that surround it arresting the Vapours as they are wafted from the Ocean unite in rendering it liable to an excess of rain; a circumstance which necessarily influences the Climature affecting it with greater coolness, and a later Season than is experienc'd in the lower grounds nearer to the Sea; hence it happens that its harvests are comparatively late, and its trees overspread with Moss and fungi – I am indebted for this observation to Mr. Treby, whom I met at the Parsonage at dinner, and it seems to be one of the three causes alledged by Horace for the Sterility of trees

> *"Arbore nunc aquas*
> *Culpante; - nunc torrentia agros*
> *Sidera; nunc hyemes iniquas" -*

If there be any similarity in the cause that produces the Idiot, between the Vallais and Cornwood – there certainly is none in the treatment, and estimation: Here they are considered as incumbrances and the worst of misfortunes – there they are held, as Blessings from Heaven, they call them "Souls of God without Sin" and many Parents prefer these Idiot children to those whose understandings are perfect, because, as they are incapable of intentional Criminality they consider them as certain of happiness in a future state " – But to return" from the Almshouses I ascended a hill, and having past by Dallamore and the Parish Church, I soon after reached the hospitable Mansion of my Friend; – At dinner I met Mr. Treby, whose Farm-seat, I had past on this side Newnham, but who was Proprietor of a very magnificent House, on the Eastern skirts of the town of Plympton. This Gentleman was a great practical Farmer; and has a claim to that Encomium to which every one of those is respectively entitled, who were Promoters of the Agricultural Society, first instituted with Us in these S.Western parts of the County.

The next day having taken an early dinner we bade a second farewell to our good Friends, and pursued our way, on our return through Ivy bridge, towards Ashburton – We were too much restricted in time to reiterate the delightfull excursions on the banks of the romantic River at this place, which

View entitled 'Bittaford Bridge', dated 1797 (DRO, 564M/F13/87)

we had formerly enjoyed, we past through it therefore without stopping, continuing from thence our route on the turnpike road. At a bridge a few miles onward, called Bitaford. The scenery was too picturesque, not to arrest my attention. Rushing by the end of a cottage, a little mountain stream was seen, broken and in foam, over it, where formerly was a small fording place, or as is exprest in its quondam appropriate name, yet retained, a "bit of a ford", a bridge of a single arch has been erected, upon which some ivy has begun to creep, that in a much more luxuriant manner has spread itself around the Chimneys and on the Western gable end of the Cottage; contiguous to it was another building of a similar cast, which was reliev'd by a group of Ashen trees, and protected from the inclemencies of the North, by a hill of considerable height.

View entitled 'Brent Bridge', dated 1797 (DRO, 564M/F13/91)

Having hastily taken the foregoing sketch, I soon overtook the Carriage, which by a slower progressive motion, had not yet master'd the ascent of a long and steepish hill, which began to rise from the eastern end of the bridge. – a short way up this hill the turnpike road from Totness, unites itself with that from Ashburton – both of them great thorough fares in the line from Exeter to Plymouth and both of them worthy of being inserted in the Itinerarium of a Picturesque Traveller, as possessing peculiar and very discriminate beauties. To him however who shall be of the character of the Person described by the Poet when He exclaimed "*I curre per Alpes*" &c who wishes for the most expeditious transit from the City to the Port, and the best accommodations – the track through Ashburton will be preferr'd!

After a few miles, we made our approach to the little town of Brent, the Scenery of whose Environs has already occupied so many pages of one of my former Volumes. The Bridge over which the Public Road ran, with its accompanying objects, of the Church, part of the town, and the conical hill on the summit of which, yet stood the little building erected by my Father, as an eye-catch from his Gardens at Ashburton. These, well harmonized together, and are delineated in the foregoing View. – the River, and the bridge at this spot however, cannot enter into competition with beauties of a like nature above the Church; the bridges there, stone and wooden, the Waters bursting in successive Waterfalls – overhung by trees, and more sequester'd are of the highest style of picturesque scenery, and are perhaps nowhere to be exceeded in the county:

We now, having past through the town, skirted the Southern Side of the conical hill, which is reputed to be extremely rich in iron ore: and travelling for several miles on a road, composed of a coarse Schist (which is the general Stratum,) at length, on our approach to Buckfastleigh, enter'd on the more profitable one of Marble. The Quarries at this place, (as I have already shewn) are of vast depth; the excavations have been forming through a series of ages, and while Lime shall be held in repute as a manure, they will continue to be enlarged, and will in consequence, become more stupendous and romantic.

View entitled 'Place Farm',
dated 1797
(DRO, 564M/F13/95)

At Dart bridge, I had to regret, that its picturesque beauties, had been wrapt in obscurity, by the twilight of the Evening; hastening on therefore to the Town of Ashburton We soon found ourselves accommodated in an excellent Inn.

After breakfast the ensuing morning, the Chaise pursuing its direct course homeward; by a more circuitous track, I went to visit some Estates which lay about a mile or two northward of the town. On my entrance into the second Farm, I had so pleasing a retrospective view of the first, that I was induced to take a sketch of it. The Farm house lying on the declivity of a hill on whose summit there is a Danish Entrenchment, has not only a pleasing prospect of the verdant Valley of Ashburton, but a very extensive one beyond it, which in its remotest part is bounded by the conical hill at Brent which may be consider'd as an headland of a chain of Wastes and commons connected with Dartmoor, which is here seen abruptly terminating, and losing itself in the more fertile tract of the South Hams. Having inspected these my two Farms of Place and Higher Way, I very soon regained the turnpike road between the first and second mile stone; the Scenery till I reach'd Bovey heath field, was rich and picturesque – the glens among the hills were often deep and well-wooded, as will always be remarked in a Country, where the predominant stratum was Marble. This was the case here! – its line of direction was from North to South, and its width, (perhaps greater than in any other part of the County) commencing between Dean and Buckfastleigh and continuing with but one short interruption, (of a Stratum of Dunstone on which Ashburton had been built) even to the Western skirts of Bovey heathfield, an extent of at least eight miles. At Bickington three miles from Ashburton, to which it is, (as that of Buckland towards the Moor) a Daughter Church, the Quarries of this calcareous rock, are perpetually obtruding themselves to the Travellers view, and in several places, are contiguous to the public Highway. One of these, which for a succession of years had been in constant work, had at length been dug back even to the very foundations of a Cottage, which I remember'd to have stood at a considerable distance from the precipitous part of the Quarry – its situation now, had it not been grounded on the rock, would have been

View entitled 'Bickington Quarry: 3 from Ashburton', dated 1797
(DRO, 564M/F13/99)

consider'd as imminently hazardous – but what it appear'd to have lost in point of Security, it had gained (in the Painters eye at least) in the accession of Picturesque Beauty; the opposite delineation will evince it to be a Scene not undeserving attention: possessing indeed most of those romantic traits, which are common to the Lime rock Quarries in this County, it had, peculiar to itself, a group of Cottages and a Church tower, one of them toppling as it were on its precipice, which added to its wild features and wonderfully heighten'd the effect. The landschapes till I got on the Heath, those especially on the left of the road, were high in the line of Rural beauty; the bridges on the Bovey river, and the Teign I have already dwelt on, and though Views of Chudleigh Rock, might be diversified, in infinitum, yet as I have abundantly expatiated on it in a former Volume, I shall at present forbear further description, but hasten home and conclude this Tour, which was done October 8th. 1796.

John Swete
Oxton House
October 3rd. 1797 [*sic*].

Fordlands

August 14th. 1797. – Mounting my horse soon after breakfast, I proceeded through the Villages of Kenne to Alphington: and having arrived opposite the Church, by a lane turning to the North I pursued my ride to Ide, through a level tract of Country in a high state of cultivation, but fritter'd into long narrow inclosures; by which means a loss must be incurr'd not only of a fifth part of the land, but of the pasturage itself. which when contiguous to the hedge becomes overrun with weeds, and suffers a considerable detraction in its sweetness. This remark may almost universally be made in the vicinity of large Towns. Prosperity there is greatly divided; and public good is render'd subservient to private convenience. Those Elmy fences also, here abundant, that contribute so much to Picturesque beauty,certainly tend not to the amelioration of this evil! Often times may they be seen, so closely interwoven one with another, as to preclude either the wind to exhale or the Sun to evaporate the foggy vapours; which condensed, are pent up within these prisoning screens, and give to the air, an insalubriousness which it would otherwise not possess, or at least not retain so long;

On my entrance to the Village I skirted the back front of the House of the late Mr. Holmes, Lord of the Manor and the great Patron and Supporter of the Sect of Methodists, which in these parts of late years had much prevailed – flourishing under the auspices and liberality of this Gentleman, who was its Presidium et dulce decus:

Having rode up the Village, whose inhabitants were chiefly occupied at their looms, at its most western extremity, I deviated from the more public road turning to the right and passing the Vicarage House and the Church – which it seems having been of yore dedicated to a Saint of the name of Ida, has imparted its appellation to the Parish. The brook which washes the lower part of the Village, and which by irrigating the circumjacent meadows, contributes so much to their fertilization is the Alphin, which deriving its source among the Whitstone hills, in its course to the Exe, receiving a number of tributary rills, and confers the honor of its name on the town of Alphinton.

Two miles of the Lane on which I was now riding, the road of which was in general indifferent, and, at times, (where by its winter torrent a small stream had undermined it) dangerous, brought me to a small grove of trees, contiguous to which, was Fordland, a Cottage belonging to Counsellor White of Exeter, whom, by previous appointment I had here, about noon agreed to meet. He had arrived just before me: and after a short rest we sallied forth to reconnoitre his grounds which I had some years ago cursorily seen, and which were now the object of my visit.

The House, detach'd a little from that of the Farm, was a shell of two rooms, one over the other, having the Windows at the Western end, in a segment of a Circle – from these, there was a command of a small lawn with a peep into two Vallies, that were separated from each other by a narrow headland which gradually lost itself, as it approached the House, in a piece of water, while over the Woods on the right, at about the distance of a couple of miles, the View was most pleasingly terminated by the catch of a picturesque hamlet situate on the crest of a hill, called Long-down end:

Over this little verdant Lawn enclosed on the right and left by plantations we past and by a rustic gate were let into the northern most Valley: The paths, branching from hence on both sides of a larger piece of Water, We took, by passing over the Head, the opposite one, which, ascending a small hill, winded through a wood of Oaks. – We had proceeded but a short way, when, by a retrospective view, I had a charming catch of the House, with its side plantations, and a Wood that rose well up a hill behind; the Eye past to these over the sheet of water, which was overhung on both sides by oaks that finely decorated its banks; on the hither side in particular they were of more consequence; they form'd an irregular Vista, through which the path ran; and threw a broad shade over the foreground of the landscape.

The Water now contracting, as the sides of the hills approached nearer to each other little space was at length left at their base for more than the narrow channel of the stream: From a Valley it became a dell, or dingle, through which the scanty rivulet worked its way, darkling, in a deep channel, which it had excavated during the winter

"At liquidi fontes, et stagna virentia musco
Adsint, et tenuis fugiens per gramina rivus"

From hence, by means of a Wooden bridge, We crost the Rivulet, and the walk led us through a clump of Oaks, which a short while ago stood in the projecting angle of a field that had intruded itself into Mr. Whites grounds – for this, with a waste on the uplands, He had lately been indebted to Sir Robert Palk, Who with his wonted liberality, had accommodated Mr. White with the part he had requested from the purchase of a contiguous Estate; This pathway soon lost itself in the greensward of a rounded knoll, which commanded from its

View entitled 'Fordland Cottage: belonging to James White Esq', dated 1797
(DRO, 564M/F13/107)

heights part of the Ide Valley, and insinuated itself in the declivities beneath, into the Southern Wood of the Valley, which extended itself to the left in front of the Cottage;

This we had but barely entered When we came to a low cavern, excavated from the Schisty rock of which the sloping side of the hill consisted and that not with the view of forming it into a Grotto, or cave, but merely for the stone that had been applied to various uses; That which however in its natural state would have been rude, and shapeless. Ingenuity, taking advantage of an old root of a tree that wreathed itself across the opening, and affording it shelter by means of a thatch covering, had given it an appearance not unpicturesque.

The gravel walk we were now on was the first formed by the Ingenious Proprietor, Who, by the discovery of new beauties, had insensibly been led on to make additional improvements, and in process of time, to bring forward to observation the interesting Scenery, which Nature had profusely lavished in every of the dells of Fordland:

After a short space We crost this, the deepest of the glens, by a larger bridge and that was more of an Alpine construction than any of those I had hitherto past; and the path, having connected Us to another well contrived Shed, made its return towards the House, winding through a more expanded Grove; and on the opposite side of the hollow, and sheet of water into which the Rivulet emptied itself.

The View of the landschape We had past through was of the most pleasing nature; and that it might be imprest more indelibly on my mind, I took an hasty sketch.

We had now made a tour of nearly the whole of this charming Spot, which may be considered as one of the most singular in the County; In the several Vallies there was not much diversification – their component parts were of a similar cast: like Sisters, Who, though differing from one another in many of their features had yet in the general traits of beauty, and in the "*tout ensemble*" somewhat by which a recognition of the Parent Stock might at once be identified.

View entitled 'Fordland Grounds',
dated 1797
(DRO, 564M/F13/119)

The Scenery was altogether Sylvan – such, in many points, as I have before observed, Waterloo would have been delighted with; and such, had there been more water (of which at this time there was a lamentable deficiency) as would not have disgraced the pencil of Ruysdael.

It was moreover sequester'd beyond any ornamented spot I had ever trod: the Stillness that pervaded the whole of this Recess might almost be felt; it might be said here to have taken up its abode " or as the Poet has it "*muta Quies habitat*". In the depths of this retirement one might fancy himself shut out from the world – He would be sure that his meditations would not here be interrupted – the birds would be his only companions, every other larger animal was excluded –

– Quo neque oves, pecudesq petuli
Floribus insultent, aut errans Bucula campo
Decutiat rorem, et surgentes atterat herbas.

To a contemplative mind, delighted at intervals to escape from the populous city and the busy din of Men, what can be more desirable than such deep seclusion? What more delicious than such an interchange; The Admirer of Nature, And such is Mr. White, feels a sort of enthusiasm whilst He beholds her, personified as it were, in her woods, and Hills, and Streams. He exclaims with rapture, while he rambles thro' the groves of his Solitary Paradise,

"Rura mihi, et rigui placeant in vallibus amnes
Flumina, amem Sylvasq"

If were easy, it would be a most pleasant task to expatiate further on the place and its Master – but I shall comprize all other Encomium in the assertion 'that I never spent a more delightfull day! –

Soon after seven I mounted my horse, making my return through Ide and Alphington at which last place Mr. White, who had thus far kindly accompanied me, left me: He proceeding to Exeter, and I to Oxton whither I arrived about nine o clock.

John Swete
October 18, 1797.

Tour to Dartmoor

The following pages will contain the result of two Excursions to the Forest of Dartmoor. The first taken during the month of August 1795 in the company of my Friend and Relation the Revd Henry Beeke; the latter during the August of the present year to which I was induced by the Personal sollicitation of the Honble Mr. Justice Buller.

The Summer Assizes being over, and having had intimation that the Judge was to be at Prince Hall for a week, on Sunday 20th of Augst at half past four in the evening I quitted Oxton. passing over Haldown, by Pen hill To Doddiscombesleigh. in my descent of a long hill to this place I had a very picturesque view of the Church and Village, seated on a knoll, and surrounded by verdant pastures.

Bridford bridge, lying at the distance of a mile and half from hence soon came in view. From a wild eminence down whose steep Northern declivity I past it was a striking object, nor was the Landschape that spread itself out in farms, orchards, and inclosures, on the slope of a hill across the glen at the foot of the common, devoid of rural and picturesque traits. Riding through the hamlet of Lee Cross, I came to the Bridge, which lay over the Teign, and though sketched in former Volumes had too many charms not to invite a repetition. The preceding Drawings were taken from the Western banks, below and above bridge.

Having crost a Mill leat, at the commencement of a hill I had a fine view of the Wear which diverted this Water stream from the Rivers bed: it has been

already delineated, as I had beheld it in a flood and when the Waters were low: in this latter state they now were, and, in consequence the dam across the Channel appeared as a long ledge of huge rounded Stones, piled irregularly on one another. The ascent, confined within a deep and narrow lane soon became steep, and there was nothing to compensate my toil, excepting it were that now and then I had it in my power to enjoy a retrospective view of the Valley through whose Sylvan thickets the River rushed, rapid and foamy.

The summit of the hill introduced me to a track of Country, which Nature had reclaimed from the hand of Man. The Vestige of inclosures continued, but the produce of the land was furze and rushes. Towering in the midst of these, having left the vast mass of Hell-torr behind I came near the Rock of Blackstone. The opposite sketch, correspondent nearly with a former one, has

View entitled 'Bridford Bridge', dated 1797
(DRO, 564M/F13/125)

View entitled 'Bridford Bridge', dated 1797
(DRO, 564M/F13/127)

*View entitled 'Blackstone Rock',
dated 1797*
(DRO, 564M/F13/131)

a few dissimilar points, in consequence of its being taken more eastward and at a remoter distance.

As I was now very near the Karn of Rocks, called Whitestone, on whose singular Rock basons I have before expatiated, I could not resist the impulse of paying it another visit. The access however on account of the growth of furze was more difficult than it had formerly been, in the renewal of the pleasure which I feel on contemplating this curious Monument of perhaps Druidical Superstition, I was amply repaid the little trouble I had experienc'd in approaching it, and the short deviation from the direct track.

The Evening was now closing in, and a thick drizling rain hastened on the Night which overtook me a short while before I entered the Town of Moreton hampstead. At the Inn I found all those comforts, which a Traveller, not fastidious, would derive from wholesome fare, neatness, and civility.

The town of Moreton, in general mean and dirty, has nothing of consequence annex'd to it, but its Church. This is seated on an eminence at the North East end, and exhibits itself in an exceedingly picturesque manner, when viewed from a piece of Water at some distance up a Northern glen: In my last visit to this Place I took a ramble up this little Valley with Mr. Beeke, and was then uncommonly struck with the diversified rural beauties of the Scene. Some of them may be conceived from the Drawing, in which the Church will be seen terminating the view in a conspicuous and pleasing manner. The Water has been here ponded for the use of a brown paper Manufactory which is carried on lower down the Valley. At that part of it also, which skirts the base of the eminence on which the Church stands, the Parsonage House is situate: it is a large, and rather handsome Pile, but lying very low, in a narrow defile, among high hills, it is necessarily subject to damps; The Living however is rich enough to compensate this inconvenience. it is a Rectory, in the disposal of Lord Courtenay, and under the incumbency of My Neighbour Mr. Clack who is also Rector of Kenn. With his Eldest Son who had just taken orders, and who, serving the Cure, resides in the Parsonage House, I breakfasted the next morning; and as there were parts of

View entitled 'Moreton hampstead Church', dated 1797 (DRO, 564M/F13/135)

the Teign at Fingle bridge which I had not seen He was so good to accompany me thither; the first part of our ride was in the direction of one that I had formerly taken when I visited Cranbrook Entrenchment: from the Northern end of the Town We began to ascend a very steep hill on a very bad road which having mastered, We found ourselves on a wild common, which was skirted however by a narrow border of Inclosures. in the midst near a Farm house I observed a vast Rock of a singular form having the appearance of a Pyramid with a blunted top – it was inaccessible, but by the aid of a ladder; and I was informed that it had a curious hollow on its summit which bore a resemblance to a Cradle, and was, in all probability a vast Rock bason – it is called Willestone.

View entitled 'East view of Fingle Bridge', dated 1797 (DRO, 564M/F13/139)

We were now riding on an eminence, from whence we had a view of the Country around Exeter beautifully tinted with a cast of blue – passing from hence by Cranbrook Farm, (above which towards the West rose high the Castle or Entrenchment) We began our descent to the River Teign. The declivity was long and steep: deep delving through Coppice and Woods, which precluded every view beyond themselves, excepting it were now and then, at the flexures of the road which being more open permitted me to get a glimpse of an opposite Mountain, and to enjoy a fine perspective defile of prominent and receding hills raising their high crests to the skies, alternately craggy and Woodland, through which, the rapid River rolled down its foamy waters; On reaching the bottom We crost a leat that ran to a Grist Mill on the right, and following the road to the left We came to the bridge.

The preceding view exhibits it, as seen from a rich stripe of meadow, irrigated by the Mill stream. It is its Eastern front, and is abundant with traits of picturesque beauty: the whole of the Scenery that surrounded it, was by far too extensive and magnificent to be comprehended by sketches taken on so small a scale as mine; This however, and the opposite one, on the Western aspect will serve to convey a tolerably accurate notion of the situation of the bridge, and of the romantic Hills that environ it.

The View indeed above bridge is of a grander Nature than that below – The Mountainous precipices, are more abrupt and elevated; and as they rise over the arches in barren majesty impress on the mind of the Beholder conceptions of Sublimity blended with others of the wildest desolation. This Picture however by a turn of the eye is succeeded by another of a softer cast. The interchange from rough crags to Woods and thickets is most delightfull, and the effect produced by one is heighten'd by the contrast born to the other; perhaps there are no parts on this River, that are so admirably beautifull and Romantic, as those in the vicinity of Fingle bridge. at about a mile or so above, at the commencement of Whiddon Park the Hills begin to be more than usually elevated, and to form themselves into those stupendous screens, and vast barriers against which the Waters of the boisterous Teign through a succession

View entitled 'West view of Fingle Bridge', dated 1797 (DRO, 564M/F13/143)

of ages have been in vain. A continuance of these magnificent features may be mark'd till the approach of the River to Clifford bridge, losing however, by insensible graduations their rugged aspect which by the accession of Woods on both sides, becomes mellower and more soft. The singular manner of these Hills receding from, and insinuating themselves into one another I have shewn in a former Volume by a sketch taken from the higher grounds of Whiddon Park and looking down the River. Fingle bridge is situate in the very midst of this magnificent Scenery, whose elevated Hills, rounded on their summits, and frequently divided from each other, by narrow glens, excited in my mind the comparative idea, of the undulations of a vast body of Waters, where huge waves were seen revolving in grand and quick succession.

At but the distance of a few paces from the verge of the River from whence I had taken the foregoing sketch, where a little trackway issued from a grove of Oaks, with but the diversification of a single object, I took another delineation of those Stupendous Hills, which rose nearly perpendicular from the bank of the Teign. Here the bridge was excluded from the sight, and an agreable interchange was presented by a group of trees, which gave somewhat of a mellow cast to the otherwise rugged and wild Scenery.

The pathway led us upwards, through the deepest defile I was ever in – the little Valley which below bridge had somewhat expanded itself here began to contract its space till, lessening by degrees, it terminated in a wedge-like point, losing itself between the River on the right side, and the Mill leat (which by means of a Wear was here separated from it) on the left.

Included between the two streams, from whose very margin the Mountainous Hills arose, lay this narrow strip of meadow, whose greatest breadth, was not a gunshot over. The Meridian Sun now penetrated this deep recess: at all other times, its shades were unpierc'd by the cheering beams; and even this transitory illumination was periodical, being restricted to the Summer Months when the Sun was in its greatest Altitude. towards the end of this strip of pasture, we found, a potatoe garden; taken in from the meadow by the Miller below which having past, the Wear and its surrounding

View entitled 'Near Fingle Bridge', dated 1797
(DRO, 564M/F13/147)

View entitled 'Fingle Wear',
dated 1797
(DRO, 564M/F13/151)

magnificence of hills and woods, burst upon us, in all its beauty. Almost the whole of this Scenery was rich and warm. The more prominent parts of the Woods, which on the Southern side swept onwards in a theatrical form, were gilded by the almost vertical rays of the Sun, whilst at a variety of spots, there were hollows, which they were unable to penetrate, and were consequently wrapt in darkness. Part only of the Hill on the right, was covered with coppice – a good deal remained bare and craggy – what there was however of this enhanced the beauty of the Prospect contributing by its contrasted barrenness and crags, to set off the verdure and luxuriance of the woods on the opposite quarter to the greatest possible advantage: in the very center of this Sylvan theatre rushed the River, foaming over a ledge of large masses of Granate; the effect produced by the Silvery whiteness of the Waters amidst the dark bosom of these overhanging woods, can hardly be conceived – it was luminous beyond any thing I had seen; and though the fall was but inconsiderable, (in height not more than six or eight feet) yet its roar was of more than proportionate consequence, re echoing from the rocks and woods and filling the whole glen with its clamorous sounds; in short, the imagery of the spot, and its associations were of no common sort – they were such, as could not fail to engage the attention of a mere admirer of the beauties of Nature! what charms then must they not possess for an Enthusiast in Picturesque Scenery?

With reluctance I returned to the bridge, from whence (Mr. Clack returning to Moreton) I proceeded onward to Drewsteignton. The road having skirted the foot of a woody Hill on the left, ascended a Hill, which ceased not, till I reached the Village on its summit. The Church and Tower were handsome in their Architecture, and materials, being large, of the Gothic cast, and composed of hewn granate.

The Parsonage house lay contiguous; with the Rector Doctor Roberts I sat half an hour – from the building itself, surrounded by Offices and outhouses there is no prospect but from a garden green on its Eastern aspect, the View (opening over the Country I had past through) had not only extent but magnificence. The Eye, was indeed unable to penetrate into the depths between the Mountains, through which the River Teign rolled its waters; and the rich Scenery of Woods that decorated their sides was lost to it. it skimm'd however over their summits, ranging unconfronted over their heath-clad surfaces, whose brown tints were here and there diversified and render'd cheerfull, by tracks of sod of the most vivid verdure – the whole was wild and grand, and though not in a state of culture, was yet admirably adapted to the maintenance of large flocks of sheep – a moreling breed! which when fatten'd in richer pastures, which the Parish also can well supply, produce admirable mutton, which for flavour, will yield to none in the kingdom; The Doctor kindly mounted his horse that He might shew me the way to Chagford, not however without previous importunity to stay and partake his dinner. On the road, discoursing of the value of the Living, He told me, that inclusive of the glebe which was large and compact, He consider'd it as worth near 700£ pr ann. but that as He wished to take up his residence on another Benefice which He possess'd in Cornwall near Mt Edgecumbe; He had offered it to Doctor Fothergill, who had the next presentation, for an annuity of 600£ a year.

On our descending a hill towards the bottom of a common, I immediately recognized a track, which in a former visit to this Parish conducted me to the Enormous Logan Stone that was situate on a ledge of rock in the bed of the Teign; this I have described as being opposite Whiddon Park, of which as we pursued our ride on the side of a Hill, we had a beautifull view; – Having past by the hamlet of Sandy Park, which had before led me to the Cromlech, we came to Rushford, where had formerly been a House of some consequence and a Chapel that had been demolish'd by its last Proprietor Major Hoare; the Estate now belongs to Mr. Fellowes on which instead of the old Mansion there is now a neat Farm House; – Rushford Bridge over the River Teign soon after presented itself, which with a Mill that I had just before past had received its appellation from the Mansion of Rushford; a circumstance, that, (exclusive of its own), annexed importance to the Place.

View entitled 'Rushford Bridge', dated 1797
(DRO, 564M/F13/157)

Doctor Roberts here leaving me, I dismounted and getting into a meadow above the bridge, was enabled to take the preceding sketch; – the Scene was picturesque – but it was altogether divested of those striking traits by which the River Teign had hitherto been distinguished; it had lost its wild association of Steepy hills, rough rocks, and overhanging woods! it was no longer a rapid foaming clamorous River! but flowing in an even tenor, and with a motion scarce perceptible, it glided through the level pastures, and reflected in its lucid bosom every object that impended over its banks! – Nothing but a distant view of the crags on the Elevated summit of Whiddon Park reminded me, (amid such a placid landscape), of the Scenery, which from what I had been of late accustomed to see, I had considered as appropriate to the Teign; these however were too remote to enter into the prospect with any degree of consequence, and served merely to fill up the View, with a good finishing back-ground. a field or two higher up, I understood there was a Wear, which diverted part of the Rivers waters to the Rushford Mill. The local circumstances however were evidently too tame to induce a visit, I therefore proceeded on my way to the town of Chagford, which lay about half a mile distance and of which I soon after got the opposite View: The Situation of the Town, on a hill sloping from the South is dry and salubrious, nor is its appearance, as thus seen from Rushford bridge devoid of some traits of the Picturesque: The Mountainous hill at its back is indeed a singularly attractive Object, whether it be consider'd as to its vast bulk, or as to its figure, which is that of a massy cone, terminating in three rocky summits, the middlemost of which is most elevated. All the buildings in the place I found mean and irregular, exclusive of the Parsonage House, which lies somewhat to the S.East of the Church, and is partly seen in the Sketch.

This Edifice is large and of Gothic Architecture, is well seated, and has within it a Monument with a concise and simple Inscription to the memory of Sir John Whyddon, one of the Justices of the Kings bench in the reign of Queen Mary – Who being a Native of this place, retained a predilection for it, and when He became possess'd of an ample fortune, purchased the Manor from the Copplestones, and a seat which was afterwards denominated from him, and retains the appellation to the present time. The place is one of the four Stannary towns of the County, and the Rectory is possess'd by the Rev'd John Hayter, whose Uncle was Bishop of London, and in whose family, the patronage of the Living has continued from the year 1742.

Having at a pothouse taken a Mutton chop and fed my horses, soon after four I quitted the town by an outlet to the N.West – but this road leading direct to Gidleigh, and as the farm of Sir Francis Buller in the midst of Dartmoor was the object I was in quest of, at the end of the Street I turned more to the West – from the ford of a Stream, the road began an ascent, which ended not till I had attained one of the Heights of the Forest – somewhat up the acclivity, I past by a grove of trees, whereon was a Rookery. This, and a road passing through it, led me to suppose that beyond, there might possibly be a Gentlemans seat of some consequence. Having the wide waste before me, I had no time allotted for a deviation from the strait road. I was therefore contented with the information that I soon after gained from a passing lad – that the place was called Way, and that it belonged to a Gentleman Farmer of the name of Conyam, in whom the Manor, transmitted from the Whyddons Northmores etc was now vested. The road was at times steep and rugged, the strata whereof it was formed, consisting altogether of a greyish species of Granate, and, where it was gravell'd, of a decomposition from it. After I had risen near two miles, at a Cross lane I was met by a Carrier with several Horses laden with Lime – conversing with him on the subject as we moved up the hill together, I found that He had been to the neighborhood of Ashburton for his manure, a distance of twelve miles, and for which He set out before day break: – Surprised at this account as I well knew, that there were calcarious rocks nearer, both at South Tawton and Drewsteignton, I yet further interrogated him, as to the reason, why he had gone to a much greater distance, for a

View entitled 'Chagford',
dated 1797
(DRO, 564M/F13/161)

commodity than there was any apparent cause for; his answer was, that though South Tawton was but seven miles, and Drewsteignton four yet that as these Kilns were situate so far inland there was frequently a deficiency of Culm; and that the assurance of being always able to procure Lime at the Ashburton Kilns, and that without long detention, which was almost always the case at the other places, more than compensated for the greater remoteness and labour: – To find a substitute for a manure, so prevalent as Lime is become, is one of the great desiderations, and should be one of the great objects with the several Agricultural Societies, that have been of late instituted in the County – for this a Premium of adequate value should be proposed for a dissertation which should best explain by chemical analysis and by Experimental facts, the nature of the various earths or soils which are met with in different parts of the County, and which should discover a species of manure, peculiarly appropriate to each of the respective soils. – Such an acquisition to this part of the County would be invaluable. Here, where for the want of it thousands of Acres lie in a state of barren Nature and thousands, (in some degree cultivated,) on account of the scanty supply are rarely found to produce above half a crop.

I now had reached the extent of the inclosed County, and passing through Tawton gate, entered on the Moor – A wide track conducted me to the brow of a hill, from which a narrower one branching to the right led away to Fernworthy, a Moor farm worth about 50£ pr ann. which lay about a mile and half off, and which had been fitted up, and used as a Hunting Seat by its Proprietor the late Sir John Davie: –

The width of road on which I rode insensibly became more and more contracted – still however though narrow it was beaten, and was marked with the vestiges of wheels. I therefore proceeded boldly onward, recollecting the old saw that the Via trita, was the Via tuta. In this however I met with disappointment, for I soon found that I had been following a Deception, which, as a Will o'the Wisp led me to a bog; – the ruts had been formed by light carts which during the Summer had penetrated thus far on the Moor after Peat which had been at this place dug and dried. I now perceived that I was got into a dilemma, from whence there might be some difficulty in extricating myself; the ground all around me was soft and boggy, so that I was obliged to proceed slowly and with caution. As I had a glimpse of the Moreton turnpike road at a considerable distance, I was not at a loss whither to bend my steps. This I set before me, as my Polar Star by which amid this ocean of Waste, I might ultimately be guided to the right and known way, by degrees riding and walking alternately according as I found the Horse able to bear my weight without sinking to any alarming depth, I gained an elevated spot, where were the remnants of what wore the appearance of Tumuli – from thence I distinctly saw the road I was in quest of at about the distance of a mile before me, to which I now made my way with greater expedition, as the surface had become less wet and consequently more firm and solid. On my approach to the turnpike, I found myself surrounded by innumerable Rabbits, and recognizing a house or two by the way side discover'd that I was at Mead's Warren. To it there was no fence but a few stones piled on one another, and ranged in a certain line, evidently serving to ascertain its limits than to preclude the Rabbits from roving: indeed on the dry hill beyond this barrier or boundary they appeared to me to be as numerous, as they were within the restricted line, whose inclosed area consisted in a good measure of old Stream works, lying deep in a hollow, and bearing a strong resemblance to the Crater of an exhausted Volcano; – Nothing could well be more wild and rugged than this spot, it was truly a "*rudis indigestaque moles*" nor was this roughness of surface confined to the Warren – the whole vicinity was deformed by deep hollows, or ravines that had been cut through the sides of the hills in several directions – clear indications of the industry of some earlier age, when the Science of Mining was in its infancy, and the Adventurer, limiting his pursuit to the surface of the Earth, had not yet dared, to penetrate into her very bowels: The "*itur in viscera terrae*" was protracted to later periods, when Enterprize aided by the ray of superior knowledge, and supported by experiment, might with security explore those unknown depths, and be directed by unerring guides to the treasure they were in quest of.

It was now too late in the Evening for me, to explore again the tin mines that were worked in a contiguous Valley. I had visited them in my former excursion with Mr. Beeke, and as I have proposed to myself to bring forward any of the remarks that I made in either of these tours (so as to throw as much light as possible on my subject), making use of them alternately "*pro re natâ*", or blending them together, I shall at present notice the cursory observations on these mines, which I had with Mr. Beeke an opportunity of making.

From a new road (which had been conducted from the public one to the Valley of tin), ere it dip'd into this Valley – we descended into a deep hollow, which communicated with the greater one at right angles. This we found had been originally Streamed, and the whole exhibited a most wild and rugged appearance – amid the clayey strata, which composed the sides of the hills, detach'd masses, and vast ledges of granate protruded themselves, whilst many of these, separated at different periods from the crumbling clay or gravel in which they had been incorporated, had rolled into the bottom and lay there in a confused jumble; in the center of this hollow stood a windlass, raised over a shaft that had been lately excavated. Of this scenery the sketch is a representation; – which though it possesses little of the Picturesque, may well be introduced among the delineations of a tract of Country, where almost every object that offers itself to the sight, is of a rough and wild Nature. The hills crested with piles of rocks, the Vallies swampy, and black with peat, and where there are no trees, insomuch that we may have a guess, that on some such bleak and dreary waste, Horace had an eye, when he exclaims

> "*Pone me pigris ubi nulla campis*
> *Arbor Aestivâ recreatur aurâ.*"

> "*In hoc loco /si fas sit/emendationem proponere voluerim: – si pro verbo*

/ pigris / substituere nigris / permitteretur, magis proprium mihi visum foret et specialiter associatum/ – Scribler "min".

View entitled 'Tin Mines on Dartmoor', dated 1797 (DRO, 564M / F13 / 173)

From this desolate spot We past on to the Eastern Valley – Here we found all the bustle attendant upon a Work where a number of hands were employed: – the Shaft that we visited, was 24 fathom deep. The load of tin lay 21 fathom so that there was not more than 18 feet depth of water – perhaps not quite so much, as the Adits mouth must be somewhat below the Mine. To raise this Water to the duct by which it was to be conveyed out of the Shaft, the Engine employed was a Water Wheel – whose power depends on its diameter, and the sweep of the cranks fixed in the extremities of its axis – the diameter of this Wheel was 36 feet – and though it was so vast, as it was actuated by a copious stream, it worked with the greatest possible ease, and turned out a hogshead of water in a minute – if the power of this wheel of 36 feet diameter, be, (as it has been conceived) nearly equal to that which is possessed by the Cylinder of a fire engine whose diameter is about as many inches – or if it were but productive of half the effect of the other, on a calculation of the expence incurred by both, it will at once be seen, how infinitely more eligible a Water wheel, commanding a continued and plentiful Stream, (where there is a deficiency of coals), must be to a fire Engine. The Adit, by which the Shaft is cleared of its water, is carried down the center of the Valley to nearly the extent of half a mile – in the digging of which, (having in the course of it met with an exceedingly hard stratum of rock) there was little expectation of its being completed before seven years were expired: fortunately however for the Adventurers, this expensive barrier was of no great length, and the Adit was brought to the Shaft before the end of the fourth year. hence it will be seen how much the success of such enterprises depends on accident – the uncertainty in which it is involved must at all times baffle the Skill and penetration of the most experienced Miner; At one spot a fathom has been driven for so small a sum as four shillings, in a stratum of decomposed Granate; at another, (when the passage was opposed by an Iron stone, a fathom has amounted to the enormous expenditure of thirty five pounds. The most advantageous stratum that can occur, is a stone that will split with a grain and this tho' it may cost 18 or 20s. a fathom, as the roof and sides of the Adit will require no timber for their support, will be found abundantly cheaper than a fathom of Adit, cut at 4s. through sand which does. The course of the Load, (as was visible from the deads heap'd around the Shafts) branched into several parts, ran across the Valley, and was ascending a hill in a line from East to West; Hitherto I understood little profit had accrued from the Mine to the Proprietor, for exclusive of the unremitting expence of 30£. pr month, at one time, the Mine, or Bal, (as it was termed) fell in, and stopt the work for half a year. – it was generally consider'd however as a productive ore, and (barring accident) likely to turn out advantageous.

The Tin, having been first drest at this place, that the expence of carriage might be abated, was afterwards conveyed in carts, to the distance of eighteen Miles on the banks of the Tamar, where it was to be smelted, and coals for the Smith's forge were to be brought back in return. The Number of Men employed constantly was 30, twenty of whom had their occupation underground; for these there was scarcely any accommodation: One little House received the Captain of the Work, and his family – nine of the Men lay in an outhouse, and the Remainder were under the necessity of repairing for shelter to the farms on the skirts of the Moor.

Passing on from Meads Warren for a mile or two the Prospect, was of the most dreary nature. The Horizontal line of every quarter was formed by the hills and Torrs of Dartmoor, a wide waste where the Eye found not a point to rest on – there was nothing picturesque, nor, though wild and rugged was there any thing Romantic.

Post bridge lies about two miles from the Warren in the road to Tavistock; and just before I approach'd it, I skirted two Farms, situate to the right and left of the way, and called, Higher and Lower Merrypit. The grass had not yet been mowed, and the Oats were perfectly green. The Old Bridge, given in the sketch was in pretty good repair, before the New one was erected a little above it. 'tis

View entitled 'Post bridge, Dartmoor', dated 1797 (DRO, 564M, F13/181)

impossible to form a conception of a Structure, more simple than this, or better adapted to the situation. It at present consisted of but three Stones in length which placed as imposts, on piers of the same kind extended from one side of the River to the other. Whatever Stones had been raised at the ends, so as to facilitate the ascent had been removed; having assisted perhaps in the construction of the New bridge. On the Western extremity the first of the Imposts, measured, in length 14 feet 6 inches and in breadth 6ft. 5in. There were two Coverers on the next and middle compartment, that were equal to each other in length being 11ft. 3in. and together extended in breadth 9 feet. The Third, a single Stone, was 14 feet 6in. long, but in width only 5 feet and a half. The whole of these lengths therefore will give the width of the River which thus appears to be about 40 feet. This Bridge, that at Dartmoor (on this same River of East Dart) with a great many others, of like structure, on Blackabrook, West Dart, Cherry brook and Swincombe Rivers, were the only Bridges on the Moor before the formation of the Turnpike roads when the three handsome ones, at Post, Dartmeet, and Two bridges, were erected. On these, Travellers on foot, and on Horseback were known to pass; and the Report of the Country is, that by the same means Carriages have crossed the Rivers. This afternoon however seems to require stronger Vouchers than I had the hap to meet with – Of this however We may be certain that the dimensions of those Carriages, whatever they might be, must be less in width, than these in present use, otherwise they could not have past over Post bridge, since it has been noticed, that the Eastern impost there, was not more than five feet and half wide;

Artless, as these Bridges appear to be, they are probably coaeval with the first travelling over the Moor, or at least, when the commercial intercourse between Ashburton, Tavistoke and Moreton hampstead commenced, and are perhaps of many Ages standing. The Stones with which they were constructed, had been neither sqared, nor joined together by cement or cranks, but they consisted of huge blocks of Granite, that were piled on one another, and somewhat like the notion which we have formed of the bulky Mezentius in the Aeneid, who (the Poet says) *"Mole suâ stat"*. So these rude Structures were kept together, by their size and ponderosity; and had from this circumstance alone been enabled to stem the tumultuous violence of these wild and rapid Rivers.

Two or three gunshots lower down the River, appeared the front shell of a large House, which I found from some Labourers, who lived in a tenement behind, had been erected to the height of the first Story, about 12 or 15 years ago, by a Mr. Warren who had been the Conductor of the Mines in the neighborhood. – contiguous to these a Smelting House and other necessary buildings had been raised: As Mr. Warren however was a Projector, whose thoughts instead of gravitating to the Earth, (where was their proper sphere of action), were always aspiring to a place *"in nubibus"* – so, as is the general event to Schemers, *"magnis ille excidit ausis"*, the Phaeton fell to the ground (for in a literal sense, on the strength of future gains, he had set up one). He was obliged to decamp, and the Smelting House so became Ruins.

When we collected this information, Mr. Beeke and I had stopt, and allured by the wildness of the Scene, had order'd some cold beef to be taken from our Wallet, that we might abate the keenness of our appetites, which had been more than common whetted by our mornings ride from Tavystoke and the effects of the Mountain air. Using one of the Imposts of the dilapidated bridge as our table, we there took a hearty nuncheon, quaffing the stream that flowed beneath us, and inhaling the salubrious breeze that played on its surface.

John Swete
Oxton House
Novr. 11th 1797

JOURNAL SIXTEEN

Devon Record Office, 564M/F14

Journal Sixteen begins with a continuation of Swete's tour of Dartmoor made in the summer of 1795, mixed together with another tour made in 1797, in which he discusses at length Prince Hall and various schemes of improvements on Dartmoor. He travelled from Postbridge and among the places he visited were Wistman's Wood, Prince Hall, Two Bridges and Tavistock.

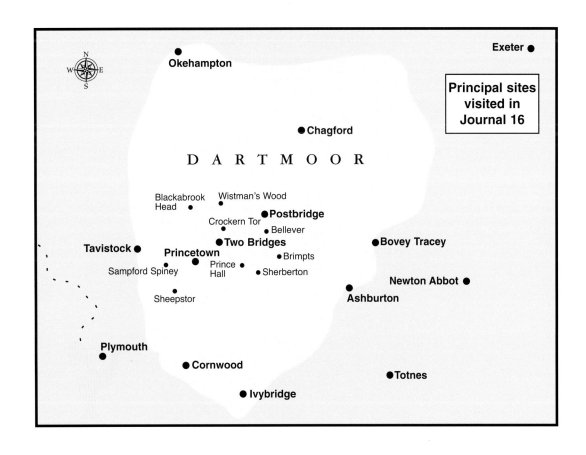

PICTURESQUE SKETCHES
OF DEVON

John Swete – Oxton House
November 11th. 1797

Tour to Dartmoor

Having finished our Nunchion; and given orders to our Servants when they had done the same to divide the klasmata among the poor children of the Miners that had flocked around us from the neighboring Houses, We strolled on the banks of the Dart, and on the skirts of the Peat bogs, which we saw in a Valley between the hills, and from whence the Miners (gaining an intermission from their subterranean labors) were busily occupied in collecting fuel for the Winter. The only object that occurred to gratify our curiosity, was the elegant little plant '*Hederacea Campanula*', which in these wet grounds we met with in great abundance.

I return now from my former Tour to my present one!

On my approach to the Old Post bridge I met with one of the Miners who work'd at Meads Warren: On questioning him as to the present state of the Mine and its produce; He told me, that the same Number of Men were employed, as had been when I was there two years ago (30) – that however it could not be said to be in a flourishing condition – for though the Ore was considered good, yet the Lodes were neither large, nor easy to be worked, and that, till of late very little Tin had been sent to the Smelting house.

By further conversation, I learnt, that the Ore was no longer smelted where it used to be, on the Tamars banks – but that it was conveyed from thence in Vessels to Penzance for that purpose: on expressing surprize at this, He said, that the Proprietors found their advantage in so doing; The Smelters on the Tamar would in return for a ton of Black tin allow but 1100 and a quarter of White; but that Those at Penzance on the same quantity had covenanted to return half hundred more. The general price of Tin (though fluctuating at times) was from 50s. to 3£ = 10s. pr 100, and as the carriage to Penzance was not more than 5s. pr 100, it is evident, that from this change the Proprietors of the Mine, had derived no small benefit. I did not learn what process of Separation from the heterogeneous mass with which it had been connected in the Mine, the Ore here underwent before it was sent off to be smelted: but I understand that the Mine Tin Ore arises at times in Cornwall so rich and pure, that it has been carried from the Lode without any intermediate purification to the Smelting House, and instances have occurred where the Proprietors, without being at the least expence, have received ten parts in twenty of it in Metal!

Pursuing my ride, I had nothing in view, exclusive of the road, that could now remind me of the labours of Man – there were neither antient, nor modern vestiges of his industry. All was wild, and unviolated Nature. The Character "*ludit exultim metuitque tangi*" given of the unbroken Filly by Horace was here reversed. The subject here might be considered perfectly passive – as one however, if suitably pressed and handled, that would be tractable enough to a Spirited effort, and make no ungrateful returns – confirmed instances of this, I had already met with in several Farms, and there was not a doubt in my mind, as I surveyed a vast tract of verdant ground, free from rocky protuberances, that fell in gentle declivities towards the banks of the East Dart, from the high Northern Karn of Long-be-torr, but that as fine a farm as any on the Moor might here be formed, and that with reasonable expectations of as good success as had resulted from any other. Other methods however must be taken than that of converting it into a mere inclosure, by erecting around a dry wall of Granate.

The New take of Bellevor which I soon after skirted, belonging to Revd John Templer, and that of Smiths lying westward of it, though consisting Each of them of many hundred acres, can never return an interest adequate to the Sums that have been expended by the Proprietors in the erection of these walls. The ground within them remains in statu quo it was in, before it was inclosed; and the sole advantage that can accrue from it is a restriction to a determinate number of Cattle and their greater Security. But I shall drop this discussion, (to be resumed in a future page,) and continue my ride!

I now came to another River of some size – this was called Cherry brook; which was so denominated probably, from its waters flowing over a bed composed of Stones and sand of red coloured Granite, and from thence assuming a ruddy teint.

I had left Bellevor Torr on my left, and a range of several more elevated ones on the right consisting of Beer yon torr, Way down torr, South be torr, and Long be torr, and soon after past under Crockern torr, continuing in the ridge of this line of Rocks and declining Southward till it terminated in a Valley of Peat near the road. But this Crockern Torr is not to be past by as lightly as those just before noticed! It has a designation more than common: – rising in appropriate consequence above the neighbouring Torrs, as Hector did above the "*Glaucus and Medon and Theosilochus*" [Greek] – or the brave Euryalus above the "*multam sine nomine Plebem*"

Fadumq Hebesumq – Rhætumq Abarimq etc.

Crockern Torr lies lower than any other Torrs in the neighborhood, and is much less compact. The Pile instead of being one congregated Mass, seems as if it had been shattered by some convulsion: it is truly a "*Montis disjectae Moles*" – whose parts, consisting of huge blocks of granite lie spread around in every direction, but more especially towards the South, where over the declivity of the hill they have rolled down, at a greater or less distance in proportion to their size appearing to have been actuated in the same manner as shodes of tin from their Lode, and possibly by a similar impulse; the largest masses lying near the Pile, and those of lesser bulk thrown off at a greater distance down the side of the hill.

On my former visit to the Moor, I took this Karn in my ride to Wistmans Wood which lies about a mile further Northward, and from the consideration that on this Torr the Stannary Parliaments had been held from a very remote age, I had formed expectations of seeing objects of high curiosity – a Judges chair, Senatorial seats, and all those other appendages which might be conceived to have constituted a theatre, where transactions of such importance might have past. – but what was my disappointment when on being told, that this was the Presidents Chair, those the Jurors seats, it was with the utmost difficulty that I could persuade myself, that there was any arrangement to be discover'd, or that these rude stones had ever been designated to any appropriated use.

It is however sufficiently ascertained that amid this wild Scenery the Stannary Courts had been held for many a Century: in later times, no business has been done on this spot; Still however some part of the antient usage was observed in the assembling together of the Official Persons – but having opened the Commission, an adjournment was instantly voted to a place of greater comfort and convenience: it has been conceiv'd that in consequence of a local sanctity, – from a notion, or Tradition that these Rocks had been consecrated by the holy mysteries or by the Laws of the Antient Britons – that in successive ages a veneration had been retained for them, and that they had been applied to purposes not altogether dissimilar, – if not as a Temple, they might yet be considered, as a Court, or Seat of Judicature.

But if these rude rocks have ever been rendered memorable by the British Cato's and Cethegi – by the rites of the Druids or the decrees of the Judge, how sad is the change! how lamentable is the consideration that their pristine splendor and honors are sunk into oblivion, and that they are now one wide waste of confused Ruin

> "Quæ priscis memorata Catonibus atque Cethegis
> "Nune Situs informis premit, et deserta Vetustas" –

To point out to the Curious Traveller a Spot once famous, and to prevent its being obliterated by the lapse of future ages, it has been an object of late with the Honble Mr. Justice Buller, to erect among these rocks a huge block or pillar of Granite, taken from the Pile, on which was to be deep engraved the following Inscription composed for the purpose by the Rev'd John Hayter, Rector of Chagford –

> "Hic ubi porrectâ surgunt Saxa edita rupe,
> Sub Jove Cornubii quondam coiisse solebant
> Danmoniig uná Patres; Stannique colendi
> Et leges, et jura dabant! – Haec saxea Moles
> Qua Praeses, veluti in solio, sceptra alta gerebat,
> Ante alios, sanctos merito sibi poscit honores:
> Fama et adhuc Saxi, si carmen forte supersit
> Bulleri jussu ventura in saecula vivet.

The Resort to this Pile ex Officio, has been, but sparing for a long time past, and this, in consequence of the few Tin Adventures which had been engaged in on the Moor. About two Centuries ago We may conceive, that such Works had been carried on with greater spirit – at least such an inference may be drawn from the Number of Persons concerned in the Mines, who, after the Preliminary matters had been "ex ordine" gone through on the Torr (assembled together, by adjournment at a House used for this purpose at Chagford (which is one of the four Stannary towns for the County) where the concourse of People was so much more than common abundant, that the Pillars which supported the room in which they were collected, gave way; and the Walls instantly falling in crushed to death the Steward with nine others; and of those who escaped with their lives there were few who were not grievously wounded.

Happy had it been for those if their habits and constitutions, bold and firm as their Forefathers, had enabled them to breast the keen air of Dartmoor, and 'pro more' to have gone through the Parliament session among the rocks of Crockern Torr! – there would have been Safety at least if there had been but little Comfort!

Having expatiated thus long on this very celebrated Torr, – I shall proceed without further interruption to Prince Hall, which tho it lay but just before me as it were, and but at a short distance, if I had cross'd the Moor, yet as it had grown late and I had some reason to be apprehensive of bog, I kept on the Turnpike road till it formed a junction with the Ashburton one near Two Bridges; and then turning short to the left, in less than a mile, I reached Prince Hall.

On alighting in the Court, I met with a sore disappointment, in finding from a Servant that in consequence of a sudden illness Sir Francis Buller had been detained at his seat of Lupton. The Source of information, which in all that

View entitled 'Fall on the Cowsick river', dated 1797 (DRO, 564M/F14/15)

related to Dartmoor I had flattered myself with the attainment of, thus appeared to be at once lost to me. The reception however which I met with from the Revd Mr. Yarde, his Relation and constant Companion in all his visits to Prince Hall, reconciled me in part to the Absence of the Judge, who apprized of my coming, had sent a letter to Mr. Yarde which He had just received expressive of his regret in not being able to meet me; In my former visit, when Mr. Beeke and myself had experienced the Hospitality of Sir Francis Buller at Prince Hall, We found Mr. Yarde of the Party and a Mr. Crooke, a celebrated Wiltshire Farmer. With these two Gentlemen, before a large Peat fire I past the Evening.

The next Morning Under Mr. Yardes escort, I mounted my horse, having proposed as objects of our ride, A Waterfall formed by the Stream that had lately been conducted to the Dock Yard, Mr Tyrwhitt's New Building and plantations, and the new discovered Tin Mine.

Having returned to the Moreton road, we descended to the Hill to Two Bridges. At this place there are two rivers, which are the West Dart and the Cowsick. The sketch above will convey some idea of the Romantic wildness of this River where with the most impetuous rapidity it rushes down a steep and confined channel, which appears almost to have been filled up by the numerous and vast masses of Granite, that at successive periods, have by accident or design been released from their beds on the precipitous slopes of the contiguous hills, and tumbled into the hollow which was altogether occupied by them and the River; on the distant ground rises a small fir plantation which has been attempted with some little success by the Proprietor of the Farm through which the Cowsick runs. This is called Bear down, and belongs to Mr. Bray, a Gentleman Resident at Tavistoke, and Steward to his Grace of Bedford for his possessions in that part of Devon. The exposure of these cultivated grounds is more than commonly wild and that in consequence of its Elevation, its site will be best conceived from the sketch which was taken at the junction of the Dart and Cowsick near the turnpike road. The fields in front of the House from which the Masses of Granite had been dug and rolled down the Steep into the River, were in high cultivation and of the most beautiful Verdure –

behind the buildings they became less and less fertile, till at length as they rose up the hill, the strong features of the Moor appeared, notwithstanding the indications of human industry which were visible in the Stone inclosures by which a vast tract, (amounting as I was told to more than a thousand acres), was surrounded.

On the public road a little Inn had been a few years ago erected by Sir Francis Buller for the accommodation of the Traveller on the Moor. The spot was most judiciously selected, being nearly at the junction of the several Roads, proceeding from Plymouth, Tavistoke, Ashburton, and Moreton hampstead, and at a central stage as it were from them all. The place had been in former times denominated from Two Bridges of the Architecture peculiar to the Moor, here thrown over the West Dart and the Cowsick; these however (tho the Spot retains its original appellation) are now gone, and in their stead

View entitled 'Bear down Farm', dated 1797
(DRO, 564M/F14/19)

View entitled ' Fall of the Dock Leat', dated 1797
(DRO, 564M/F14/23)

just below the conflux of the two Streams has been erected the other of the three Bridges – which I have before noticed. Without stopping longer at present at "Two Bridges", I shall proceed onwards to the Dock Leat. Taking the road to Plymouth, which diverging to the South, here separated itself from that which led to Tavystoke, We past round the side of a hill, which soon after by a gentle descent brought us to Blackabrook. This was a rapid Stream with the same character of Wildness and obstructions in its course by means of large stones of granite, as all the other Moor Rivers have in common. Its channel here was deep between quick sloping hills; at but little distance however above, these declivities lost themselves in the more expanding Valley, and from thence was derived the commencement of the Dock leat. This, as we advanced we cross'd, and quickly after past by two Lodges erected by Mr. Tyrwhitt as the entré to his farm and Mansion. We had from thence a mile onwards to a Valley harrowed up by Stream works thro' which ran a shallow streamlet – This we forded, (having greater Mist Torr above us on the West), and following its course soon after came in sight of the Bridge and Waterfall we were in quest of. When we crost the Rivulet on the Plymouth road, We were properly without the precincts of the Forest of Dartmoor. We had enter'd the Northern limits of a vast tract of Common; part of the Parish of Walkhampton, and of the demesne of Mr. Heywood of Marystow Who was Lord of the Manor. These coarse grounds consisting of 10,000 acres, differ'd not in the least as to external appearance from the Moor we had quitted – it was alike wild, boggy and strewed over with rocks, among which was a Karn of a singular figure on the side of a hill, formed of huge laminae or ledges, which might well have been conceiv'd to have been the effect of Art, if the magnitude of the Mass had not superceded such an idea. The spot from whence I took the preceding sketch, was in the center of the Valley which not only continued to be deformed by the antient Stream works, but exhibited some sepulchrale reliques, – the remnants of Tumuli, one of which (probably of more eminence than the rest) had been encircled by large upright Stones several of which were yet erect, and compose the foreground of the drawing. The Leat having been conducted for two or three miles through a level track,

View entitled 'Subterrane on the Dock Leat', dated 1797 (DRO, 564M/F14/37)

making a circuit round the Eastern side of a hill, was at length brought towards the S.Western aspect, where by a steep and abrupt declivity the Eminence lost itself in the Valley. Down this precipitous slope, a rugged Channel had been dug for the Waters, which as if glad to escape from the placid tenor in which they had for so long a way been compelled to run, hurried down the steep with impetuous violence, leaping tumultuously over the rocks that lay in the channel, and exhibiting themselves in one vast body of foam!

Thus they descended for a space upwards of 200 feet, and then at about twenty feet above the level of the Valley they were received into a duct formed on an embankment which had been raised athwart the bottom; this solid Mound however towards the center became converted into a bridge consisting of one arch, through which the Rivulet that ran through the Stream works, was permitted to pass, and which I was given to understand, had occasioned the considerable expenditure that had been incurred by the erection of the embankment and the bridge. In regard to this Stream there was a Noli me tangere! a prohibition to mix with its waters, or to divert its course, for it was the head of the Other Leat, which the celebrated Sir Francis Drake had above two Centuries ago, out of his great munificence and love for the Place conducted to Plymouth, from which circumstance I conceive that this Rivulet must be the Mew, which in Mr. Marshalls tour is erroneously observed to take its rise at the foot of Sheeps torr. – but this Torr lies considerably lower down in the Valley, and is the rounded rocky hill seen at a distance on the left in the sketch. The contrivance of conveying one stream over another is a very ingenious one, but Mr. Grey the Projector of this work can lay claim to no merit on this account except in the adaptation of the plan to the present exigency – if I mistake not to Mr. Brindley the Conductor of the Duke of Bridgewaters Canals in the neighborhood of Manchester the origin of this singular device is to be attributed: and it occurs to me that the most extraordinary one of the kind perhaps in the kingdom is to be seen in the road between Burton and Derby, about a mile or two (I think) from the former town. As I rode over a County Bridge, I observed another running parallel to it a short way below, which had been thrown over the same river and consisted of thirteen arches. Upon this Bridge the Canal from Derby to Burton had been conducted and, it fortunately happen'd, that at the instant in which I was admiring a contrivance (at that time so novel to me) a barge passed over this bridge.

Nothing could answer Mr. Greys purpose better than the introduction of such an admirable contrivance at this spot – it was possible indeed on the supposition that the two streams had been here united to have erected a dam across the bed of the Valley and therein (having ascertained the quantum of Water possessed by the Plymouth stream before it became mingled with the other) to have contrived a floodgate with an aperture of such dimensions, as would exactly let out from the Leat a body of water equal to that which it had received. As this plan for preventing the inconveniences that would have attended an intermixture of the two Streams, (and that at a trivial expence) must have been sufficiently obvious to so clever a Man as Mr. Grey so, I must conclude, that in the construction of the Mound and bridge He must have had in view other advantages, one of which might be, the gaining on the opposite side of the Valley a level higher than the bed of the Plymouth stream, of from ten to twenty feet. In the Sketch this Water is seen winding round the side of a knoll, and losing itself at length behind it – on the right appears a mountainous hill (Leather torr), crested with rugged rocks, at whose foot in the widening Vale, sheltered by a grove of trees rose a farm house with here and there patches of cultivated ground, whilst on the left in a still more remote point, rising gently from the Valley came in view, the very conspicuous Sheepstorr, which was well descried from the higher grounds in the environs of Plymouth, and which in my former ride from Cornwood to Shaugh, I had remarked as an object of wild and Romantic beauty.

Having returned to a gate which gave access from the Moor to a few inclosures, in which I observed several tolerable crops of oats, just got into Ear, We struck across the Valley, taking advantage of a beaten pathway which the Wandering herds had formed, among the rugged mounds thrown up from the Streamworks. The operations at this part and indeed throughout the whole of this Valley, are of immense extent and magnitude; and, to have given adequate compensation for so much labour, must have been attended by Success. The whole bottom bears a resemblance to the entrenchment of former times, being thrown into Valla and Fosse's – the excavations however are so prodigious that they very much excited my surprize, not having before had a conception that any quantity of Shode tin could have remunerated such toil and exertions. I saw here the Remains of a number of Huts, consisting of thick walls, which probably afforded shelter to the Miners during their occupation, indeed they could be applied to no other purposes, for in those earlier days, before the discovery of Lodes, there were neither Buildings for Engines – for stamping the Ore, nor for smelting it – this last operation was effected by simple though not be aeconomical means: for there was a profuse consumption of wood and doubtless a great waste or loss of metal. A pit was dug, into which were thrown layers of Shode stones and layers of Wood alternately, and when this last became consumed a succession of the same fuel was heaped on the ore, till it melted. These Stream works I have observed must have been very rich, and as the Shode stones are ascertained to be the Briel or loose top of a Lode, which were separated from it and carried down the Valley by some torrent of Water (probably the Deluge) – I am at a loss to conceive why, (wherever these Antient Stream works appear to have been rich) Adventures have not been formed, – and spirited searches made after the Parent Lode – from what I have learnt on the subject, there cannot be a doubt but that an Experienced Miner would infallibly make such discovery, and if the Parts separated are found to be of value, an inference may be drawn that the Mass itself must be of equal, if not superior worth.

It was with some difficulty that we scrambled out a way through these rough and irregular mounds: which at length having effected, we ascended the hill over whose Western declivity the Waters of the Leat had been precipitated – along the banks of this Stream we now proceeded for some space, and when to take advantage of a level it began to make a flexure round a hill, we crossed it, that we might find a readier way to an opposite eminence, where we were to meet it again at its subterrane. To do this we had to ride along a ridge from whence the Elevated ground began sensibly to decline and to lose itself at a distance in those lower cultivated Lands which lay spread out at the foot of Sheeps Torr.

This was a fine Spot for a Moor seat and farm, at least to those, who wished to have some of the wild objects by which they were surrounded blended with the picturesque. – the features on either side were grand, and the foreground as that of a good Painting, bold and full of Effect – in the middle view was the winding Valley – whose barriers on the East and West were high and rugged Torrs and beyond all, the eye conducted over Sheeps Torr took in the Plymouth Sound, the Tamar and at a break of the hills, the Nodder spread out as a luminous mirror in the bosom of the Cornish Hills, 'A beautifull and enchanting prospect !! – from this ridge we were soon obliged to depart and to take our way again towards the interior parts of the Moor; this tract was very wet and morassy and accidentally touching on a new road (, which we afterwards learnt, was carrying on by the Proprietors of Tin works on Fox torr meers to make the approach to them from the West accessible by Carts). We took advantage of the peaty turf being shaven off and proceeded on it at times rather more commodiously.

Having again forded the Leat dipped into another deep hollow of Stream works, and ascended the hill beyond, We at once came in sight of the aperture from the Subterrane through which the Waters rushing, fell almost immediately four or five feet and formed a pretty little Cascade: the Hither end of the hill, through which the excavation had been made terminating in a slope, shewed on the parts above the opening, the natural face of the country, here, in rather a shelter'd spot, overspread by patches of heath and long grass. The green and purple tints of this straggy covering, being intermingled with the ruddy colouring of the sub soil – added to the effect produced by the dark cavern and the falling Waters; and altogether formed a singular and picturesque Scene.

We now mounted the summit of the hill, and following the course of the Subterrane (in which We were guided by the deads that were heaped round a succession of Shafts) We came to the other extremity into which the Waters made their entrance. Here as the interrupting eminence had at first a gradual acclivity, the ground had been opened to the level and the leat having been formed by large superincumbent slabs of granite, had been (to some small depth covered over again by the gravel that had been dug from the hollow; but when the Hill began to rise to a greater height the Engineer was obliged to have recourse to another mode of proceeding –

> "Abstrusae per inhospita viscera terræ
> Fossor in occultos duxit vestigia flexus:"

and that He might more easily get rid of the rubbish or as they are called in mines "the Deads", He found it expedient, every five or six land yards to make a shaft or opening to the grass, through which what he had dug, were drawn up and formed those heaps that We had lately past by; these operations must have been attended by considerable expence, for, both in excavating the passage for the waters and the Shafts, several strata of moonstone had been met with which lay scatter'd about the ground in numerous fragments: the whole length of this Subterrane, was, as near as I could guess, about a quarter of a mile, and had not this Hill, which rose from 20 to 30 feet above the level of the Water, been perforated, the Leat must have made a circuitous range of great extent, by which a much larger expenditure would have been incurred.

Having satisfied ourselves with the inspection of a work, which seems to have been no less ingeniously contrived, than admirably executed, We turned from it towards the West, and at no great distance thwarted, a trackway, which from want of use was now nearly effaced, whereon We found a very large Granite Cross, firm and erect, which I was informed was called Nun's Cross.

On the southern face had been graven the figure of a Cross and there was also a scroll of ornament, or letters that were in a great measure obliterated – there was no decision to be made, whether it had been an inscription, or intended for decoration. We now made our way towards Mr. Tyrwhitts plantation, the wall of which we saw rising the hill before Us – but in our progress We met with very boggy ground, and the little Morasses lay so close together that we found no small difficulty to advance with security, or to thread the intricacies of this insidious labyrinth – to the mossy texture of the vegetable surface, and the brighter verdure which it wore, we were enabled to work out our safety – and this tint which would have led an unwary traveller into danger – the practical experience of my companion knew to be, if not, "Suppositum cineri doloso!" yet with perils that one would wish equally to be guarded against. We had now gained the summit of the hill, and had reached some Labourers who were working on the Wall that was to surround the grounds. On questioning one of them, I found that He had taken the Wall at 6s. pr land yard – that He was not only to build it, but to collect the materials, which by the efforts of Oxen and a slide He procured from the contiguous parts of the Moor. Whether that these were more persevering than horses or that they had been more accustomed to the morasses, it was a confirmed fact, he told me, that they would go through their labour with greater facility and with much less expence. The mode of erecting this wall, was the most judicious I had observed on the moor, – and was particularly adapted to the present purpose. The Walls, as they are commonly raised consist of granite blocks, as large as human Strength can manage with the aid of a lever, which are lain on one another according to their natural forms, whether they have angles or not, and in general adjusted with considerable skill; still however without the wall be of great thickness, there will frequently appear large open interstices, through which the cold horizontal Winds blow, and continue their ravages – this is termed a dry wall, that is without cement, and is common to all wild countries, where there are Stones ready at hand. On the interior part of the Wall here erecting, a strong mound of the superficial black spungy soil had been raised, which by insinuating into the interstices, and by opposing a mass of bulk and weight, not only gave strength to the Wall itself but administer'd shelter and warmth to whatever might be within side it. Protected by such a Nurse the Plantations, which consisted of firs and forest trees, have doubtless a fairer chance for a prolongation of existence, if not of Stature. They may live for a few years, but whether they will grow, must be left to the decision of Time – in general beneath the light spongy earth there is found on the moor at greater or less depths a sub soil, of a reddish colour and of a more adhesive nature, at times incorporated with a sharp gravel – this has been raised at I should conceive a considerable expence and on it the young trees have been planted: – I was sorry to see that their appearance did not promise to falsify the conjecture I have just made! –

As we descended the hill (having been introduced within the wall by means of a hurdle) the ground by degrees became more firm, which was evidently occasioned by thick layers of Granite sand, which by incorporation, and by pressure had in general rendered the surface more solid and compact. This was certainly a good commencement in the reclaiming this boggy land; where however there was Peat of any depth it was not productive of the same success, as we found even within a landyard or two of the front of Mr. Tyrwhitts house, where the horse of Mr. Yarde, sunk beyond the knee, and had some difficulty to extricate himself. But if the state of the ground was bad around this Moor seat, there was but little encomium to be given to the Building, and less to the site; whether it were considered in regard to the circumstances of things in its immediate vicinity, or, as to the nature of its prospect, had it fallen to me to have fixed on a Spot on which a House for the residence of a Gentleman was to be built and around which a farm was to be formed, I would not have selected a situation to which the inconveniences were attached of a contiguous mine and Smelting house, a Leat of water which ran at the distance of a few gunshots from the windows, and where the only view that was presented to the eye was that of a valley of Peat, whose appearance could never be meliorated. The Leat of water in itself indeed, if conducted by the hand of taste, would have been rather an object of beauty than deformity: but as it had been executed before Mr. Tyrwhitt had made choice of a situation, so Mr. Grey had consulted how to conduct the stream to a given spot at the least possible expence, and not by its windings to give it that picturesque grace which the Proprietor of the place would have wished – there was moreover a circumstance which yet further detracted from its beauty; the line that had been observed, was of course regulated by the level and to obtain this, any little rising of the ground that lay in the way, had been cut through and every depression raised. – hence, in both cases, little banks had been necessarily formed, and in that of the latter (the materials that had been used being light and porous, and liable to the accidental inroads of cattle), the Water constantly oozed through, and occasioned pools, of a black cast, and of course not very pleasing to the sight.

Those grounds (which I have before noticed) looking down the Sheepstorr Valley, (according to my conceptions) would have claimed a decided preference, or if the View was to be concentrated within the horizon of Dartmoor, there was no spot which (as far as I had seen) held out greater attractions of Torrs, and a River (the chiefest local beauties) and what in an interested view, was certainly an object of more moment, a finer expanse of glade, for pasturage or for the other productions of Moor culture, than that part which fell gently from Long be torr to the East Dart and Post bridge. But I know not what privilege I am entitled to, thus to turn Critic! – I shall therefore shelter myself under the old adage of "*de gustibus non est disputandum*" and proceed on my ride.

Having encounter'd the perils of another bog, as we quitted Mr. Tyrwhitts Premisses We ascended a short hill to a shaft where we saw two Men at work with a windlass. The Lode which they were pursuing had been discovered about three years by mere accident in cutting the channel for the Dock Leat, and had turned out so productive, as to induce the Proprietors (Mr. Grey and others) to erect a smelting house and stamping Mills, in the bottom beneath on the banks of a small stream, which emptied itself into Blackabrook. This Mine was called Batchelors Hall, employed 16 Men, and with those of the Warren and Fox tor Meers, comprized the whole of what were now worked on Dartmoor:

At other places indeed Tin has been found at different periods in great abundance. The Works that are visible are in general to be referr'd to Antient times, before the mode of penetrating the depths of the Earth, by shafts and adits had entered into the daring imagination, which is restricted perhaps to the space of [blank] years. Of course We meet with little on the Forest but Stream works – and how frequent these occur I have already noticed! On the Eastern confines, where the high barren grounds constitute part of the Parish of Holne; there are shafts, and I have been informed, that from the Lodes there found, the richest Ore has been drawn: a ton of Black tin having produced thirteen hundred and [blank] of White; which is perhaps superior to any other, discovered in this County or in Cornwall! Why this mine was discontinued I was unable to learn: it was perhaps exhausted, or what is more probable, inundated. At Brimpse, nearly opposite to this quarter, in the Parish of Widdecombe, (one of the best Moor Estates) Mr. Sanders of Exeter, the Owner and a Gentleman of considerable information, whom I fortunately met at Prince Hall, informed me he had collected pieces of Ore, which he considered to be rich in Metal, and which might instigate him to commence 'Adventurer', as he conceived from the Specimens He had found, and their locality, a Lode must necessarily be at a short distance.

On the more Western part of the Moor also, at a place called Rendals Streamworks, a few Persons have of late, from the success of their researches, met with sufficient inducement to adventure somewhat farther, and to sink a shaft – about the commencement of this work an accident happen'd to two Miners, (who, by the falling of a Shelving bank (under which they had taken shelter) were crushed to pieces), that in the day of Superstition would have been considered as a bad omen and have stopped the enterprize – in the present times however We seem to be hastening to an opposite extreme and their leading trait is, to "unshackle the mind, and emancipate it from the bondage, by which it has been so long enslaved" – As these Dogmata of the modern Philosophists want that confirmation which Time and experience give; with some it may yet remain "*in dubio*" whether there may not really be some inherent excellence in those systems of government, morality and Religion, which have been venerated by our Ancestors, and sanctioned by their adoption and practice – "it would have been better perhaps to have purged the old leaven, and to have retained the more valuable part"!!

But to return to the Mines! – I have noticed all those of Tin that have reached my knowledge – a few miles however from the last mentioned one, on the skirts of the Moor in the Parish of Sampford Spiney there have been mines work'd of late Years, and in particular, one of Copper. A Miner (Who has long been A Labourer with me), informs me, that between 20 and 30 years ago, as He was pursuing in this Parish on an estate belonging to Mr. Tolcher of Plymouth a Copper Lode (that was of the Yellow kind, and valued at about 7£ pr ton) on a sudden by striking his pick axe into a sort of Gossan (which was (as it were intermixed with the Lode) a body of Cobalt fell, and with it a quantity of Water, of which this Gossan) being of a loose and spongy nature, seemed to be the Conductor;

As from Cobalt the different sorts of Arsenics, zaffre and smalt are produced, it had long been a desideratum, instead of importing it, to have it discovered in our own kingdom; For the encouragement of such research The Society in London in the year 1774 offerr'd a premium for the Best that should be found in England, (according to Dr. Borlase) but as I have learnt, for the production of a Quantity, which should amount to a ton; This was obtained by Mr. Beauchamp of Gwenap in Cornwall, who however did not come up to the stipulated quantity, being able to transmit only 1750 weight.

From this Copper Mine however of Sampford four ton at least of Cobalt was taken; of which 1700 lbs was sent to London and sold; but what the return was I have gained no information; an inference however may be drawn, from the Remainders having lain, and perhaps even now lying on the ground there neglected; that the emolument resulting from the sale must have been inconsiderable; indeed the English Cobalt has always been consider'd inferior in value to that which is dug from the Mines in Germany Saxony and Bohemia; The German contains a quantity of Bismuth, so did that found at Gwenap – the Bohemian is impregnated with Silver – so was this at Sampford, and that in a singular manner; for it appeared here, as hairs or tassels of the purest Silver which easily separated from the Cobalt, and were of such flexibility, as to allow their being wound, in the manner of a ring, round the finger; – from among the Cobalt and Water that burst forth together, the Miner collected a handfull of these Silver filaments, or capillary Efflorescencies – about an Ounce in weight; some of them nearly of the size of a straw, and about an inch and half in length.

I shall here conclude this little detail of what I have been able to collect relative to the minerals that have been discovered in Dartmoor, and on the commons that, lying contiguous to it have little dissimilitude as to appearance and natural productions, but in their appropriation to other Parishes, and the assumption of their respective names; –

View entitled 'Entrance to Prince Hall on Dartmoor. Seat of the Honble Mr Justice Buller, dated 1797 (DRO, 564M/F14/59)

From the Shaft, of Batchelors Hall, we made our descent towards the bottom where the Smelting house had been erected, over a communicating road of the best stile, for it had been formed of the finest materials in the world decomposed Granite, or sand of Granite, before a union had taken place, so as to have assumed the appearance and reality of a Stone: Let Philosophers decide which, I have no pretensions!!

We had whiled away so many hours in this our ramble, that I had no opportunity of inspecting the Smelting House – it was four o clock, and we were yet at a distance from Prince Hall.

Leaving these Buildings therefore a little to the right, we descended yet further to the River Blackabrook which on account of the vast masses of rounded Granite in its channel, We had some difficulty in fording. from thence, We made our way, with what speed we could, over a morassy track to two Bridges, where we found The Landlord and Others busily engaged in the erection of Booths, and Standings for a fair which was to be held there on the morrow. These having past through, we soon finished our excursion, and being joined by Mr. Crook sat down to our dinner with appetites not a little whetted by the keen action of the Mountain Air.

The next morning I made a survey of Prince Hall Farm, and was pleased to find that some considerable improvements had been effected since my last Visit. The opposite sketch I took from a rising ground by the side of the Road that leads into the Courtyard; the House is seen in its back front, almost the Whole of which has been built by its Present owner Sir Francis Buller; the remainder on the left, is part of the old Building which was on the Farm, when it was sold by Mr Gullet the last Proprietor: The View from the Southern Windows varies but little from that of the Sketch, and by it, as favorable a notion may be gathered of Dartmoor Scenery, as (I think) can be gained from any other point – the winding of the West Dart, is well descried, and the rapids on it, (which may be easily raised into greater consequence, without violating the wild genius of the Spot) give life and animation; which one seeks for in vain among the dreary Hills that rise in a succession of heights beyond.

View entitled 'Front of Prince Hall', dated 1797
(DRO, 564M/F14/63)

The Torr observable on the highest Eminence on the right, is that of Hessary: on this hither side of which, too depress'd to be discernible from hence, is situate the Villa of Mr Tyrwhitt. The House stands at the upper end of a large meadow, which tho' a productive one, and of fine verdure, by further draining and pressure may receive very material improvement; This by a gentle descent loses itself in the River, over which with a view of forming a communication with Sherberton another of his Farms, and with the opposite Hills, The Judge, has just raised a Wooden bridge, which at either end is grounded on walls that are composed of immense blocks of Granite; At less than a gunshot below this the River makes a quick bend, and rushes down a small declivity, forming a wild and tumultuous Waterfall – the whole bed of the River consists of a jumble of prodigious Stones, here stopt, as it were, from proceeding further, by a contraction of the channel and exhibiting an appearance not dissimilar to that delineated already on the Cowsick river.

I shall forbear expatiating on the culture of this Farm, till I have gone through a detail of other excursions, and occurrences on the Moor – and as those were of more moment which happened at my former visit to Prince Hall, with Mr Beeke in the August of 1795, I shall refer myself to them. On this day was the anniversary of the Fair which had been this time two years instituted by the Judge: – it was rather a singular circumstance that by mere accident I should have been present at both; At this latter fair, the appearance of Sheep and Cattle was pretty nearly the same, as on the former – the only difference arose from a number of Scotch black Cattle which Mr Crook, had introduced on the Moor; and which having in a great measure fattened during the Summer on Smiths new take, which he rented of the Judge at £40 pr an., he sold at the rate of 7 or £8 pr head. Sir F Buller however had some years before procured a few of this breed from Scotland, having inferr'd, with his wonted acumen, that An Animal which had been bred on the bleak downs in North Brittain would easily assimilate with a pasturage of the same Nature elsewhere, and that where the Climate (by verging some degrees of latitude nearer to the line) was necessarily warmer, the probability was in their favor, that they would improve, and eventually turn to greater advantage.

In the yard at Prince Hall there were several of these Milk Cows, and I understood that they were found to answer better than the indigenous ones of the neighborhood. As these however were from their size by no means calculated to undergo the drudgery requisite for the culture of the grounds, the Judge had ordered others to be brought from his Estate at Lupton. When I returned from the fair with him in 1795; he told me that a Young Bull of three years old had been introduced to the farm; but that as there was another Bull already there, two years older, it was absolutely necessary He said (ere they were yoked together,) which was his intention) that there should be a decided superiority on one side or the other, and that, this matter could only be adjusted, by a combat. He therefore ordered the Hind to bring the Young Bull to a large field where the older one was grazing with some cows, and, induced by the novelty of the thing, the whole company which were invited to dine at Prince Hall, assembled on the spot. When the Young Bull was introduced the older one was at the upper end of the field and it was therefore some time before they caught each others eye. At the instant however this happened, (which was perceptible to the whole Party) they began to advance towards one another – the approach was absolutely grand: it was slow and solemn! The Eyes of both, were intensely rivetted on each other. They took not the least heed of the Cows (who were seemingly interested in what was going forward), nor of the Crowd of People that were ranged on the higher ground; in an oblique line they made their advances, untill that they were got near together, when in an instant, as if actuated by one impulse, or obedient to a given signal, they turned their heads direct, and rushed impetuously against each other. The shock of their meeting foreheads appeared to be violent – the aim however did not seem to be that of goring one another, but of vying in point of Strength – thus their horns spreading over their fronts, and locked as it were together, they strove, which should force the other to give way, and by mere pushing with their foreheads, to cause each other to be retrogade in his motions – Thus for a quarter of an hour the conflict continued without any manifest superiority excepting what the older one seem'd to possess, from the circumstance of being on the higher ground; at length the Young Bull, by a persevering push of the Other having been nearly brought on his knees, gave up to his Antagonist and slowly moved away. Whilst the Conqueror, evidently, elate by his victory, held his head erect, and silently followed;

Considering the disparity in their ages, (the Old one being five years old, and the Other only three) it was rather wonderfull that the contest should have lasted so long – nor did it appear less extraordinary that on their first approaches to each another, and in the whole of their exertions, no roar or threatening sounds should have been emitted; all was still, and solemn silence; – During this transaction I endeavored to recall to my memory the picture Virgil had drawn of a similar fight but the whole of what I could recover, was the circumstance of their engaging with their foreheads *"conversis frontibus incurrunt"* and of the roaring that reverberated from the Woods and Mountains; – The motives however that instigated these Wild Bulls of the Poet, might originate either in their more ferocious manners, or in rivalship for some beautifull Heifer, who might have been Spectatress of the fight. Such as that which Another Roman Poet himself saw and thus describes.

> *"Vidi Ego, pro niveâpugnantes conjuge tauros*
> *Spectatrix Animos ipsa Invenca dabat."*
> > *Ovid*

Mr Townsend in his description of a Bull feast at Madrid gives an account of an engagement between a Picador or Horse Combatant and a Bull, the circumstances of which are in most respects similar to those I have related. He says "As they draw near, they stop, then move a few inches, surveying their Antagonist with a fixed attention each in his turn advancing slowly, as if doubtfull what part to take; till at length the Bull, stooping with his head and collecting all his strength, shuts his eyes, and with impetuosity rushes on his Adversary". – In this relation we have no notice taken of any bellowing, Such as Virgil gives, but we have an additional circumstance which is wanting in the Poets description, that of the Bulls, invariably closing his eyes on the immediate onset.

Having recurred to Virgil on this occasion for his Bull fight, I find there are two, one in his Georgics and the other in his twelfth Æneid, which I shall introduce – both on account on their beauty, and as they may serve to illustrate, what I have myself related – that of the 3d Georgic runs thus:

> *"Pascitur in magnâ Sylva formosa Iuvenca*
> *Illi alternantes multâ vi prælia miscent*
> *Vulneribus crebris: lavit ater corpora sanguis*
> > *– Versaq*

> *"Versaq in obnixos urgentur Cornua vasto*
> *Cum gemitu, reboant Sylvæ et magnus Olympus*

The Other, occurring in the 12th Æneid is no less beautifull:

> *"Ac veluti ingenti Silâ, summove Taburno*
> *Cum duo conversis inimica in prælia Tauri*
> *Frontibus incurrunt, pavidi cessere Magistri:*
> *Stat Pecus omne metu mutum, mussantq juvencæ:*
> *Quis Pecori imperitet, quem tota Armenta sequantur:*
> *Illi inter sese multâ vi vulnera miscent,*

*View entitled 'Tavistoke Abbey',
dated 1797
(DRO, 564M/F14/75)*

*Cornuaq obnixi infigunt, et Sanguine largo
Colla, armosq lavant: – gemitu nemus omne remugit"*

There are in these descriptions two circumstances (which did not happen in our field of battle), both of which may well be ascribed to the greater ferocity of their natures: The roar of the Bulls in the first, and the bloody wounds which they mutually inflicted. In every other trait there was a striking similarity. – and in particular that picture, finely delineated of the other Cattle standing fixed, and silent, gazing on the Combatants, was justly realized *"Stat pecus omne metu mutum"*. –

The experience of those times also had taught the Master of the Herd, from these contests to look for consequences similar to what were now expected. Victory having decided in favour of One, the other either resigned himself to subjection, or withdrew himself to a distant region. –

"Alter Victus abit, longeque ignotis exulat oris" –

To my present enquiries, as to the effects of the fight, and the condition of the Bulls at this time, I learnt, that the Young One had never since dared to enter the lists with his Conqueror, but had submitted himself passively – that they had been frequently yoked together, and what was contradictory to the antient usage *"Nec mos bellantes unâ Stabulare"*, had been foddered and bedded in the same.

Reserving the detail of the culture of the Farm of Prince Hall, and its Natural productions, to the general discussion of the History and State of Dartmoor, with which I shall close my remarks, I shall, (by a reference to the former Tour) proceed with my friend Beeke from the hospitable mansion of the Judge, to the town of Tavistoke.

In our way thro two bridges, between six and seven We found the Fair, at its height, in point of revelry and pastime – the Women, however not yet emboldened by use, had in a great measure withdrawn, and the amusements of the Men seem'd to be confined to Wrestling and drinking.

Passing Cators farm, the evening Mist debarred all after View, and Night preceded Us to Tavistoke. The Abbey drew me early from my bed the next morning; the fine Remains of this Antique Edifice could not fail of causing a reiteration of the delight, I had formerly felt in viewing them; and for two hours I continued my researches, in defiance of a drizling rain, though the result of them was attended by little Novelty. I discovered parts indeed that I had not before seen, but in their yawning ruin, and mercenary dilapidation, where there were few, if any Vestiges of original magnificence, the sensations that agitated my mind were tinctured more by regret and indignation perhaps, than by pleasure.

I cannot refrain from some warmth in my emotions when I find, that the Reliques of the Architecture of Antient times, have been undermined by Avarice or convenience – had the *"major e longinquo Reverentia"* actuated the minds of Men with that influence which it holds on those of Taste and liberallity, We should now have beheld in various parts of the kingdom, numerous venerable Structures, which have been permitted gradually to moulder into dust through neglect; or at once to be hurled to the ground, and laid waste, by Ignorance and indiscriminating devastation. – Abbies, and Antient Castles (So few as there now are in any degree of preservation) should be vested in the Antiquarian Society – or at least they should so far become Public Property, as to be placed beyond the depredations of a tasteless or mean spirited Individual – I would have them, neither laid desolate by the hand of Avarice, or Time: or subject to the trim decorations of a capricious Fancy – They should be preserved as Monuments of former times – as specimens of Antient Architecture; and I should be happy to have it in my power to say to a selfish Proprietor of any of these Reliques of Art and Taste

  "the shared; don't say yours alone." [Greek]

To the Sketches which I have already given of the Remains of this once rich and famous Abbey, in the 4th volume of these Tours I have added another, which at one point of view comprizes almost the whole of what is worth notice. Its History also I have there expatiated on: so that I shall quit it for Dartmoor, to which, as soon as Breakfast was over, We began our "retour".

The environs of the Town, now cleared by the Sun of the Mist that had enveloped it, I found to be extremely picturesque – Our way at first led us by the banks of the Tavy, which offered to our view several very pleasing traits, and from the heights, which were soon after gained We had the command of a most rich and beautifull Valley through which the River winded its foamy streams, where the Town exhibited itself finely in the midst of the surrounding hills, and chiefly in its most western part, where the fretted turrets of the Abbey rising above the rest arrested the eye by their singular and elegant appearance.

From the pleasing and the Picturesque however the Scene was soon shifted to that of a more rude and wild Nature. – We had now ascended Commons, which bordering on the Forest, partook of its aspect, and this grew more and more savage in proportion to the advances that we made. On Merrivile down we had a view of a singular Torr on the right called Vixen, and beyond, the Downs of Sampford Spiney and Walkhampton; from this by an unpleasant descent we came to Merrivile Bridge and hamlet. The River Walkham here tumbles for a very considerable space over as rocky a channel as can be imagined, forming throughout the whole of his course a succession of Waterfalls: the Scenery was wild and barren! but though it consisted of foamy waters, rough grounds, and innumerous Rocks, it was in no degree romantic. near the 5th mile stone, on the Southern hang of a sloping Eminence, I observed a very considerable number of Circles consisting of large stones piled on one another similar to those which I have before described on the Cornwood Hills which are but a continuation of the wild tract that descends from Dartmoor; I shall pass these now, reserving them for future discussion. – At Pily brook to which we soon after came, where its stream crossed the turnpike road, I remarked with admiration one of the most excellent Pavés I had ever seen composed of flat Granite stones of massy bulk; contiguous to which, was Randals Stone and those considerable Streamworks, denominated from it, where the accident happened to two Miners, of a Mass of Earth falling on them and crushing them to death, which I have already noticed.

By previous appointment, (which the Judge had yesterday taken the trouble of making for Us) we were here met by an Old Man of the Name of Cator, whose cot I observed by the way side, as we passed from Prince Hall to Tavistoke. This Person having resided long on the Moor, and being well acquainted with the whole of it, We had engaged as our Ciceroni, to point out to Us what was remarkable on the Forest, and to be our Guide, across its N.Western parts to the town of Oakhampton. – to our great disappointment it happened that for the last hour the Fog had been returning: and the Misty Vapours now so thickly envelopt the Torrs on every quarter, as to shroud them from our view. These the Old Man told Us were his only Land marks, and without they were visible, so that he might be able to discern their several bearings to each other, He would not dare to hazard our safety, by making an attempt to conduct us across a trackless and dangerous waste. Acquiescing in his reasoning, which was too evident not to bring conviction with it, we gave up our scheme, and proceded onwards with Old Cator to his Cottage.

In the course of our ride We were much entertained by the old Mans garrulity, and shrewdness of observation: He was possess'd of much Anecdote, and his loquaciousness induced him to give vent to whatever came uppermost. He told Us that He was 77 years old, that He had a large family of Children and Granchildren but that He was well able to maintain himself by his own labour without their assistance; His Honour the Judge told me one day (said He) that thus Old as I was I ought to lay down my spade, and that My Children should take it up, to provide me a maintenance for the remain-der of my days. No No, please Your Honour, cry'd I, that will never do: though a plain unlearned Man, I have been accustomed now and then to make observations on things, and from what I have remark'd in Nature, I have in some cases learnt how to order my own actions and opinions. thus in a Rookery, which I have often seen and admired on tother side of the Moor, I never once saw an instance of the Old Rooks being fed by the Young Ones – on the contrary these had all their food brought them by the Old Birds.

"Tho there was no inference to be drawn from hence to the present case, yet as the Old Man appeared to plume himself on his sagacity in making the application, we were not so ill natured as to expose to him the fallacy of this his "*Mentis gratissimus Error*".

I have placed out (continued He) two of my Sons, in little farms like my own and at but little distance from it; and I have grand–children at home that look to me for their supplies, and they shall have them, for , thank God though I am near fourscore, I am yet strong and heart whole, and when I set about it with Spirit, I can earn 4 or five shillings a day by cutting turf. few people however have worked harder than I have done in my day! when I first under-took to look after the roads on Dartmoor, I took a good deal of them to make by the job, and as I found that a great deal of time was lost by going at Night for shelter to some house at many miles distance, and returning again in the morning, during the summer Months, wrapt up in a rugg and with a wisp of Straw under my head I have lain myself down to sleep under a dry bank; and have always slept as sound as a top."

On such a narration how readily do the applicable Lines of the Poet recur to Ones memory:

"Nec pudor in Stipula placidam cepisse quietem
Nec fænum Capiti supposuisse fuit"

Ovid

And how strong an exemplification is this of the truth of another Roman Poets remark, who was in no less degree an Observer of the operations of Nature,

View entitled 'Cottage on Dartmoor', dated 1797 (DRO, 564M/F14/89)

and admired its effects whensoever they became obvious to him, whether in his Visits to the Imperial Palace, or in his more sequesterd walks around his Sabine farm – Thus exclaimed He.

> *"Somnus Agrestium*
> *Lenis Vivorum non humiles domos*
> *Fastidit, umbrosamque ripam".*

The Winter however, continued the Old Man, at length set in, and as no constitution can weather that, at least on the Forest, I bethought me of raising a sort of a House or shed, which might give me Shelter. Accordingly, I got a grant of a New take here (we were now arrived at his Cottage, just by the head of Blackabrook, and by degrees I worked up with my own hands, some Walls, which I covered over with turf and long grass, and this little hovel, has by additions which I have since made to it grown to what You now see; Here I have lived for the last seventeen years. I have brought up 9 children in it; and I have besides these 36 Grandchildren – the farm that lies around my house has been formed by my own labour, as have also been in a great measure those other two in which my Sons now live."

This Story of the Old Cator, related, tho' with some exultation, yet with the most artless simplicity, was in itself highly interesting. I admired him first, and I then turned to admire his House – I found it, in one part to come within the description given Us by Virgil *"Pauperis et tuguri congestum cespile culmen"* – it was composed of turf and Peat; and in another (which was now the chiefest habitation), such as has been handed down to Us by Livy, of the antient mode of erecting such sort of Buildings: whose walls were formed of Stones, not cemented by Lime, but having their interstices filled, by mud, or by some what analogous to it, as here, by peat.

> *"Cæmenta, non calce durata, sed interlita luto; Structuræ antiquæ genere.*

Such was a cottage at Rome, and such is Old Cators on Dartmoor. – rough and shattered as it was, it yet possessed much of the Picturesque in its appearance – insomuch that I was induced to take the Sketch delineated in the foregoing page; a circumstance that seem'd to give no small satisfaction to the Veteran Architect and Proprietor.

Having finished, I gained permission to visit the interior of the Cottage which I found to correspond in every respect with the outward appearance. The door enter'd into a portion appropriated to the Winter reception of Cattle belonging to the farm, from thence I past directly into the Kitchin, which was lighted by a sort of Window, (seen in the middle of the Building in the sketch) – at the further end was a large Chimney in which blazed a cheerfull Peat fire; of which fuel, as it rose at their door they did not seem to be sparing. Near the entrance I observed a Ladder which I concluded, must lead to the bed chambers; up this I ran, and found it to be so, in the singular number – for it consisted but of One, about 20 feet in length and half that space in breadth; in which as close to each other as those in the long chamber of the College at Eton there were ranged five beds in which, without the interposition of Screens or curtains the Old Man, his Son, and others, amounting to four Men, and five Women, every night took their rest. What purity of thought and manners must there not be in this family! How Patriarchal and in the antient stile of doing things! – indeed I understood that the Old Man, was yet, the Cock of the roost, – that the whole Household regarded him with affection and respect and that He had the appellation of Grandfather, given him by All indiscriminately. –

In this picture of primitive Simplicity and Purity, with the circumstance of Cattle being sheltered under the same roof with their Master, converting only Spelunca into tugurium, (Cave into Cottage), how well may we discover the prototype in the first lines of Juvenals sixth Satire – where describing the antient manners, He says

> "Credo pudicitiam Saturno rege moratam
> In terris, visamq diu; cum frigida parvas
> Præberet Spelunca domos, ignemq, Laremq,
> Et pecus, et Dominos communi clauderet umbrâ;
> Silvestrem Montana torum cum Sterneret Uxor
> Frondibus et Culmo, vicinarumq ferarum
> 　　　　　　　　　　　　　　　Pellibus. –

The last part of strewing the couch with leaves and with the furry skins of wild beasts that had been slain in the neighborhood, however it might have been (when among the woods of the "Forest of Dartmoor Bears and Wolves prowled) could not now indeed be applicable without some allowance, for the only Wood extant was that of Wistmans and every Wild beast was extirpated excepting the Fox which now and then was found among the Torrs, a solitary Savage! –

Such was Old Cators Cottage, which resembled Nothing that I had seen before, more than those I had met with in the Highlands of Scotland, especially in the inner equipment and arrangement – it might however be considered as holding a place amongst the higher order of those, where the central hearth, had been superseded by the mural chimney.

Having thus gratified my curiosity as to the House, I was next led to consider the Farm that lay around it, and which had been reclaimed from the Common by successive inclosures and the culture in vogue among the Foresters. The crop of Potatoes was a good one, and tho' the Oats were but moderate the Old Man had reason to boast of his grass. – "This Valley, Sir said He, when I took it in hand 17 years ago, was black and boggy as most of the other parts of Dartmoor: I, and my Sons have made it what you see. I have here three farms as good as most of those possess'd by little Farmers. Where there is plenty of money, the lands may be made better; and I remember the greater part of Prince Hall, before his Honour the Judge came there, in a much worse state than mine. We told him, We should be glad to see his peat pits, and his method of cutting it, if it would not be too much for him! 'too much for me', no no Masters, though I am past 77. I have not lost so much of my strength, but that I can get, without much trouble 3s a day at that work. We old fellows, can get as much as some of your young ones now a times: – Why yesterday at the Fair I met with two hearty old Cocks of the Moor of my acquaintance, and as we sat and drank a pot or two of ale together, we summ'd up the ages of Us three, and I dont tell You a lie, when I say that they amounted in the whole to 13 score years! – Still however though the Air of the Forest is excellent, We cannot expect to live for ever, and I think old Farmer Leman of Dunnabridge was too bold in his strength when at the age of 85, He order'd particular grounds for a course of tillage of three years, of which He expected to see (tho He didn't) the last harvest".

As the Peat lay contiguous to his fields, and close by the road, the Old Man, who had taken his instruments with him soon began his operations. He first pared off about 8 or 10 inches of an upper superficies, which consisting of mere vegetable matter, was considered as little worth, and generally thrown away – the body that now appeared, seem'd to be of a closer contexture, and more fat or bituminous: – the cut which He now made was 15 inches long, 6 wide, and 2 thick – these were sold by the piece, and when dry, He carried 20 of them to Tavistoke (6 miles) for 2d. the third layer, or rather the second of Peat was the finest, the cut made of this, (excepting one inch of greater thickness) was of the same dimensions as the former, and for 6 score of these, at the town, He was paid 15d. On enquiry I found that He rarely cut more than two spits deep, and that, in a long space of years the pits fill up again, tho' the produce is never Peat; in this however the Old Man had not been sufficiently accurate in his observations, for without the Mass of Peat be severed on every side, and dug through to the gravel at the bottom, in a certain course of years (,how long has not been ascertained) a body of the same matter occupies, and fills up the place. . and this was a strong circumstance with Dr Anderson, (Who made a carefull Analysis of Peat) in addition to its other qualities, its decomposition and final decay, to confirm him in the opinion now generally assumed, that it was a vegetable substance, a Moss, recent and "*sui generis*" – from a superficial observation however we should scarcely be brought to such a conclusion, for it certainly bears a stronger resemblance to a mass of putrid vegetable matter, than to a real living substance: – this indeed with Naturalists would be an argument of but little weight as they would produce similar instances, or nearly so, in Spunges, trufles, and several other sorts of fungi.

There are Persons who imagine that Peat consists of the Sphagnum palustré and some kinds of Conserva in a certain state of preservation; And Monsr de Luc in his Geological letters holds it to have its origin altogether in the spoils of herbaceous plants – "These vegetables says He, at first simply withered form a spongy mass always soaked with water, on which new plants, some of them aquatic grow in great abundance and with much rapidity. . but if it be a fact, that when cut to a certain depth (, not quite through as I have before observed) in a period of Years, of itself, without any accession of the "Spoils of Vegetables", there shall be such a reproduction, as 'again to fill up the pit from whence it was dug, this theory of Mr de Luc's must be ungrounded. And that it is a fact we have the utmost reason to conclude from Dr Andersons experiments, which clearly prove, that if cut half through, it vegetates again so as to fill up the excavation with similar matter "but if it be severed from the substratum, no peat ever appears there again; and that from hence, no inference can be drawn but that it is a plant, perhaps a Moss, (as indeed it is often called) ' sui generis, produced by a gradual increment of a vegetable matter, still alive, and in a growing state.

The collateral testimony of Dr Platt seems to give confirmation to this hypothesis. – discoursing of Peat dug at Staunton Harcourt in Oxfordshire, from its peculiar properties He thinks it to be a Subterranean Plant. At this place, He observes, after the Peats are taken out they fill up the ground again with the grassy earth that was first cut up, and at Cowley, where they also dig them, they usually leave the depth of one "Spade-graft" at the bottom, as a foundation whereon they may grow again which in the space of 20, or 30 years 'tis observed they will do in the north of England" . . At another place Mr de Luc, says, "it is perhaps owing to an Antiseptic quality in some of these plants, that there happens such an accumulation of their "Spoils" constantly penetrated with water without their undergoing any putrefaction. a circumstance that essentially distinguishes Peat lands from Marshes, for the air is always salubrious.

But – if Peat be considered, as a living Mass, we need not refer ourselves to any antiseptic quality that may be inherent in it, for its not becoming putrid. – perhaps, there may be another reason why the exhalations that arise from the immense surface of watery ground on the Moor, are not noxious as the, miasma, from Stagnant Marshes; and that may be from their being impregnated with the Vitriolic acid. The streams that exude from these Peat or Mossy bogs, are generally tinged with dies, purplish, red, and black; and this must be occasioned by the action of the Vitriolic acid on some astringent Vegetables:

As we know therefore that all Mosses yield some colour or other, (the Archel on these very moors is particularly famous for throwing a most beautifull and vivid Scarlet) and many of them, Such as are specified to tinge these waters, in this circumstance, we may find other support for the conjecture that the vegetable part of Peat must belong to the Class of Mosses.

In some parts near Prince Hall I observed the Water to be slightly tinted with purple – this was owing perhaps to the colouring matter being greatly diluted: at other places it appeared to be of a black, which shew'd the nature of the bog to be abundant in green Vitriol: "as it is the characteristic of those plants whose astringency is soluble in water, as galls of Oak, its bark mosses etc to strike a black with chalybeate vitriol. – in short, one might conceive the Waters to be a kind of ink, which gives a purplish or black cast, as it is more or less diluted. The experiments produced by Lewis in his Commercium Philosophico –Tecknicum made on Galls Copperas and water give confirmation to the foregoing observations.

Peat bogs, are in many countries esteemed of great Value, on account of their ashes which are held as an excellent top dressing, and for fuel, which they afford. – the best sort, which is the second spit, makes a most admirable fire, adapted to culinary uses, and when charred in order to dissipate its fuliginous and sulphureous parts, is of estimation for the nicer sort of chemical operations – and as it strikes a stronger heat, has been used in the Smiths forge and for the smelting of Minerals.

The Hills around Old Cators farm being covered over with Peat ricks, had a singular appearance– they resemble an opening fir Cone, the several layers being spread hollow over one another so as to permit the air constantly to ventilate them. in this state they remain till they are perfectly dry, when as occasion serves, they are either carried away for sale or deposited under the Farmers shed for the Winters store.

Our Curiosity having been now amply satisfied, We thanked the Old Man for his attentions, and remunerated them with a Crown. – We then left him, not however without the strongest conviction on our minds, that Happiness was a Plant, that depended not, for its nutriture, on Situation, soil, or the accessions which it might derive from the elegancies and luxuries of Opulence, for We found it here, luxuriant in an Old Mans breast amidst the apparent uncomfortableness, of a most miserable hovel, and surrounded by a Scenery whose wildness, dreariness, and deformity could not well be exceeded by any part of the globe. Contrary to the character Horace gives of an Old Man *"Multa Senem circumveniunt incommoda"* – this Veteran if He knew them at all, appeared to rise above them.

The Poet says, *"res omnes timidé gelid*[que] *ministrat"*. He is *"Dilator – spe longus, iners, Difficilis, querulus"* – Such in truth the generality of Old Men may be but Such Old Cator is not, for every thing that He takes in hand, He executes with energy; his activity even yet keeps pace with an alertness of mind – and, contented with his lot, He goes through its exacted labours without murmur or complaint, – nay, He talk'd of them so cheerily, that I was almost inclined to think that He rather considered them in the light of amusements than hardships.

> "How smiles each Object! when the peacefull Mind
> Rests on itself! Wheree'r the Eye shall rove
> It joys, delight on Natures face, to find;
> Whether with gold the Sun-beams tinge the grove
> Or plays, the brighter, purer stream of Love!
> Such to the Soul refined! – Nor, ev'n to Him
> Who breasts the beatings of the scowling blast;
> Whom Labour braces in each manly limb,
> And Industry provides a scant repast,
> Will any Charm with surer influence last!
> Content! 'tis thine, above all other Power,
> To cheer with blissfull throb the Peasants breast:
> Feathered by thee, flits fast the day's light hour
> And Peace at Eve conducts to softest rest:
> With this Sonnet, whose inspiring Muse Was the cheerfull Old Man of Dartmoor, I bid him adieu!

From hence to two Bridges the distance was about two miles. Of this place we got a view from the brow of a hill, and in the course of the descent, passing by the most Southern inclosure of Mr Brays farm of Bear down, I observed within side the hedge, another, at about 15 or 20 feet distance running parallel to it, this was formed of turf, and athwart the area included between these two fences were other mounds raised, dividing it into small oblong compartments. in these spaces had been planted a number of firs, of various sorts, which appeared to flourish beyond my expectation. The leaders which they had thrown out since the last Spring were strong, and their verdure exhibited such signs of health as indicated no aversion either to the soil or situation. – what inference have we to draw from hence but that with similar protection, or one adequate to the peculiar exigencies of the different trees that might be planted, Dartmoor might once again, become a woody Forest – which, there is some probability in supposing it once was. – That Oaks will grow on the Moor, we have manifest proof in the fine Wood overhanging the East Dart on the grounds of Mr Saunders at Brimpse. Tis true this wood lies on the shelter'd hang of a hill towards the East, from which quarter, the more fatal winds do not blow, and being in the Parish of Widecombe, may be said not to be on the Forest of Dartmoor: – but a boundary of this nature capriciously, or interestedly fixed, effects no change on the soil and aspect of the Country, and in no respect does it influence the climature. The extensive Wastes, of Widecombe, Holne, Walkhampton, and the many others that lye around the Moor, as I have already observed, are not distinguishable from it, and have no sort of advantage over it, but that for the most part they are less elevated.

We have indeed besides this Wood of Brimpse other instances to support the hypothesis that the soil and Climature of Dartmoor was not so unfavorable to the growth of trees and especially Oaks, as it now seems to be. – that very extraordinary Wood, known by the appellation of Wistmans situate in the very heart of the Forest, however low and stunted it may be, shews that it must have been a production, not of Art but Nature; and if indigenous, it must have originated from other trees of the same species which grew in the vicinity and here scatter'd their acorns: Risdon, having recorded a charter for the limits of Dartmoor ascertained and enacted in consequence of a Perambulation taken during the reign of Henry the third, afterwards adverts to the antient Tenants, called Fenfield Men, and to the prescriptive rights and priviledges with which they were invested.

Among which is the following clause "And they shall have in the said

Moore, all that may do them good except green Oak, and Venison." – If a prohibition of this kind should lead us to conclude that Oak was not in great abundance, it yet informs Us, that there were oaks and that of such consequence, as to be entitled to the protection of the King; the circumstance also of Deer being found on the Moor, brings a sort of collateral evidence that there were woods on it, not scant, or stunted as that now extant of Wistmans, but such as might at the same time afford the herd shelter and provender; – if I mistake not it is a general Opinion, that almost the whole of the Island was at one period covered with Woods: – The Greek and Roman Historians, who have described this Kingdom give us grounds for such a supposition. – Delighting in the hill country, as being perhaps less exposed to ravenous beasts, to waters and bogs, the Britons, who were the Aborigines of the Island, most probably at an early period there fixed themselves, and in process of time, as is now the usage in the uncultivated parts of America, cleared away the Woods and thickets around their rude dwellings, – thereby rendering themselves less liable to the sudden attacks of any prowling Wild beast, and gaining pasture adequate to the maintenance of whatever cattle they might be inclined to keep. – The occupation of these Aborigines (Who had left the maritime parts to Strangers, who were in all likelihood Merchants and Husbandmen) was that of Herdsman: who lived on the produce of their flocks and herds: – which circumstance indeed is confirmed by Cæsar who says *"Interiores plerique frumenta non serunt sed lacte et carne vivunt"* –

On Dartmoor then, we may well conceive Many of such Stations may have been; – those circles so frequently met with in great abundance and contiguous to one another, may have been the habitations of such herdsmen, or sheltering places for their cattle by night – Dartmoor on this supposition must have been well covered with woods for it would otherwise have been highly uncomfortable if not impossible, for those Herdsmen to have taken there a continued residence. Nor from its present denuded state can any fair deduction be made, that it must have at all times been thus waste and devoid of trees – there surely can be no reason for such conclusion if it can be proved, that Hills, more elevated, and more exposed, (now also in the same naked state,) have at a former period been cloathed with Woods. And this I think can be done in the instances of Salisbury plain, and Karnbre Hill in Cornwall. – Stonehenge it seems to be allowed, was a British temple; and if so, every consecrated Edifice, among the Druids was encompassed by a grove *"Nec enim sacra fuit Ædes sine Luco"* – and this is confirmed by tradition – for though the whole plain, (of much greater elevation than Dartmoor) is now, without the vestige of a tree: and in particular not a stump visible in the vicinity of Stonehenge Yet it was once a Forest *"Si fides accolis habenda Qui tractum Sylvestrem in totâ illâ, planitie usque ad Ambresburiam fuisse perhibent"* – Keysler –

In allusion to which Mr West in his poem of the institution of the Garter has this fine passage – " consecrated hills

> *"Once girt with spreading Oaks, mysterious rows*
> *"Of rude enormous Obelisks that rise*
> *Orb within orb, Stupendous Monuments*
> *Of artless Architecture, such as now*
> *Ofttimes amaze the wandering Traveller*
> *By the pale Moon discerned on Sarums plain"*

But the Cornish Hill, was a spot, infinitely less likely to have been crested with a Wood than the plain of Salisbury, or the Forest of Dartmoor: by a quick rise from a valley in which the town of Redruth is situate, Karnbré lifts its summit to a considerable height, buffeted on all sides by storms, and cutting winds, which vent their violence upon it from the British Channel, and the more boisterous Atlantic thus isolated and exposed, it is found to have been the theatre of the British Superstition and to possess most of those Monuments appropriated by the Druids to civil or Religious Uses. – We must therefore in consequence, conclude that these consecrated Rocks, were secluded from the public

Eye by incircling Woods ,and accordingly Dr Borlase tells us "that the Spaces between and below these Monuments were, in the memory of the last generation filled with a grove of Oaks – now (he continues) there are no trees, but the places, where those trees were charked (or burnt into charcoal) are still to be seen".

Having, myself been on Karnbre, I am competent to form comparisons between this Hill and Dartmoor as to their local qualities, and their respective fitness, for the growth of antient Woods, or present plantations, and I cannot hesitate to give my decision in favor of Dartmoor – from the present aspect, of the Forest and the Hill, there appears little to countenance an opinion, that on either of them Trees ever grew – but as we have it ascertained as a recent fact that the latter was at no distant period covered by Groves of Oak – there can be no improbability in supposing that the former, in an earlier age was alike circumstanced.

But superadded to the arguments and the Vouchers which I have offerr'd for substantiating my Hypothesis that Dartmoor was at one time cloathed with woods, I have yet another to produce and that is, in the trunks of Oaks that have not unfrequently been found, among the bogs and the Rivers. – From an intelligent Miner, who had resided many years on Dartmoor, and on its skirts; both on the Western and Eastern parts, I got information that Oaks of different magnitudes had been thus found. That their hue was of a deep black, their texture when first taken from the ground or water, soft; so as easily to be cut or abraded, which after a while grew so hard as to resist strokes made on it with an Axe – that with them hazel bushes had been sometimes found, with vast quantities of nuts; from which circumstance taking it for granted, that they had been thus deposited by the Deluge, he drew a pertinent inference, that this great inundation happened in the commencement of the Autumnal season.

The discovery of trees in Peat bogs, and morasses, has been recorded by many of our Provincial Historians, and, in particular Dr Plott in his "Oxfordshire" adverts to a similar curiosity, of Oaks, Hazel bushes and their nuts being found together under a pond at Watlington Park in vast quantities and high preservation, for he quaintly tells, that the Nuts were sound and hard, "which Times iron teeth had not yet cracked" – He further remarks "that the Wood of the Oak was as black as Ebony, and that at some places they were covered over with a blueish substance much of the consistence of flower of Sulphur, and not much unlike to the finest blue starch" – This observation brings to my remembrance the Experiments made by Dr Watson with green Vitriol on Galls, which gave a purplish or black tint in proportion to the quantity of water by which the mixture was diluted and those, on the bark, the sap, and the Wood, of the Oak, the heart of which, after an infusion into which was poured an equal quantity of a solution of green Vitriol, gave one of the most vivid blues he ever saw: – from such a combination, it may not perhaps be rash to suppose, proceeded the Cæruleum nativum of Dr Plott; and from the operation also of the Vitriolic acid, (but little diluted), on the astringent property of the bark and timber – may, with greater probability be attributed the conversion of the natural brown tint of the wood into black – to the same cause acting upon similar principles, has already been ascribed, the purple and black colour of the Waters on the Moor. –

But to return to the Subterranean trees, – Which being thus found bedded in the bogs of the Moor, are an indubitable proof that they once grew there, and that being laid prostrate by a subsidence of ground, or violence of winds, on the surface of the bog or moss, they were either submerged by their own weight, or overgrown by the rapid accretion of the spongous vegetable.

If I have thus brought a proof that Dartmoor, in its antient title of Forest, had no vague ascription – that it was covered with trees, or at least had considerable woods on it; it may be required that a reason should be assigned why it has suffer'd such a denudation, insomuch, that exclusive of Wistmans wood, there is not a tree to be found on any part of the Forest properly so called.

To speak to the whole of this waste, in its full extent, is more than I shall attempt, much however may be imputed to the quondam Inhabitants, in their Agricultural exertions, and more perhaps, to the profuse consumption of fuel, in the original smelting of Tin ore. "Some late discoveries, says Dr Pryce (where the charcoal, and dross of the metal have been found mixed together) have given us an idea of their process, which was, to dig a hole in the ground and throw the ore on a charcoal fire, which probably was excited by a bellows". Agreably to the simplicity of the times no notion was entertained of confining the fire, to make it act more forcibly on the substance to be smelted: no furnace either simple or reverberatory had ever been made use of – the natural consequences of this were an improvident consumption of fuel, and a great loss in the produce of the Ores.

So long as an undue quantity of Woodland rendered its consumption necessary for the purpose of purifying the air; and to make room for more usefull productions (and such undoubtedly was the situation of this country in the earliest period) so long was it a practice highly commendable to employ the superabundant fuel to so beneficial a purpose; but when we behold a wide and barren waste extending itself throughout the whole Mining district of this County, without a tree to intercept the fury of the wind, we have no reason to commend the prudence of our Ancestors in thus depriving their demesne of its necessary shelter".

What Dr Pryce has thus observed as to the cause of the demolition of Woods in Cornwall, may in every respect, be applied as to their consumption on Dartmoor; the face of the Country about Redruth (where the Doctor lived), and indeed throughout the whole of the Mining district, is, to the full, as wild, and naked as Dartmoor – and if this desolation has been occasioned by the Mines, and smelting the Ores, before the introduction of Coals from the opposite coast of Wales, why may not the deprivation of Woods, (which the Forest has now to deplore) be ascribed to the same source. In former times the Mines in Devonshire, (and these were chiefly confined to the Moor) were more extensive and productive than those of Cornwall: but these in a manner had ceased to be worked about the middle of the last Century when coal was imported into Cornwall for the purpose of Smelting, and the devastation, whatever it was, had by that time been effected.

Having thus endeavored to support my Hypothesis that Dartmoor was in an early period overrun with Wood, and in some degree accounted for their demolition and present deficiency; I shall finish the discussion with a more particular notice of Wistmans Wood to which I have already adverted. – From Crockern Torr it lies directly North at near a mile distance, and is situate on ye slope of a hill rapidly falling to the West Dart, which hurries down a rugged Channel immediately beneath it. – exclusive of this Wood being found in the midst of Dartmoor The trees themselves, in their external appearance, indicating extreme old age, are a most singular curiosity – what their age may be, no records, or tradition are at hand to ascertain; their knarled branches however, hastening visibly to decay, and the Parasitical excrescence, Moss, with which many of the limbs are envelopt, even to the thickness of a foot, are manifest testimonials of their antient birth – perhaps they may have claim to an origin, of a remoter date than that which many Representatives of old families are known to plume themselves on. – I will not say, (whatever reason I might have for so saying) to as little purpose!! the age, the number, and the dwarfish Stature of these trees have given rise to a Witticism which is in the mouth of every Moor man in the neighborhood: "that there are a thousand trees, a thousand years old, and a thousand feet high", by which nothing more is meant than that each tree being a foot high, the aggregate height of the 1000 trees would amount to a 1000 feet.!

Whether Virgil be correct or not when he asserts, that in proportion to the height of the Oak, (however elevated it may be) to as great an extent below ground do its roots stretch themselves: I think there can be little hesitation in holding it for a truth in the present instance, where, from the medium altitude of the Oaks they would not be expected to thrust down into the earth their tap roots more than ten or fifteen feet at the utmost. – Whether it be (however) from this circumstance, or from the huge masses of Granite, which defend, and prop them on every quarter that these trees have been enabled to withstand the rude buffetings and shocks of the Forest winds for so many ages, I am not competent to determine – had the Wood but consisted of the Species of Oak alluded to by Virgil one would almost have imagined that the Poet had it in his eye when he wrote the following beautifull description. –

> *"Æsculus imprimis, qua quantum vertice ad auras*
> *Ætherias tantum radice in Tartara tendit.*
> *Ergo, non hyemes illam, non flabra, neque imbres*
> *Convellunt; immota manet, multosq per annos*
> *Multa Virûm volvens durando sæcula vincit"*
>
> *Georg. –*

It is hardly possible to conceive any thing of the sort so grotesque as this Wood appears, with their branches just spreading themselves over the enormous blocks of granite among which they are intermingled; and their upper lateral roots twisted around their bases, and in the most fantastic wreathings insinuated, whereon a recess, or interstice offered themselves – from the visible decay of their branches, their having long ceased to produce acorns, and the encroachments of the Moss, their destiny seems to be near, and in the 4th part of a Century, they may be conceived to say *"Actum est nobis"* – indeed this Moss, (in the common way so injurious to trees,) must, in the voluminous mass in which it is here found, have hastened on the ruin of the trees; – from the branch of one of them, I peeled of the Moss for a foot or two in length, and having rolled it once round my hands, it wore the appearance, though it exceeded in bulk, the largest Muff that I had ever seen. – among the Oaks, a few shrub like trees of the *"Sorbus Aucuparia"* or mountain ash, and an immense quantity of the Fumaria claviculata (small climbing Fumitory), rather a scarce plant, appeared to diversify the scene: – there was however a sort of solemn awe that pervaded it! Silence seemed to have taken up her abode in this sequestered Wood – and to a Superstitious Mind some impression would have occurred approaching to dread, or sacred horror: –

Though this remark of mine might seem to originate from the gloom, and wild Solemnity certainly brooding on the spot, I am aware at the same time, that it may in part have arisen from what I have heard concerning the notions entertained by the Foresters of this Wood.

Most of those, I believe, who have not to boast that their minds have been enlightened by an intercourse with the towns that at some distance lie around the Moor, speak of this Wood, with an apprehension that cannot be concealed. – there is a bug bear, resident among the recesses of these old trees, which though their Imaginations cannot personify, they yet stand in dread of:

> *"Stat Vetus, et multos incidua Sylva per annos:*
> *Credibile est illi Numen adesse loco"*   *Ovid*

"Nor does it in the least excite my wonder, that so Antient and singular a Wood, situate amongst mountainous hills, in a wild and dreary Country, thinly peopled should have inspired the Inhabitants of their vicinity with some Superstition about it – "In the infancy of the Mind of Man, it has been remark'd, (and whoever has well considered the history of Savage Nations must necessarily assent to the truth of the observation) that a belief in the supernatural agency of Invisible Spirits, has in all ages, and in all countries, been a substitute for Philosophy; known effects, from inattention, or inability, are attributed to sacred or mysterious causes; and indolence is the Nurse of Ignorance: – habituated to delusions which have been transmitted from one generation to another, Mountainers like these on the Forest, hardly dare to think that they can have originated in Superstition, or misapprehension – and in consequence, every uncommon occurrence is looked upon as a deviation from the laws of Nature to which the operation of some unseen Being alone is adequate; – from the same source also are derived those other fantasies, alike visionary, which have an equally strong hold on the ignorant mind and exhibit themselves in the form of omens and Charms. At the fair, at two bridges, I saw an old Rustic with the exuviæ, or skin of a large snake, wreathed as a band round his hat; I had the curiosity to enquire whether he thus wore it for ornament, or use; he replied that he never went without it, for that if by accident he had taken into his flesh, a thorn or prickle, the application of this Snakeskin would operate as a charm, and instantly extract it. If this Man told truth, He could not be altogether a Moor Man; – for if so, as there were no thorns on the Moor, he never could have had an opportunity of putting the virtues of the Skin to a test.

Taking leave of Wistmans wood, or Wishtmans, as it is as commonly called, in which latter appellation, (if the real one,) we may discover an appropriate signification of the opinions entertained of it by the Old Inhabitants of the Moor, Wish't in the provincial dialect being a Synonym to Melancholy or of what one has some sort of apprehension, – for instance – "it is a Wish't place"! – one that I do not care to go to, haunted, or otherwise dangerous: –

I shall now advert to the circles of Stone, which I have before noticed in my way from Tavistoke, near Randals Stone, and which lie between this Wood and Crockern Torr in abundance. – Most of the Reliques of Antient times either in their pecularity of figure, composition, situation, or things that have accompanied them; have afforded some clue to the Antiquary in his researches and have enabled him, if not to determine their absolute designation, yet to throw such light on them, as to bring it within the bounds of rational probability – The Cromlek, Barrows, Rock basons may be produced as instances: On the present subject, as indeed on almost the whole variety of Circles, there is little left but Conjecture; and how unsubstantial a foundation this is, must be well known to those, who have had the patience to labour through the numerous and discordant Hypotheses which have been fabricated by Antiquarian ingenuity, when a subject of discussion has been "*in dubio*".

The appearance of these circles, formed of large stones, and at times connected in the manner of rude walls in a state of dilapidation has suggested the several ideas, of their being Sepulchres of the Antient Britons, inclosures for their flocks and herds, or Houses for their residence: – had there been an Opportunity, I would have ascertained the first Supposition, by getting the areas of some of them dug into – had there been bones, or ashes or utensils discovered in any of them, as has been the case in some of the Stone chests, or Kist vaens (which are also encircled by large single Stones) on the skirts of the Moor, on the Buckland and Widdecombe downs the matter would no longer have remained "*sub judice*" – But as this did not fall within my power, I have nothing left me, but to join issue with those, who have considered them, as remnants of Houses and inclosures. I embrace both conjectures, from the circumstance of the different sizes of the Circles – for though the major part were about 15 feet in diameter, there were several that were at least 60. These last could in no respect have been Houses for no method can be conceived, by which the rude Inhabitants of the Moor could have covered so large an area with a roof. These then I shall suppose were Pens wherein the Cattle during the Night, or very inclement Weather, might be kept both safe and Sheltered. When these inclosures were erected, the flocks and herds had every thing to dread, in these desert, and perhaps Woodland regions – from the Savage Animals that prowled around; The fox and the Bear in those days infested the Island, and the Wolf, their most ravenous foe, was at all times plotting their destruction.

> "*Tum Lupus insidias explorat ovilia circum*
> *Et gregibus Nocturnus obambulat*"   *Georgic:*

As it may well be conceived then that the Herdsmen however bold and vigilant they might be, with the assistance of their Mastiffs, might often times have found it a most hazardous and not unfrequently an impracticable business, to preserve their flocks, from such gaunt and daring assailants; it must, after a time, unavoidably have occurred to them, that to raise stone inclosures, contiguous to their own dwelling Houses, would be the means of providing for them the best security.

Of this description I shall take it for granted were those large Circles, generally found contiguous to the smaller ones, and which upon the same grounds I shall consider as places, of the Herdsmen's abode. Mr Whitaker in his description of the houses of the Britons, tells us "that they were round, the foundation walls of Stone, which supported a sloping roof of Wood formed of Skins, or reeds". This however I should conceive to have been a mode of Architecture, resulting from a state in a degree of civilisation: for in the earliest age of the Aborigines, I cannot give them credit for habitations superior to what a Cavern or huts, wattled with underwood, or twigs and reed and having their interstices filled up with earth, peat or clay as either of these materials were at hand – the appropriate appellation which in one of my dissertations on this subject I had given to these rude fabrics, of Wicker work – has induced Mr Whitaker to make use of language inconsistent with his Character, and that it may be presumed, because the Opinion I had hazarded, but which if occasion served, might be well supported was not perfectly accordant with his own – but the truth is that I think he has mistaken the whole matter. I do not disagree with him that the Britons had their houses of the form and construction which he has conjectured but I think this mode of Architecture was not the Earliest in the Island; it was probably introduced in a second age, when they had a more mechanic knowledge and a greater degree of ingenuity, acquired by observation and a wish for greater comforts. – then perhaps were the round Cabins erected, of which these rude circles may be the remains – and upon these walls of stone a few feet only raised from the ground, roofs may have been formed, like the present ones of the Kamskat kans, of long poles resting their larger ends on the Walls, and converging to a center, over the middle part of the area which they inclosed: and these were doubtless covered with whatever was readiest at hand, and would but answer the intention of providing shelter and security from the Weather; whether it were skins, or reed, or what is most probable, turf. – this last was obvious, and to be had in abundance, and that it will make a good and protecting roof, may be evident, to any one who will give himself the trouble to inspect a couple of Huts, lately erected on the other side of the Cowsick River by the Tavistoke road, whose walls are composed of squares of Peat and their roofs of turf, yet in a state of vegetation and as green as the sod-roofed Houses, recorded by Olaus Magnus to have been in use among the Ancient Goths. He is giving an account of a town straitly besieged by an Enemy – wherein the Citizens being, amongst other Evils, sore oppress'd by famine make a desperate Sally – and meeting with success *suripiunt commeatum, præsertin pecudes, quas secum abductas, in herbosis Domorum tectis pascendas imponunt.*

Among the Memorabilia of these Wars the Grave Archbishop, with the greatest Historical precision, relates how these houses are erected with their vegetable roofs, and how the Cattle are fed on them, but he does not narrate how they are prevented from falling from the high roofs and breaking their bones. The picturesque design at the head of the Section, shews that the roofs were of an inclined plane and rather steep, on which, the herds are seen in the very act of feeding, and such is the accuracy of the representation that

> *Quæ sunt oculis subjecta fidelibus, et quæ*
> *Ipse sibi tradit Spectator*

cannot possibly be misapprehended. I should rather however conceive that the Ingenious Designer must in this respect have committed a blunder – and that instead of giving those Houses a sloping roof, he should be covered them with a flat one. Having finished my discussion of the Houses on the Forest of Dartmoor, I shall again advert to those of Olaus and dignify one of my pages with an extract from his most wonderfull description. He proceeds –

Quod autem in tectis commode pascuntur Pecora, ritus Gothicarum gentium in primis est attendendus. Ædificant enim Domus lapideas, sublimes, ac amplas, ligneasq: quas tignis abietinis, et corticibus arboris betulæ (birch) exquisitâ industria tegunt, terram herbiferam, quadratâ figurâ a campis excisam, superimponentes; quam submisso avenæ vel hordei semine, firmioribus radicibus nectunt; quo fit, ut tecta hujus-modi pratorum virentium speciem et virtutem æmulentur: Sed ne herbæ tectorum, priusquam evellantur, arescant, vicissim cum pluviis, domes-ticâ diligentia aquas asperguntita Neassitas homines fortes instruit, ut supra humanas vires Obsidentibus resistant et illudant; ac penuriam omni contempta adversitate superent.

Of this account We get a confirmation from Dr Withering, who tells Us, that the Norwegians, on the rafters of their houses, place layers of Birch bark, and cover them with green turf three or four inches thick; but as to the sowing on them Oats or barley for a crop, and thereon depasturing Cattle, the Doctor is altogether silent.

From this marvellous Outlandish description I shall again return

"celebrare Domestica facta"

and having begun this long digression from my journal, at or near Two Bridges, I shall there resume it; and this, the rather, as I wish to introduce a view of the Bridge and Inn at Two Bridges from a sketch which I then took of it in the year 1795. In the vicinity of this spot, as I have already noticed, there has been cultivated by its Proprietor Mr Bray of Tavistoke a farm of respectability, whose inclosures, notwithstanding their high situation, are

View entitled 'Bridge and Inn at Two Bridges', dated 1797 (DRO, 564M/F14/141)

found to be as productive, as any on the Moor. The Buildings on this Estate were the only ones in view from two Bridges untill the erection of the present little Inn, which was completed a few years ago, by Sir F. Buller, on the Western extremity of one of his New takes, distant about a mile from Prince Hall.

How well He exerted his judgement in the selection of this particular spot, must be evident to those who have knowledge of the superior beauty and convenience that are attached to it, and are at the same time appraized of the accommodations which, on account of its central situation, it offers to the Traveller taking his way over this long and dreary waste from the several towns of Plymouth, Tavistoke, Ashburton, and Moreton – from the first of which it is distant 16 miles, from the second 8: and from each of the others 12.

The great object with the Judge is the cultivation of the Moor. in this pursuit all his thoughts seem to be absorbed when He is at Prince Hall, and that not more (as I conceive) for the promotion of his own private emolument, than that a great advantage may ultimately accrue from it to the Public.

I shall defer my sentiments, as to the probable practicability of such an Event taking place, to another occasion; and observe in the interim, that the erection of an Inn on such a judicious spot was commencing the plan "*felicibus Auspiciis*" – the Hope to be cherished, is that the Single House, will grow into a hamlet, the hamlet insensibly increase to a Village, and the Village "*longo quanquam intervallo*" raise itself into the importance of a Town. –

In the same ratio as are the advances of the Buildings, so will necessarily be the culture and melioration of the Surrounding ground – were it infinitely more barren than it at present appears to be – did it lie under more disadvantages than it now labours with, (and it must be allowed) that they are not a few) – the industry of Man, stimulated by his Wants, would soon render the former fertile and provide a remedy for the defects of the latter.

Manure, the great desideration, in Agricultural improvements, would be here at hand, in the article of Dung, while the caustic effects of the Winters frosts (now generally fatal to almost all Vegetables,) would be mitigated, and become less severe in consequence of the warmth communicated to the circumambient Atmosphere by the Village, its numerous fires, smoke and the breathings of Men and Animals.

And that this is not the Waking Dream of a mere Projector may, I think, be already evinced, since that during the interval of my last and present visit, another decent House, (A Smiths) and two turf composed Cottages have been erected. Mr Tyrwhytts Seat also, and the Smelting House of the Batchelor Hall mine are but at a short distance; and whilst I was at Prince Hall, the Judge had a proposal made to him by a Gentleman at Tavistoke, which if carried into execution, will have a stronger tendency to expedite the improvement of this part of the Moor than perhaps could have resulted from any other – the purport of the offer was, that, having a particular spot of ground, just below two bridges allotted to him for a lease of lives, the Person (Who was in the Clothing line) would expend the sum of £2000 in the erection of Buildings, and the Establishment of a Factory – that is, a Mill, on the principle of the Arkwright machinery, for the spinning of Wool. Of the Judges acceptance of this offer, I can have no doubt, and should the enterprize take effect to its full extent, the immediate advantages accruing to the Moor, in offerring it here a home Market for its Wool, and procuring the requisite supplies for the subsistence of the Children occupied in the business, would be, I might almost say incalculable!

From the Fair, instituted, by Sir Francis Buller at Two Bridges, (of which the present, was the second anniversary) much benefit, as to the improvement of the breed of Cattle in the neighborhood, and a readier and less expensive, sale, might reasonably be expected; so also, in consequence of this Factory, the flocks of Sheep, fed on the forest would be more attended to, and the fleece taken greater care of. Nor will it be perhaps one of the least advantages resulting from it that the Inhabitants of the Moor thereby gaining a more familiar

View entitled 'chapel for Dartmoor', dated 1798 (DRO, 564M/F14/149)

intercourse with the Farmers of the inclosed Country, will by degrees acquire greater knowledge, and be stimulated to the utmost Exertion. – In the course of conversation also, during my stay at Prince Hall, I understood, that it was intended, as soon as it could be got ready, to offer a Bill for the sanction of Parliament, of which the leading Articles were to be, the Separation of the Forest of Dartmoor, from the Parochial jurisdiction of Lidford and conversion into a Parish of itself – a general Division into farms, and the erection of a Church at Two Bridges. By such a public co operation with the enterprizing schemes of Sir Francis Buller, Mr Tyrwhitt, and Mr Bray, the Entire Town of Two Bridges would make rapid advances to maturity and become a Sun-like Center, from whence the radii of Cultivation would spread themselves around, and by a gradual acquisition of Power, year after year form a more extensive, and discriminated periphery.

From a plan of the intended Church, which I saw at the Judges, I took a copy of the Western Elevation which when built of hewn granite, (its appropriate stone) will be no inconsiderable Ornament to the Moor, and give a greater degree of dignity to the Exercises of Religion, which are now, once a Sunday performed within the unconsecrated and humble Walls of a Barn at the farm of Mr Bray.

I shall now make my return again to Prince Hall where though many an Agricultural improvement had been made, since my last visit, it was obvious there yet remained an ample scope for more: the first Inclosure within the Lodge (lately erected and occupied by Labourers) in which as the Judge told me 14,000 Larch brought from Scotland had failed, and which had then on it a very fine crop of Potatoes, was now in a sad fallow state, being covered over (where the black spungy Earth did not make its appearance) with the larger Senecio, foxglove, Rumex acetosella in great abundance with here and there a thistle; the whole aspect of the field was an indication of the utmost Sterility and wretchedness; the great obstacle at the commencement of melioration of the ground, is its wetness and light spungyness – these render the cultivation by means of the plow almost impracticable: and consequently protract the acquisition of a greensward, which is the grand desideration: – this however had been within the last two years effected, on what had now the appearance of a fine verdant meadow, and as seen from the house, had added greatly to soften, and enrich its view.

The chief instrument in contributing to the improvement of this pasture, was a Stream of Water, which notwithstanding it had been collected from the oozings of a Peat bog had yet, either by pressure, or the conveyance of nutrition to the grass, covered the land with a matted sod, and given it considerable firmness. Water indeed it is well known, is the most effectual Reclaimer of light porous ground – and I conceive, that of whatsoever nature they may be (without they are Chalybeate which are always more or less Enemies to Vegetation) they must be beneficial.

The several modes for converting these loose and springy lands into good pastures, which have had the sanction of the most scientific Agriculturists appear to have been adopted. Mr Tyrwhitt has begun with his grounds, by laying large quantities of granite gravel on the natural superficies – the Judge has rolled his with an immense ponderous roller (it having been ascertained by experiment, that a Body of this kind of three tons and a half weight, incumbent on a square rod, acts just as a Press does on a cheese, and effectually cures a Soil, so remarkable for its retentive quality), and He has also as I have already observed brought a stream of Water over them All of which, have been productive of very visible good effects. – more advantage however might, I think be made of this latter, than at Prince Hall they seem to be aware of – for, if I am not mistaken in the level of the West Dart (from the cursory view which I had of it) it appears to me that many hundred acres of the waste ground above, and on the Farm itself, might be floated with a park, or even (if it were required) the whole of that River, – a few wears would effect this, which while they were contributing to meliorate the pasture would at the same time, create Objects of picturesque beauty, which in the environs of this Forest seat, would doubtless be a desirable acquisition; One or two in particular, half formed to the hand, might be introduced to the front windows of the House, as may be conceived by an inspection of my first sketch of the place which by gaining an accession of consequence, would forcibly attract the eye from thence and every other point where they might be visible.

But, previous to the carrying any of these plans into execution, the preliminary step must be taken of Draining. Without drains to carry off the water, neither condensation by sand, the Roller or by the River, would have any effect – in a country abundant in stone and Peat there can be no difficulty in making such preparations: Granite is always at hand, and there are few parts where peat may not be procured – and had the drains in the front meadow been judiciously formed of this latter material, it would perhaps have had less spunginess than it now possesses. Peat, when dried is of the first excellence for making drains – excepting charcoal no other substance will perhaps be of equal duration: and on this account and where from the quick accretion of extraneous matter or the insinuation of the fibrous roots of vegetables, Drains are subject to be choaked. Dead Peat is of superior value, because its nature is admirably calculated for the percolation of Water.

The consideration that ought to be of chief moment with a Dartmoor Farmer is with the utmost expedition, to clothe his lands with grass. This and Potatoes should be his primary crops – I would have little to do, with Corn, excepting it were for its straw: – the nutrition which the Stalks of Corn derive from so light a soil is neither equal nor permanent – it becomes oftentimes so dry in the summer in consequence of the Exhalations of the Sun and the winds, that it is thereby rendered almost incapable of nourishing any usefull Plant whatever – Sometimes Oats spring up well, and arrive at maturity, forming a good heavy crop, and if the harvest be not late, so as to be affected by Autumnal rains, the Farmer reaps considerable advantage from them. Oftener however, tho it be seen to shoot well into Stalk, it fails of filling the Ear and, withering before there are kernels in the grain, becomes, what is termed a deaf crop. A similar effect from a different cause is not unfrequently met with in strong old ground on its first breaking up. This, I myself experienced, for having converted an Orchard of four acres into arable, as preparatory to laying it down into grass, from a crop of Wheat which most abundantly covered over the whole ground and which had advanced on to maturity in the greatest luxuriance, I did not thrash ten Bushels. – so that I had reason to join in the wish of Virgils Husbandman

> *"ap nimium ne sit mihi fertilis ista*
> *Neu se prævalidam primis ostendat aristis"*

Little then would be my expectations from a Crop of Oats at present – but were the subsoil, which generally consists of a red gravel mingled with a kind of Argillaceous Earth turned up, exposed to the frost and Sun, and then well incorporated and blended with the black light Earth, possibly a good loam might be thus formed that would have consistence to retain a due moisture and strength adequate to the carrying on the grain of any sort of Corn to maturity and excellence: At Mr Tyrwhitts, and at Prince Hall, this subsoil has been brought to day, but neither mixed with the upper black stratum, nor sufficiently long, exposed to the influence of the air, before that it received a plantation of trees. A Year or two will exhibit proof of the experiment. In the interim I confess that I have my apprehensions: for exclusive of this circumstance, I cannot but think, that every Seedling that is planted on Dartmoor, should not only be raised on the Moor, but planted on the same soil, (or better if procurable) than that on which the Seeds first vegetated. This was the Error which became the instrument of failure to the 14,000 larch, which, I have before noticed, had been brought originally from Scotland, and planted in one of the largest inclosures.

He therefore who shall plant on Dartmoor, let him first ponder well, the admonition of the great Georgical Poet who says

> *"At si quos haud ulla viros Vigilantia fugit*
> *Ante, locum similem exquirunt; ubi prima paretur*
> *Arboribus seges, et quo mox digesta feratur:*
> *Mutatam ignorent subito ne Semina Matrem"*
>
> *Georg. lib 11*

At Prince Hall there are two or three inclosures, in the whole not an acre, which are occupied by Plantations – one of them near the New barn and Farm offices, is of 20 years standing – there may be from ten to twenty firs, chiefly spruce and Larch, which have the appearance of being about 6 years old, tho' several have leaders, shot out very lately above a foot in length – *sed hæ nugæ*! Was Prince Hall mine, and had I, with the spirit of Enterprize that actuates the Judge, the same ability, I would proceed on a larger scale, – I would devote the whole of the grounds that rise behind the house to Plantations – and my plan should be this: having incorporated the subsoil, with the upper black earth, and burnt whatever there might be of vegetable matter intermixed, I would let it be exposed to the Summers Sun, and to the frosts of a Winter – in the interim I would raise (with masses of Granite, and with the aforesaid mingled mass of Earth, clay, and gravel), large Mounds, similar in every respect to a double Devonshire hedge, which should thwart the grounds in such a direction as to be opposed to the violence of the S.West Winds – to these at but a short distance others should run parallel so as to give the whole, the appearance of a vast entrenchment, fortified with high Valla and deep fossés. – on the summits of these mounds which for the better protection of the plants should be scooped to the depth of two feet, I would with seedlings of Oak, Ash, Willow, Sycamore, larch, Scotch fir and Mountain Ash, sow the seeds of the same trees – thus an experiment would be made on a variety of Plants, and the sorts that seem'd best to be assimilated to the Soil and to have born the brunt of the Storms I would propagate in larger quantities, that they might supply the failure of the rest. In the inclosures formed by these Mounds I would raise thick Plantations which at first should be my seminary – from thence I would gradually and equally draw those supplies for the tops of my hedges; thus the Plantations would successively become thinned – at least so far as that no one Plant should detract from the nutrition of another.

On my first visit to Dartmoor this struck me as being the most effectual mode of commencing Plantations, especially in the immediate environs of such a Seat as Prince Hall: and I am confirmed in this my opinion, by the corresponding Sentiments of the Agriculturist Mr Marshall, who in his view of Dartmoor discussing the subject, observes "that such a Mound, (nearly at least as I have described) is an immediate fence and Shelter; and the coppice wood as it grew up could not fail, from its relative height above the subjoining lands to improve their Climature; and encourage in a particular manner the "growth of herbage" beside being at the same time singularly friendly to pasturing Stock." Mr Marshall is here speaking of the general improvement of the Moor, and at the close expresses his doubts "whether the expence of raising these high mounds would not overbalance the advantages that might be expected from them:" – I do not hesitate in the least to say that it would very far exceed them, but this tho' an unsurmountable objection in the large scale of improvement would have little weight with any one who had at heart the melioration of his own Farm and especially the immediate environs of his house, whereby He might obtain, amid so bleak an exposure, protection and comfort.

Still however these, and all other attempts for the improvement of particular spots, will, I am persuaded be abortive, or answer only to a certain degree, unless the Whole or the greater part of the Moor be drained, or deprived of its superficial Water. Whoever has explored the Forest must know that there is scarcely a spot not in culture, that is not saturated with Water – hence arise thick Vapours, at almost every season of the Year, and the cold which is their natural consequence becomes in the Winter, so severe, as to destroy almost every thing that has vegetable life. The Moormen call this frozen Vapour, rime, which they say has the same effect on plants as if they had been scorched by fire. indeed it has been ascertained that the extremes of heat and cold are productive of like sensations – the one burning as the other, a contact as it were of dissimilar Powers conjoined in the same circle. But these Mists, though they are thus at times found noxious to Plants, have no deleterious effect on the Inhabitants of the Moor: the atmostsphere to them is salubrious, whether it be light or dense; dry or impregnated with moisture; Exhalations that arise from Fens and marshes are always injurious, bearing with them pestiferous miasmata; but I understand that the Vapours that are exhaled from Peat bogs, are very different from these, though the great chill that is frequently felt on Dartmoor, and especially after a hot day, and thick fogs, may give occasion to Persons to entertain notions of their being unwholesome.

But this Cold is caused by quick Evaporation of the Water through this porous spongy soil, for nothing generates cold like Evaporation; and as the air incumbent on Peat bogs is very dense, it of course holds more water in solution than a more rarefied air, which Water being dissolved by the heat is in the cool of the Evening precipitated; and thereby Mists are formed. Monday, (on the Evening of which I reached Prince Hall,) had been at times exceedingly hot. The whole of the day that I had past in the Vallies had been clear and cloudless, but while I traversed two or three of the last miles of the mountainous heights, I perceived in different parts grey Mists which had begun to sweep along the distant summits. It was rather cold when I dismounted from my horse and when introduced to the Parlour, I was not displeased at the sight of a chearfull Peat fire; I had sat but a short time, when on looking towards the Windows, I perceived that they were rendered so opake by the condensation of the internal air in consequence of an increasing Cold without, that no object, neither the distant Hill, nor the nearer meadow could be distinguished; and this I found also to be the case, in my bed room, where no fire had been lighted. the Windows were there also spread over by a thick adhesive film, which having originated in the precipitated Vapours of the Evening, had pervaded every room in the house, and had suffered condensation on the Glass as being there more easily, and more visibly affected by the Night cold, than elsewhere.

From hence, and from what I have before observed on the subject, I infer, that without the Moor be drained in a great degree of its superficial waters so that the source of this vast evaporation be destroyed and the pernicious Cold, its natural consequence; but little reasonable Expectation can be formed that its Climature will be ameliorated, so as to admit other crops than those which are at present in use, or that even these will be brought onward to an earlier maturity.

Under the subsisting inconveniences, it seems to me that the measures that have been adopted to alleviate them, that of converting as speedily as possible the lands into Herbage, are the best that can be devised. – Several of the Meadow pastures, and the artificial grass lands, on Prince Hall farm would be considered as creditable to many of the best Estates in the South Hams. For these, a top dressing is used of Peat ashes, for the burning of which Sir F. Buller has erected a Kiln on a peat bog South of Crockern Tor with contiguous Sheds, for preserving them from the influence of the weather; I did not understand however that Experience of their effects had brought them into high estimation. As these indeed differ in proportion to the degree of Strength possessed by the Alcaline Salts of the Ashes, so it remains to have it ascertained by experiment, what quantity the Lands would require so as to derive from them the greatest possible advantage. In Berkshire They enter much into its Husbandry: insomuch that near Newbury an acre of Peat to be burnt and used as manure is considered as being worth from 50£ to 100£. These are found to answer well as a top dressing on Clover Saint foin and other grasses, but caution must be taken in their application, for as they are of a hot and corrosive nature, if lain on, as soot, in a large quantity and thick on the herbage, it will be infallibly destroyed.

In contradiction however to this practice, so general in Berkshire and Hampshire, Lord Dundonald condemns the usage of burning the peat, affirming that a great deal of its most useful parts are thus dissipated and converted into Vapour and gases.

Still he holds it to be good manure, if in its crude state, it be mixed with Lime completely slaked under cover, in the proportion of six pounds of peat moderately humid to one of Lime. in this state the heat generated will be moderate, and never sufficient to convert the peat into a carbonaceous matter, or to throw off in a state of fixable air, the acids therein contain'd – As this Mixture for top dressing pasture ground is particularly recommended by his Lordship, it would certainly be worth while to make an experiment of it on Dartmoor, if it were only to ascertain the comparative effects of this preparation with the Ashes.

Every hint should be caught at by the Farmer, Especially in these parts, that might be the means of introducing to them a new manure. While discussing this subject one Evening with Mr Crook, having adverted previously to the inhospitable Climature for the keeping on the Moor, sheep or Cattle during several of the Winter Months, I said, that as the Potatoe plant seemed to be more than any other assimilated to the Moor, and to be in general productive, that had I the farm of Prince Hall, I would erect a very large Piggery, which having consumed the Potatoe crop and attained some maturity, should be annually sold to the Drover – thus (I continued) without the trouble and expence of carriage, I should have great profit returned for my potatoes, and with the aid of Oat straw, I might be able to collect an immense quantity of Manure. "Sir (says He) I approve of your scheme vastly, and think it might turn to the best account; but, in the construction of the Styes, I would have a flue to run through the chief Wall, which might communicate warmth to Styes that might be erected on each side: Warmth "Sir is of the first importance' it is as necessary to an Animal as his food, and there is none perhaps to whom it is more delightful than to Swine;" – however fanciful this addition to my proposed plan may appear, I am convinced it would be not less excellent than feasible; I think it has been observed that in Scotland (where in the country Hovels the Poultry roost in the Kitchen, and in common with the human Inhabitants partake of the influence communicated by the Hearth fire), the Hens are in a constant routine of laying Eggs during the Whole year and it is a truth generally allowed, that the effect of considerable cold is to check Animal as well as vegetable growth; Here therefore it would be essentially requisite, where during the Months of Summer a fire is not unwelcome, and in those of Winter, the Cold without a counteracting power to those who have not been inured to it, would be intolerable: Here doubtless the artificial warmth of a flue, attempered and regulated by a thermometer would be, As Mr Crook observed, of the first importance – and in carrying it into execution, there would be but little draw back in point of expence. Stones rise on the spot, and the fuel will be administered by every Peat Bog.

But then as to the Manure, it may be asserted by those who are well versed in the lore of Antient Agriculture, that tho Ashes may be allowed to be good dressing, the soil from Pigs is not: and to confirm this their assertion they will of Course quote Palladius, who in his Chapter "*de Sterquilinio*", after numbering up the several composts, concludes at last "*Porcinum pessimum: Cineres optimi:* But with the utmost deference to the superior information and experience of Palladius I cannot but conceive, that this is one of the best possible Manures for cold wet lands, and this opinion (by any person who will take the trouble of inspecting them) will be found corroborated in several parts of the "*Bath Agricultural Memoirs*".

But on the supposition that the Soil from the Piggery was not of the first quality, where almost every kind of manure was wanting, this would necessarily be in request. The Earths in general naturally supply but little pabulum to the few indigenous plants that vegetate on them – I find that the black peaty one on this farm spontaneously produces the Rumex acetosella (Sheeps sorrel) and a Polygonum "*the Persicaria vulgaris*" (common Arsmart) – from which last plant, taking a hint, I should make an Experiment, and by analogous reasoning, having sown the seed of the Fagopyrum, (Buckwheat) which is of the same Class 'Octandria trigynia) should expect to reap a good crop. What the natural produce of the reddy subsoil would be has not yet been ascertained. I was told as a singular circumstance, that though both the black and red Earths individually were dead to the action of acid of Vitriol, yet that when mixed an effervescence would be created: the Experiment was made – and in their union I could barely perceive a faint ebullition. – On some other parts of the Moor however in addition to these, and a fine clay which I saw near Mr Greys subterrane, I learnt that there was a loamy soil, sometimes discovered of a depth adequate to any sort of Culture, and which perhaps, if the situation would admit might be found to make returns more answerable to the expence laid out on them, than the peaty grounds.

Messrs Frazer and Marshall, in their surveys of Dartmoor though they join issue, as to the vast advantage that would accrue to it, if by means of Canals a communication was opened between it and the lower lands, yet have no agreement as to the profit derived from it, in depasturing Sheep and Cattle. In the article of Sheep the Farmer thinks it "a most unprofitable species of management, so much so, that He says the most intelligent Farmers in the neighborhood have given up the practice altogether, convinced from experience "that it is infinitely more profitable to keep a less stock well on their own inclosed grounds." to support him in this assertion, he appeals to Messrs Ball and King, two Persons very respectable in this line, whose estimates certainly give it strength and plausibility – and the deduction which He draws is "that those rights of common on Dartmoor as far as they respect Sheep, are by no means profitable to those Who exercise them, and that a good Farmer would not make use of them, even if he had it in his power." The subject was touched on, the Wednesday (which was the day of the Fair) after dinner at Prince Hall, where among a number of reputable Farmers was present Mr King who, though the major part of the company were his opponents, gave a statement similar to what Mr Frazer has done, and said that he had formed his opinion, from conviction on the result of his Experiments.

In regard to Cattle, Mr F. continues "There are still Many who send cattle to pasture on the Forest, particularly in very dry Summers, when their low lands are short in grass – but the reasoning held, respecting stocking with Sheep, applies in every respect with more force to Cattle. The Best Farmers send none".

We will now hear a word or two from Mr Marshal, a Pleader on the other side of the question: Having stated the use the Moorside Farmer made of the Forest, by pasturing his flocks and young herds on it during the Summer, He observes "The Present Value of these Lands appears from this general view of their application to be far from inconsiderable. I had not an opportunity of estimating the aggregate of the Stock they support, but an eye accustomed to observations of this nature may readily discover that in a Political light, these uncultivated lands are at present of some Estimation; for admitting that a Moorside Farmer by the Assistance of these lands in supporting his stock nine or ten Months of the Year, is enabled to rear, and forward to market, twice the number of Cattle and Sheep (or even one fourth of such additional number) than He could without their assistance – the aggregate increase of produce to the community would be found on calculation, to be worthy of public regard."

"*Non Nostrum inter Vos tantas componere lites*
Et Vitulâ Tu dignus, et Hic" –

I have indeed but little to remark on the subject – so far indeed I can say upon the assurance of Mr Crook, that the Scotch Cows, which had depastured during the Summer wholly on Smith's New take which he rented at 40£ pr ann. from the Judge, were found (when driven to be sold at the Fair) to be nearly fat; – an inference also may be drawn in favor of the pasture of the Moor, from the price which so experienced a Farmer gives annually for his new take; – nor can I ever be persuaded, but that, during the Months, when his fields are lain up and cropped with Hay and corn, it must be highly advantageous for the Moorside Farmer to unstock his inclosures, and permit his store flocks and herds to graze at large on a Down so abundant with Herbage where they subsist without expence, and where, if they do not get fat, they most assuredly increase in growth and strength; –

If in cultivated lands subsistence can be procured for a number of sheep or Cattle equal to what are maintained on the Moor, there cannot be a doubt but the returns made from them would be attended with the greatest emolument. it follows not however, that from the others no profit would be derived! – The Antient Herdsmen and Shepherds of the Moor doubtless drew no small advantage from their Herds and flocks – and they had no inclosures, no cultured grounds for the purpose, no sheds perhaps for protection: their system and usage was as that of the Numidian flocks – "

"*Sæpe diem, noctemq, et totum ex ordine mensem*
Pascitur, itq pecus longa in deserta sine ullis
Hospitiis; tantum campi jacet"   *Georg. 3d*

I shall now finish my Agricultural discussions on which I have perhaps too long expatiated: exclusive however of the last topic they have been fixed on Subjects, untouched, or but slightly by Mr Marshal's or Frazer's pens, and may therefore serve as Addenda to their Surveys of Dartmoor, which are fraught with ingenious remarks and most valuable information.

I shall now turn to some of its Natural productions, its Minerals I have already brought forward, and in regard to its Fossils, but little, that has fallen within my notice, is worthy recording.

On Dartmoor the fossil that obtrudes itself almost in every part on our notice is the Granate – with this the tops and sides of Hills are thick studded, and this, from its being invariably found on wastes and Moors, is universally called Moorstone. Those torrs which give so wild and Romantic an air to the summits of the Eminences are, without doubt terminating parts, or apices of immense strata which at times spread themselves under the surface of the Earth – the detached masses (which, scattered on the slopes of hills give the country so barren and rugged an aspect) appearing, As I have before observed, to be nothing else than a sort of Shode stones, separated from the vast Mass above them.

The sort chiefly met with, and predominant at Prince Hall is of a greyish ground, charged with cockle, a few micæ, and with large toothed, oblong bodies of quartz, – there are other kinds found however on different parts of the Moor, and probably indeed all those varieties which that able Naturalist Saussure discovered on the Alps. of this Stone, all the rude Monuments of Druidical Superstition in these Western parts of England are formed – the Cromlêks, Logan stones, rock basons, idols, Kist vaêns; and in the present times, at least On the Forest and its Environs it is applied to the erection of Houses Churches Bridges, and those stupendous Walls which form its inclosures – too often also they constitute the chief part of the Roads, which, when the gravel that had been lain over them, has been driven off by the violence of Winds and Waters, appear rough and prominent and render travelling on them both incommodious and dangerous. – When this gravel has been spread to a sufficient depth, perhaps it forms a road which for compactness and a smooth surface is not to be equalled, most assuredly not exceeded, in the world. – This gravel is found on every part of the Moor, on the high, as well as the low grounds – which seems to counteract the commonly–received notion of a decomposition from the Granate Stone. Dr Borlase certainly coincides in this opinion, for he says "I should imagine these Sands to be natural (that is instead of having been dissolved or fretted from blocks of Stone) and some of the Primary concreted materials of which Moorstone appears to have been formed: and that Moorstone consists only of the same grit, cemented into Stone by a Crystal basis. – that the basis, which forms all stone was more abundant below in the bowels of the Earth, than near the surface; and that from a deficiency of this Cement near the Surface, as well as the interfering powers of air heat and cold, this sandy grit never was fixed into Stone, but always remained in its present incoherent state." Where so admirable a material is every where at hand it seems somewhat extraordinary that the great roads over the Moor should be in so neglected a state. – Old Cator no longer farms them at an annual stipend, but repairs them, when set to him, by the yard – the only part of the road now in order, is that, of near a mile in length (which extends from the Lodge at Prince Hall, to Two bridges, and this is of the first excellence – besides the granate there is another Stone frequently found, scattered about in nodules of no bulk, black and grey of a very hard nature in which large masses of opaque Chrystal or Quartz are generally embodied. I have heard it also asserted that 'Schist' is frequently met with on the Moor and that Lava having there likewise been found, it must have proceeded chiefly from a fusion of this Stone. – tho I will not positively contradict the reality of either of these discoveries, I will say that there do not seem to me any good grounds for even suppositions of this nature, and that at the several times in which I have been on the Moor I have neither seen, nor heard of either Schist or Lava's being found. – That Schist, (as has been of late remarked in Scotland) may pass under the granate is very probable, and indeed on one of Moors on the Western side of the Forest in the parish of Sampford Spiney, Schist has been found as if proceeding from Dartmoor, at the depth of five or six feet – but, as is observed in Goughs 2d Edition of Camden "in no part has it been traced to any considerable extent, or considered so minutely, as to enable us to draw any conclusions from it respecting the origin of either Stone."

From this Parish of Sampford I had brought me some years ago by a Miner (who has long had the management of my roads and Water works) a Mass of Chrystal, singular in its form, and very beautiful in its appearance. It was discovered by him on Sampford, (an Estate the property of Mr Hall of Manadon) connected with the moor, in fissures of Rock, extremely hard and of an iron cast, filling these fissures up, from one to nearly five inches in breadth; its exterior part approaches towards an Hexagon, tho' not generally, or regularly so; whence it should seem that this Chrystal had a tendency to form Pyramidal bodies, but was prevented from shooting into regular ones by the quantity of terrene particles with which it was debased: The planes of this Hexagon are of different breadths, length's and inclinations, yet, tho' not determinate in form, unite in a blunted apex; the basis is a white opaque Chrystal or Quartz.

The beauty of this Chrystal consists in a purplish metallic tint, which bears a strong resemblance to the gem, and particularly emulates the Amethyst; this however is not equally diffused thro' the whole Mass, but commencing at its base with a lighter tint, grows deeper the further it recedes till it acquires a cast of the darkest purple. – Sometimes it is found in detached Masses (as in a piece in my possession, where among other rude and imperfect forms, a congeries of Hexagons clustered together on the surface, and of various sizes may be distinguished:

In a perpendicular Section of this specimen there appear to divide these purplish Strata (for sometimes these crusts or strata are double, triple, or of more successive Orders of different breadth's throughout) Veins of the white opaque Crystal; which partaking of the inequality of the Stone to which the Crystal is affixed, and of the arrangements of the several Hexagonal prominencies on the superficies (which tho' forming one Whole are obscurely and irregularly striated towards a center) do not run in a uniformly transverse order but in general extremely slanting, wavy, and oblique exhibiting salient acute angles, some projecting considerably more than others, and displaying a curious, and at first sight an apparently exact ichnography of one of Monsr Vaubans fortifications. This Chrystal breaks rough and uneven, is hard, heavy, not easily scratched, and admits of an indifferent polish. it strikes fire with steel; – doth not calcine in the fire; – doth not ferment with Aqua fortis. In the experiment I made on it in the crucible the only effect produced was a deprivation of colour.

January 12 1798
John Swete
Oxton House

JOURNAL SEVENTEEN

Devon Record Office, 564M/F15

Journal Seventeen continues the Reverend's Swete's tour on Dartmoor in which he discusses at great length the nature of Dartmoor. He travelled across the moor from Sampford Spiney to Ashburton where he stayed at his former home which had been converted to an inn, now the Golden Lion. He shortly afterwards returned to Oxton. The journal ends with a discussion of places along the Exe estuary.

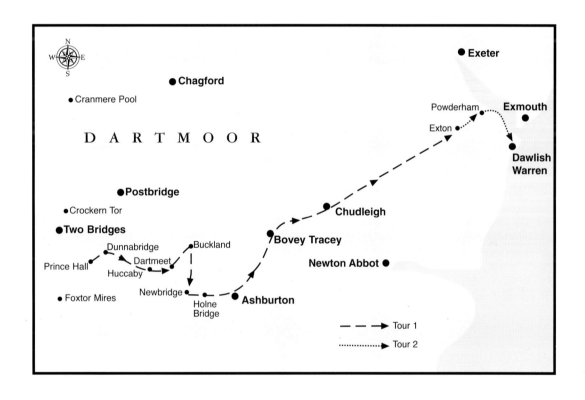

PICTURESQUE SKETCHES
OF DEVON

John Swete,
Oxton House
January 12th. 1798.

Continuation of the Tour to Dartmoor

This Parish of Sampford Spiney seems to abound with Minerals, and curious fossils: for besides the Amethystine Crystal, among the Cobalt (already noticed) were found a quantity of other Crystals (upward of a thousand,) of regular forms, being all of a short thick column with tapering pyramidal ends; they were composed of eighteen planes, six on each of the Pyramids, and six on the columns. The Specimen given me by my old Miner is in form and size like this icon. And seems to be the *Brachy-telo-stylum* of *Hill pyramidibus brevibus, columnâ brevissimâ*; differing however in this particular that throughout the whole body both of Column and pyramids, the Planes in dimensions of width and length regularly answer each other. Crystals of this species are (tho' found in Germany and the East Indies) rarely discovered in England – they are always met with (as in the present instance) in parcels in the same place, generally separate and single, tho' sometimes a few of them, cohering with one another. That which I have is crusted over, but they are in common beautifully transparent, and of extreme brightness – so hard as not be scratched, freely giving fire with steel, and not fermenting with *Aqua fortis*.

Having thus given an account of the different Fossils that occurred to my notice, the produce of Dartmoor and the circumjacent Commons, I shall next advert to the Plants which I observed there, of which the greater part if not all, are indigenous.

The first, as seeming most to claim attention is *Eriophorum – Gramen junceum Canatum of Park* – Cana or Cottongrass. This is a kind of Grass which grows on most of the Morasses of the Kingdom – its stalk is of the reedy nature, and it carries a tuft of down very much resembling Cotton – in the isle of Skie poor people stuff their pillows with the down and with its pith make wicks of Candles. – A Gentleman whom I met at Prince Hall asserted that a Waggon load of it might be gathered near the Moor farm of Cater in the parish of Widecombe. if so, when the spinning Mills shall be erected at Two bridges, it may be an object (of curiosity at least to have it Manufactured.

It is excessively White, and consequently often introduced by the Northern Bards, in their similies concerning the beauty of Women – thus Ossian "if on the heath she moved, her breast was whiter than the 'down of Cana" - (*Triandria Monogynia*)

2 *Myrica – Gale*, Dutch Myrtle, it grows in boggy grounds and diffuses to a distance a most agreeable fragrance. The catkins boiled in water throw up a waxy scum which, if gathered in sufficient quantities would make Candles. – This is of the Class – *Diæcia tetragynia*

3 *Anthericum Ossifragum* – Bastard Asphodel – of a greenish yellow tint, sweet smelling, grows on turf bogs. *Hexandria, Monogynia*: – August

4 *Campanula Hederacea* – Ivy leaved Bellflower, Wet places. *Pentandria, Monogynia*.

5 *Fumaria claviculata* – climbing Fumitory, a rare plant except in Devon. Here

found frequent, and in great abundance in Wistmans wood. – *Diadelphia, Hexand*:

6 *Erica Vulgaris, Erica cinerea, Erica tetralix* – the three only Heaths discovered in this County.

7 *Potentilla reptans* – creeping Cinque foil

8 *Polygonum – Persicaria* – common Arsmart.

9 *Rumex acetosella*, small sheeps sorrel

10 *Senecio viscosa major*; large stinking groundsel

11 *Sphagna varia:* Mosses, Lichens!

12 V*accinium – Vitis idæa, fructu nigricante*, common Whortleberry. I met with them among the rocks on the highest and most exposed torrs.

13 *Rubus. idæus fructu rubro.* Raspberry, found in Mr Saunders Wood at Brimpse. We had a large plate, full of this fruit, somewhat smaller than the garden ones. As a Moor desert one day at Prince Hall, – a present from Brimpse! *Icosandria – Polygynia. –*

The Chamæmorus Cloudberry, which grows on Peat mosses – (of this Class and Order) might be expected to have grown on the bogs of the Forest – they have not however been discovered on it. – Mr Clack however has intimated to me that there is a Plant, apparently a Heath which bears a berry, and which grows on the part of the Moor, West of the town of Chagford – these berries, he says, are gathered and sold to Apothecaries at Moretonhampstead, who apply them to Medicinal uses. – to my enquiries about them on the Moor I could get no kind of information, – and I cannot conceive what the Plant may be – without it shall prove, the Heath *Andromeda – Daboæcia – Erica Cantabrica flore maximo – Raii: – Vaccinnium Cantabricum* = Hudson: or Irish Whorts. The fruit of this is a Capsule with four cells and four valves – it hath all the appearance of the Gardrobe (:*Andromeda*) but the numbers of the Heath thus Withering who observes also that it grows in spongy wet uncultivated soils: – *Decandria, Monogynia.*

14 *Genista spinosa vulgaris* – Furze on the lower parts of the Moor.

There are besides these to be met with of the tree kind – *Quercus* = Oak. – *Fraxinus* = Ash – *Sorbus Aucuparia*, Mountain Ash – and one or two Salices: –

These are All the Plants which occurred to my notice on Dartmoor that I made a memorandum of, or can call to my recollection. As to animated Nature I have very little indeed to capitulate: – Trouts and Eels are abundant in both the Darts, for want however of the quantity of nutritious pabulum which is met with in streams slowly winding through loamy meadows, they are in little estimation – Salmon, after its wonted, though almost incredible exertions is frequently found within the confines of the Moor, having forced its way thither up a thousand rapids, and over innumerable ledges of rocks on the sandy shallows to deposit her spawn – but She is often intercepted in her course by the fly or spear of the Moormen, the generality of whom use both with an adroitness that can only result from frequent practice. Quadrupeds are confined to a very few species: of Foxes there are a few that haunt the torrs: Hares at times in plenty – Rabbits, none "*feræ naturæ*". there are two Warrens however well-stocked with them.

In foxtor Meers there is a large pool much resorted to by Wild ducks, and other aquatic fowls – the Snipe, breeds here, and is found at every season of the year. – the Ring-ouzel also, "*Merula torquata*" here forms her nest and rears her Young, making her arrival in this wild region during the Month of March and emigrating from it again towards the North of the Kingdom about the latter end of September. – As they are found also on the peak of Derbyshire, it should seem that they have a predilection, for barren mountainous regions, where it is most probable they meet with their food in greatest abundance. In Derbyshire they are called Tor Ouzels, but on Dartmoor their common appellation is, Maryland Tor quakers: a strange assemblage of words, for which I cannot account without it be a corruption of "*Merulæ Torquatæ*" which it strikingly resembles; and if this be not its "*Etymon*" it must be owned, there is a whimsical coincidence.

My Forester, from whom I collect my information tells me, that it is a fine-tasted Bird, of a dusky greyish colour, with a white streak under its throat, – from which description, and the circumstance of its frequenting the torrs, I should have conceived it to have been "*the Merula Saxatilis*" had this ouzel ever been seen in England.) He tells me likewise that it is somewhat larger than a black-bird, And that when it first reaches the Moor, it has so little shyness that he has frequently knock'd it down with a stone; "the whole of this account corresponds with the several details on the subject given Us by that minute though agreeable Naturalist Gilbert White in his history of the Parish of Selborne, where in his 38th letter he says 'Come from whence they will (whether from the North of Europe or the northern parts of this island) it is plain from the fearless disregard that they shew for Men or guns, that they have been little accustomed to places of much resort. Navigators mention that in the isle of Ascension, and other such desolate districts, Birds are so little acquainted with the human form, that they settle on Men's shoulders; and have no more dread of a Sailor, than they would have of a goat that was grazing. On Dartmoor (and indeed from Mr Whites observation) it appears that they congregate in flocks or coveys. From whence it should seem that their nature is more assimilated to the fieldfare and Redwing of the class of Turdi, than of the thrush or black bird.

I shall close this little list of Animated Nature with the Alanda, (sky lark) which I shall introduce here more on account of a very pretty Sonnet that was written on one which had take up her abode on the Forest than as considering it a Denizen here, who, winging the liquid air might transport herself in a few minutes from these upper regions to the more frequented scenes beneath.

The Author, (an old acquaintance), seems not to have had the most distant idea, that, from so desolate and barren a tract as Dartmoor, so much entertainment could have been reaped, as has fallen to my lot to enjoy, whether in my visits to its bogs, and rivers and rocks, or in scribbling thus their description – these were his reflexions! "The Genius of this place wears a settled and eternal frown; Barren, rocky, savage, the wearied eye recoils from the waste, but the active mind yet urges it to roam along, to try if hill, or dale can afford it one intervening charm to rest upon – but in vain!!

The Lark was the only pleasing object I beheld, and his song was the more welcome, as being a sprightlier strain than I could hope to hear in so deserted and leafless a region. His having communicated the only pleasing sensation I felt in a progress of 18 miles over Dartmoor gave birth to the following effusion.

Sonnet
To the Lark on Dartmoor

"*Sweet soaring Minstrel of the wild, I hear*
    The pleasing music of thy tunefull throat
As welcome o'er the desart to mine ear
    As to benighted kinds the matin note;

I thank thee, Warbler, for thy cheering lay; –
    But why in such a barren lonely dell
While other Scenes the vernal sweets display
    A wing'd recluse, art thou content to dwell.

O' yet I trace the motives in thy song,
    For freedom now the lofty burden bears,
And now a tenderer strain is pour'd along
    And love is breathed with all its charming cares;
"Thus, though ev'n here sequester'd, dost thou prove
    Life's dearest blessings, Liberty, and Love".

Having thus long expatiated on the nature and productions of the Forest of Dartmoor, and exhausted the memoranda I made at Princes Hall; ere I take my departure from it, by way of giving a kind of finish to the sketch, I shall add a few observations, of a general cast, which will be chiefly drawn from the Surveys of the Moor, taken by Messrs Marshal and Frazer.

As to its Extent, there is a wide difference between the two: The Former computing it at more than 200-000 acres, the Latter at 80-000, or at the utmost 100-000. To this last calculation, (whether erroneous or not) I cannot say (The Country has commonly assented; – and from such concurrence of opinion there is greater probability of collecting truth, than from vague conjecture.

Mr Marshal's reasoning is from a circle of twenty miles diameter, which comprizing at least 300 square miles of Surface (he observes) will amount to more than 200-000 acres. but in this computation, it should not be suppress'd, that he includes all the open lands in this part of Devon.

As to Elevation He gives no definite idea. He says "the Sea washing the foot of the mountain, its positive height is inconsiderable, compared with that of many less Mountain-like Masses which occur in the most central part of the Island". Where however a height has not been ascertained by the accuracy of Geometrical observation, some sort of calculation may be formed – from the extent and current of the Rivers that have their source in it: and the ratio of this latter will be in proportion to the rapidity of its descent.

From Cranmere pool about 8 or 10 miles north of Prince Hall spring the Dart and the Okement – they both take a contrary course – the latter towards the Bristol channel – the former to the English. This eminence may therefore be considered as one of the highest on the Forest. And the Dart pours from his urn a full stream of waters, which hurry on tumultuously foaming over their rocky beds, till they arrive at the level track between Buckfastleigh and Staverton – where receiving a check to the violence of their career they after-wards glide on gently for the remainder of their course. Notwithstanding this, the height of Cranmere is by no means so considerable, as, may from hence be imagined, for Mr Frazer says "The Sources of these Rivers are computed to be not more than 8 or 900 feet above the level of the Sea" – on what authority Mr Frazer vouches this computation, I have not heard, but it must be a palpable error indeed, if it be true, (As there is a circulating report) that Mr Mudge has ascertained its extremest height to be no less than three thousand, instead of 900 feet. In respect to the tenure of property, or the peculiar priviledges which some Proprietors of Forest lands possess I shall briefly remark "that those who have a right of common are called Venville Tenants, or sec Risdon "Fen field" – These pay an acknowledgment of three pence a year for as many Sheep as they chuse to send, and two pence a head for Cattle. – But from those not in venville, it is customary for the Lessee to take for cattle, one shilling or one and sixpence pr head and one shilling for every score of sheep. – and the whole of the Revenue arising from hence to the Prince does not amount to more than £43 pr ann. Another Priviledge, which is restricted to those who are Proprietors of Antient tenements, (which in the whole are 37 and half) is of a very singular nature. Upon Death, or alienation these consider themselves entitled to what is called a New-take, which upon application to the Reeve and Jury, is set out on any part of the Moor that shall be selected; of this the strict allowance is but eight acres. – but as the specification of these is 'that they shall be free of rock and bog" it has not unfrequently happened, that the eight acres have risen to several hundred." In consequence of the idea entertained of such encroachments, much obloquy has been attached to a few of the chief Proprietors – the matter it seems has been taken up by the Princes Council, and I understand *"ne quid detrimenti in futurum capiat Foresta"*. Such claims are to be altogether abolished.

On this head Mr Frazer declares himself indignant. A few years ago, who ever thought of Dartmoor that it was considered as an unproductive waste, and that it would be but a step removed from Madness or idiotism, for any Person to attempt its cultivation "it is the late improvements of the Honble

Mr Justice Buller that have given even an ideal value to the lands of Dartmoor. I should be glad if his Royal Highness had half a dozen more such Tenants".

The warmth exprest by Mr Frazer, as to what regards Mr Justice Buller, which in part perhaps may be imputed to a sense of hospitalities received at Prince Hall, is in my opinion not less creditable to him, than are his sentiments as to the advantage which has, and must yet further accrue to the Forest and consequently to the Community from his many and expensive experiments: – What was done before Sir F. Buller purchased Prince Hall, was done sparingly and cautiously. The Farmer "*timide gelidèq ministrans*" attempted no improvement without a certain assurance of attendant Emolument, he broke up but little ground: his inclosures were small and insignificant so that, I think, with but little modification the Lines of Virgil may be well applied to the enterprizing Proprietor of Prince Hall, – " – *Ipse colendi*

> "*Haud facilem esse viam 'reperit', Primusq per Artem*
> *Movit agros –*
> *Ante 'Illum' nulli subigebant Arva Coloni*
> *Nec signare quidem, aut partiri limite campum*
> *Fas erat: in Medium quærebant*"

"To the Exertions of this Gentleman as to the cultivation at present, and what may in future be made on Dartmoor Not only the Prince, but the Country is most highly indebted; No profits that can arise from any of his Farms, I am persuaded, will at any period balance his expences: He might have purchased fee simple lands in the best part of Devon, and productive of a greater income, for a much less Sum than has been expended in reclaiming these waste grounds from the worst state of Nature, and bringing them to the degree of culture which they now possess.

If the Man therefore who makes two blades of Corn grow, where but one grew before, deserves well of his Country, what should not his Praise be, who amidst the cheerless bosom of a wild and barren region has introduced beauty and fertility – If these lands under so unpropitious a Climature, He was unable

> "*To bid with fruitage blush or wave with grain*"

He has attained in many respects to such a degree of perfection, as, amongst the few competitors he has at present on the Moor, must entitle him to the plaudit which "*Detur Digniori*", and will doubtless hold out encouragement to other enterprizing Spirits, who by considering What Sir. F. Buller has done, may be instigated to attempt similar improvements.

I shall forbear to discuss The various arguments brought forward for the introduction of Canals to Dartmoor – the benefit that would result from them doubtless would be of the first consequence; but the obstacles in the way are great, and the Expence that would be incurred, even on the ingenious plans of Mr Fulton, would necessarily be enormous. – I shall forbear also to detail Mr Frazer's other scheme of settling in Villages on the Moor Colonies from the Highlands and Western isles of Scotland – or his calculations on the culture of this and other waste lands in the County of Devon, which amounting to at least 300-000 acres, might (he conceives) be so improved as to be worth at an average 10v pr acre, and of course return an annual profit of £150-000, additional Rent!!!

But having said a word or two, on the Scenery I shall recommence my Tour. – From the various descriptions which I have given in the course of this my Survey, a strong idea must have been entertained, of the local Character of Dartmoor. To a vastness of extent, which attaches to itself a degree of Magnificence, the higher swells of the Forest have also in themselves a peculiar trait of solemn and savage Grandeur: there are but few Picturesque Scenes, and these are restricted solely to the Rivers, and their foamy tumblings over inartificial masses of Granate, rudely piled by the force of torrents on one another – these however are strongly blended with the Romantic, which cast is more predominant, pervading indeed the greater part of the Moor and becoming most conspicuous, on the cloud-capt Tors, which either rear their craggy summits aloft into the air, or fractured into huge blocks spread themselves around the Parent Rock, which not unfrequently assumes the air of an Antient Castle, and frowns a Ruin over the dilapidated fragments.

The Scenery that presents itself to the Eye of the Beholder, wheresoever it shall be cast, is in its composition grand and wild. Nothing has been here frittered, or lain out on a trim or narrow scale: Here the Disciple of the great Picturesque theorists – the Enthusiast who Would

> "With Price, and Knight grounds by Neglect improve
> And banish Use for naked Nature's love"

would find it impracticable to deteriorate the surface of the Country so that it might assume a more rugged aspect – Prepared to his hands He might here find

> "Rocks' forests' Rivers' in one landschape drawn
> "His Park , a County, and a Heath his lawn"

With this quotation from that keen and elaborate Satire, the Pursuits of Literature" I finish my sketch, and return to my Tour.

On the Thursday Morning soon after Breakfast I took my departure from Prince Hall, and turning my horse eastward travelled on the road that led to Ashburton, having on my left a wide expanse of uncultivated Moor, and, on my right a wall running parallel with the road, a considerable tract of which, formed an inclosure which had on it an apparently fine crop of Potatoes.

Having made nearly the progress of a Mile, I forded the River, Cherry-brook, which in my first days ride on the Moor I had crossed when travelling on the Moreton road. Here the Farm of Prince Hall had its Easternmost

View entitled 'Trilithon – In Dunabridge pound', dated 16 Jan. 1798 (DRO, 564M/F15/25)

boundary And the Wall of inclosure, turning quick towards the South continued with the Streams course, till, after a short space it emptied its waters in the West Dart. The crop of this hithermost field was hay, which the Hind, and his Attendants, taking advantage, of the fine morning were exposing to the Sun. It was now August the 24th, and not above half the Moor's hay harvest was over. . . Not far from hence I came to Dunabridge pound, a large wall'd inclosure for the safe detention of Cattle, just within whose gate was a rude kind of a seat, oer-canopied by a single flat stone of considerable dimensions, of which the foregoing is a sketch. – Contiguous was a pot house and in front of it Farmer Lemans well cultivated Estate. On my first Visit to the Moor, I rode through this farm, which for the greater part I found in high culture. The meadows in particular, which were irrigated by the wash of the Court Yard, were perfectly sound, and in the richest verdure; In this Yard, a large body of Water issues from an inclosed Area, whose covering stone, of a rounded form, oblate, and considerable in size, was the identical table that in former times had been appropriated to the Use of the Stannary Parliament at Crockern tor. The Original Cultivator of this Estate, (at least the Person who enlarged it and brought it to a state of respectability was the Old Man alluded to by my "*Narrator temporis acti*", Cator, for having had sanguine expectations, even in extreme old age, of seeing the last harvest of a set of fields which he had ordered to be put into a course of husbandry for three years; – Such hopes, however ridiculous they might appear "*Abnormi Sapientiæ*" ot Old Cator are not uncommon to Old Age. – its Prototype is finely given us by Horace in the portrait which he has drawn of a wealthy Architect, who tho' tottering on the verge of the grave was projecting plans for other Edifices

> "*Truditur dies die*
>   *Novaq pergunt interire Lunæ;*
> *Tu secanda marmora*
>   *Locas sub ipsum funus; et Sepulchri*
> *Immemor, struis Domos; – "*

This Farmer Leman was at first a Laborer on Dunabridge Estate at fourpence pr day – but scraping up by the severest economy a small sum he purchased an Ewe, then two; in process of time a Cow, all of which, by a natural increase, enlarged his Stock. At length he became Master of a new take, and by the loan of a small Sum made a purchase of Dunabridge Farm, for £400, which by a perserverance in the same industry assisted by a keenness of Understanding that led him to the best mode of improving a Moor Estate, he had more than quadrupled in its value at his decease. At present its worth is estimated at £150 pr ann.

On gaining the Ascent of a Hill from the Pound I had a fine retrospective view, wild and Romantic to an extreme; – full in front I beheld the West Dart, descending from Prince Hall, diversified in its appearance one while with masses of Stones that seem'd to have block'd up its waters, which however at others were seen covered by them, and breaking them into foamy sheets and innumerable falls. The fields of Farmer Leman, falling with a South exposure to the River, highly verdant, tho with the different tints that were occasion'd by crops of Oats, turnips, and watered Meadows, most delightfully attracted my eye – nor on the opposite side of the River was the Scenery less beautiful: On the Northern bank, was Dunabridge farm, on the Southern another, which under the wild side of an high hill spread out a few cultivated inclosures – terminating in a bold headland this Hill extended itself to where the West Dart formed a junction with the Swincombe River which originating in Foxtor Meers descends through a defile among the Mountains in a South westerly direction.

Foxtor Meers I have already noticed when on my excursion to the Dock Leat, I approached them on the Western quarter – in the opposite sketch they lie over the summit of the highest hill, spreading themselves out into an extent

View entitled 'Sherberton –
Moor Farm of Honble Justice
Buller', dated 1798
(DRO, 564M / F15 / 31)

of at least a thousand acres – near the center of them, is the Pool, to which Ducks and other Wild-fowl make their resort, and close by it, is what is termed a Market place, at which in former days the Miners used to sell their tin – around this are a considerable number of Granate rocks, the surfaces of which are excavated into holes, wherein ere the invention of Stamping Mills, the Miners, according to the tradition of the Country were accustomed to pound or (as the phrase is) buck down the ore for sale – Whether this be the real fact, or whether these cavities are Rock basons once appropriated to Druidical rites, not having had an opportunity of visiting them, I cannot determine.

In the preceding view, I have endeavored to delineate the Scenery on the Swincombe River, which after a descent a short way further pours itself into the Dart, – the farm seen on the high ground on the right, is that of Sherberton, between which and Prince Hall, the Judge, whose Property it is, is about to form a communication by means of the bridge just erected over the Dart at the bottom of the Meadow in front of his house – the group of buildings on a prominent part of the Hill, surrounded by a clump of trees, has a more than common degree of respectability among the Dartmoor Farm Houses, as it is seen at least from the road. – The whole hangs as it were over a precipitous declivity, dipping rapid to the Rivers bank – which however is thrown into inclosures, in one of which appears a thriving plantation consisting of Ash or Sycamore. Beyond this also on two other declining headlands are visible thriving plantations of fir, which contribute to soften the scenery, and render the harsh features of the Moors by which they are environed more smooth and picturesque; this Character indeed predominates here, blended however with the wild and romantic, which exhibit themselves in the rocks, and mountainous eminencies that hem the narrow glen in on every side. – towards the upper part of the River as it is seen in the sketch, stands over its foamy Waters one of the antient Bridges of the Moor by which the farm of Sherberton is rendered accessible to its more Eastern parts. – This (I believe) is one of the chief of Sir Francis Bullers farms, and with six others, are what He possesses of the 37 and Antient tenements of the Forest.

At but a short distance from hence I skirted on the right a well cultured Farm belonging to a Man of the Name of Norris – it is called Hucaby, and through it, diverging from the Ashburton road, is another which leads towards Holne – here on the Dart which also runs through Hucaby crossing the Holne road at right angles, was another of these antient Bridges, but this had been superceded by a more safe and commodious one. – There are few, if any of the Farms on Dartmoor that have not derived their appellations from some significant circumstance belonging to them; a Name is rarely affixed at random: One is determined by that of the Lord of the Forest, Another by its local connexion with a bridge, a River, and a third by its vicinity to a Tor: – This however of Hucaby seems to baffle all conjecture: – could it but be allowed me, (but I fear there is no Itinerarium in my favor) that the Romans had formed any of their Roads, across the Moor, then indeed I might hazard an Hypothesis. I might suppose that from the more Southern one which passing over Teign-bridge led on to Totness, there might have been another which tending to the Northern parts of Cornwall had been carried athwart the Forest via Ashburton to Tavistoke, Launceston (where in the Castle is a tower erected by that People) or yet further, to unite itself with an acknowledged one of theirs at Stratton (Street town) 'via Strata' situate on the North Coast of the Province Dunmonia – and indeed as some authority for this supposition, I might quote Mr Polwhele, who in his Historical Views gives an extract from a Letter of Colonel Simcoe, wherein it is observed "that as in each of the two districts, formed by Dartmoor there must have been a distinct road, lain by the Britons before the arrival of the Romans, so a third must have penetrated the Mountain to afford a ready conveyance for the tin, which abounded in these regions".

If then before the Roman conquest the Natives had constructed over these rugged hills, a liège road, – what difficulty can there be in conceiving that the Romans, who laid their rapacious hands on every thing that was valuable in the Island (among which Tin, at this period a most precious article must be included) made use also of the great roads which were ready made to their hands? If this then be allowed, We will suppose that by this People (sicut mos erat) were at stated distances erected "Milliaria" and at the commencement of every road branching from the great one, "Directoria" or, as they are now called, Directing Posts. Here then at a turning, leading to other Mines, might have stood one of these Posts. Here, as on their Monuments placed by the road side the Passenger was addressed, Sta! siste gradum Viator so it might have been their usage on the directing post to introduce the place to which the road led with the prefatory address, "Huc Viator, Hucabi!

Whether such was the Original of the present appellation of the Farm Hucabi, or Huckaby (for it may be spelt either way, the Pronunciation being the same in both) I will leave to more profound Antiquaries than myself to decide, – thus far however I will venture to observe, that the Etymon corresponds in the minutest point, nay even to a letter, which is a matter according to my humble judgement, too lightly attended to in the many valuable disquisitions of this nature which have been given to the world from the Antiquarian Archives. Here I was about to close this interesting discussion, but having had occasion to mention the name of Polwhele, with it at once became associated his Armenian Hypothesis, which I understand, (notwithstanding the critique of his best Friend the Historian of Manchester which attempted to subvert this Doctrine) is yet cherished by Himself, and as it is asserted, Another – Hence then I began to consider with myself, whether its derivation (as we are told, most of the Promontories and Tors in this County are) may not be deduced from the Armenian language. We find Astaroth or Astarte, who was perhaps a Goddess of the Armenians as well as the Phænicians giving her Name to the "Start" point, and to bring the matter more to the Spot we are informed that in Bellevor Torr (almost contiguous to this farm) we have the Rock of Bel or Belus, in Hessary torr the rock of Hesus, in Hams torr the rock of Ham or Ammon: – All these Torrs, not to forget also the headland deriving their Names from the East (it matters little whether from the hither or more remote

*View entitled 'Antient bridge
near Dartmeet – Dartmoor',
no date given
(DRO, 564M/F15/43)*

parts of Asia, from Lybia, Syria, or Armenia), if it were possible to produce a word from either of these Countries similar to the present one on the tapis, I think, it may give ground to invalidate its attribution to the Romans – and add another testimonial to the support of Mr Polwheles original Hypothesis – this then (fortunately I have it in my power to perform – I can on the authority of Mr Maundrell, produce the Word "*Occaby*" which (making a trivial allowance for a difference in the idiom of the two Countries or perhaps, in the bare addition of an aspirate to the word which, during a succession of so many ages is but a slight deviation,) must be acknowledged to be the very word itself.

Mr Maundrell says that in his route from Aleppo to Jerusalem, one of his first stages, was a place called "*Occaby*" – whether however it was situate in Armenia or Syria I cannot absolutely determine, but I rather think, as he soon after says he touched on the Coast, which was doubtless the Mediterranean, it must be part of the latter Country."

*View entitled 'Brimpse – Moor
Farm of Sanders Esq.',
dated 1798
(DRO, 564M/F15/47)*

I have thus ingeniously as I flatter myself, sifted the derivation of Farmer Norris name of his Estate on Dartmoor Hucaby – and having brought specious arguments on one side that it may be taken from the Roman *"Hucabi"*, and others, having perchance equal probability that its original may be the Eastern word *"Occaby"* I can only say to the Reader *"Utrum horum mavis, accipe"*.

On this Estate there are many beautiful meadows, declining to the Dart with a western exposure – the River winds in a most picturesque manner around it, and by its quick flexures incloses it nearly on every side. – part of the adjoining grounds, belonging also to Farmer Norris, stretch themselves on by the side of the road, running parallel to the more Southern inclosures of Brimpse, till they receive a boundary at the Easternmost point by the River.

This Estate of Brimpse, the Property (As I have already noticed) of Mr Sanders, a Banker at Exeter, under his judicious management, has been rendered perhaps the best cultured and most productive one on the Moor – its aspect indeed is in many respects better than most – which is sufficiently demonstrated by its power of producing good red wheat, (of which I now saw a fine field bordering on the road) and of nourishing up to Maturity a large wood of Oaks. The opposite sketch is of the Remains of an old Bridge already delineated and described in the third volume of these Tours. It has some little diversification from the drawings there made – takes in the whole of the Ruin with part of Brimpse Wood overhanging the East Dart, a high mountainous hill opposite, crested by a Torr and having the Ashburton Road winding up its side.

The New handsome Bridge of two arches just below the antient one, was erected in the year 1792. And I conceive was indebted for its Existence to the influence of the Proprietor of Prince Hall. – in whom originated not only this, but almost every other improvement that of late has been effected on Dartmoor: – The East Dart here runs in a deep narrow hollow between two hills between whom by means of this bridge a good communication is formed: it passes on but little more than a gunshot, when it embraces the River West Dart, and considering her afterwards as *"Dimidium sui"* forms with her an indissoluble union; at this instant cease the discriminating adjuncts of East and West, by which they had hitherto been distinguished from each other, and thus incorporated they form one Whole, the Dart, which begins to roll down the narrow glen with accelerated impetuosity and greater consequence as a River.

From "Dartmeet" bridge I began at once a mountainous ascent which from the verge of the Rivers rose steep, and to a very considerable Elevation. Having mastered about two thirds of the Eminence I had a good prospect of Brimpse, and of the East Dart pursuing its wild course from afar. – Attracted by a collection of large stones, which indicated the remains of an honorary Barrow, I past a little way from the road towards the left that I might examine it, I found it to be the Reliquiæ of a large one, and possessing from it a finer view of Brimpse than I had yet seen, I took the opposite sketch. The Whole Farm, with the House in the most central part, lay spread out before me, as if it had been delineated on a Map. This beautiful illustration of the efficacy of Art and Industry exemplified by the high culture of numerous inclosures that were surrounded by a wild and mountainous region yet retaining its original features, was productive of a most pleasing effect – it was in a certain degree Picturesque, though the predominant trait was a savage Sublimity.

On these Hills, I observed a number of tumuli such as I have introduced into the foreground of the preceding Sketch – and further onward on the less elevated Eminences a great abundance of Kistvaens environed by large upright Stones. the whole of these which occurred to my Notice had been opened, and the cavity was rarely of larger dimensions, than what might be adequate to the reception of a Human body.

The unfrequent occurrence of Tumuli, and the almost total absence of Druidical Monuments on Dartmoor (for I know of no Vestiges of them but Rock basons on some of the Torrs) are a sort of indication that the Resort of the

Druids was not on the more exposed and mountainous parts. – On the Commons circumjacent, we discover a great variety of their Monuments. – On these Widecombe downs, there are tumuli and circles of several kinds. Rock basons are met with on abundance of Rocky Masses, and on the North East verge there is a Cromlêh, Logan stone, and numerous Stone Pillars erect. We have to regret that No Antiquary was found in these parts, to have recorded the Druidical Reliquiæ before they were subverted and removed by the incroaches of Culture on the rugged natural face of the Country – for I have not a doubt, but that (by an inference from what appear at present) I might be warranted in the supposition that Monuments of every denomination of the Specimens given Us by Borlase might have been found in this country; especially in Drewsteignton, which (as that of Karnbré) seems to have been in a more especial manner appropriated to the Mysteries of this Antient Superstition. Those who first made inclosures, doubtless took the Stones that were readiest to their hands – and what could be more fitted for their purpose, or more convenient to removal than those large Monumental ones, which being above ground were at once lifted by levers into the Wall, or clove, during successive periods by Stone cutters, into Posts, or hewn into arches for gateways, chimney pieces, steps, or Cyder pounds; of which We have immense numbers in every parish whose distance from the granate rocks did not render the expence of carriage imprudent if not impracticable.

From this tumulus, having regained the road and ascended to the summit of the hill, I stopt to look around me: the immediate environs especially towards the river were grand, but the retrospective view was not only singularly romantic, and uncommon, but of very great extent, for it comprized almost the whole range of the Moor that, in my several excursions, I had visited; full before me lay Brimpse, the two Darts and Hucaby – then came in succession, Dunabridge and Sherberton Farms – beyond these through an opening on the line of Hills, I was able to descry the roof of Prince Hall House, and had a perfect view of the Lodges; the Horizon was finely broken, to the right commencing at Bellevor Torr, it stretched onward, trending to the West, taking in the Torrs (before enumerated) descending as on a ridge to that of Crockern – the House of Bear down, cresting the rounded Eminence above two bridges was next discernible and the Tavistock road leading on to Old Cators. This was the Western most point, and as I turned toward the South – Hessary Torr, that rose behind Mr Tyrwhytt's [house] marked the tract of Country through which ran the Water Leat that supplied Dock – the Chain of Mountains in its hills and Vallies – exhibited specimens of a smooth and rugged Country – all the diversities of wild and savage Nature dotted with patches of inclosures, and blended at times with the Magnificent.

Proceeding on my way, I skirted a farm or two on my right, one of which in particular, appeared seated on a bold projecting Eminence, fronting an immense Mountainous Mass, that rose all but perpendicular from the waters of the united Darts that rolled far beneath in the intervening bottom; Eastward was before me a high pointed Karn, above which rose the aspiring Sharpstorr.

The road now entered between the inclosures of the small farm of Old brim, that lay in the way. it was now the 24th August, and the Farmer was in the act of mowing one of his little fields, for the provender of his Winter flock – in two other inclosures the Hay was in swaths – backward however as was this Harvest, yet the appearance of a small field of wheat was a sort of indicating Symptom that the Climature was less severe than that which was experienced towards the more central part of the Forest – this Farm of Old Brim lay as it were in a sort of Circle, whose diameter having quickly traversed, I again got on the common by which it was encompassed; the extent of this however was but short, and having soon gained the extremity I was about to bid adieu to Dartmoor and its communicating Wilds, when by the aspect of a Torr a little to the right, I was induced to think there might be Rock basons on it, and to pay it a visit.

On my approach I found it to be a most singular pile of rocks, on the uppermost of which, as seen in the sketch, I found indeed a pretty large hollow, but

View entitled 'Rocks, near Uppercott', dated 1798 (DRO, 564M/F15/55)

not sufficiently determinate in figure, that I could pronounce it to be a work of the Druids; there were many other Karns visible from this, but on Mil torr only, (which I have amply described in a former Volume) have there been discovered any Rock basons. Among the deep interstices between these rocks A number of Cattle had secreted themselves, and every now and then, as I leaped from the surface of one disunited Mass to another, a terrified Bullock bounced from some hollow beneath and scampered over the heath, as if it had been stung by a Gadfly. On the descent of a steep hill, under the Eastern hang of the Commons I had past I had a rich and very beautifull View, of a pasture'd slope in the highest verdure dipping towards a glen thick set with Woods; there were interspersed several Farm houses and Cottages, which greatly added to the picturesque enrichment of the Valley: A Hamlet called Uppercot which retained a good deal of the meanness of the common Buildings on the moor lay at the foot of this first descent from the Forest – through this I past, and very soon after began another dip by the fir Plantations of Park, which I recognized as old Friends, many of which (having planted and watered them) I may say, owed to me their Existence – and leaving the Lodge on my left, I quickly reached another little group of Farm Houses and Cotts called Pounds gate. Among these Buildings were scatter'd Sycamore trees and Oaks which gave the spot a pleasing rural air; through them also there were openings of the Country towards Buckland, Widecombe and the high Torrs of Buckland Beacon and Azell; the whole of which Scenery was uncommonly wild, picturesque and romantic. I now came to the ridge of a long and Steep Hill down whose rapid side, the road wound in quickly-repeated flexures. For the mutual accommodation of myself and my horse, and that, more at my ease, I might enjoy the very delightfull Scenes, that were spread out before me, I dismounted and began my descent on foot; Close by on the left, I past a vast pile of towering rocks, which, if view'd at some little distance when rendered somewhat indistinct by a haze or at the *"dubiæ crepusculo lucis"* might very easily be mistaken for the Ruins of an Antient Castle, the magnificent Remains of other times! – the other fine features of this picturesque Country I recognized with wonted delight, in the Chace woods those of Buckland and Park, the River – Cot and New Bridge.

View entitled 'New bridge on the Dart', no date given (DRO, 564M/F15/59)

On this latter object in particular my Eye rested with increased delight, and when I reached it I could not resist the inclination I felt, again to delineate it. In my third Volume I have expatiated on this Bridge and the surrounding Scenery, and as the Sketch there introduced was of the lower part with a back view of Sir Bourchier Wreys Cot and Woods, so the preceding one is a Representation of its Upper front, taking in, in the middle ground the road I had descended, winding up the slope of the high Hill, on the declining ridge of which appears the Pile of Rocks before noticed, which the late Lord Ashburton from its being the frequent Resort of the Bird used to call Ravens Castle and which consists wholly of a very hard stone whose field is a dark blue, intermixed with large veins of Quartz so as to give it, on a cursory inspection, much the look of Masses of Marble. from the direction post on the ridgy point of this middle ground a diverging road leads thro a valley to Park, and to Buckland, whose Church tower is seen in the more distant grounds, relieved by a grove of tall Elms.

The whole of this scene is fine and beautifully Picturesque, it struck me as being equal to any I had before met with; but my conceptions had a higher zest perhaps in contemplating the Objects now before me, in consequence of the Contrasted Scenery on which they had for the several last days dwelt – had I come upon this view from the East, it would have been through a succession of Picturesque beauties, some of which I have already acknowledged to be on an equality with those at New bridge – the effect produced on the mind by the impulse of any pleasure is in this, as in every other instance not only in proportion to the Quality, but to the frequency likewise of Delightfull impressions by which it has been agitated before. The Traveller passing through a Country abundant with Romantic and Picturesque objects, feels himself struck with admiration and delight, whilst arrested by their novelty, and their beauty, he contemplates them in every point of view, and can hardly persuade himself to pass on to others, which he sees before him in his way of similar attraction, – by a too frequent repetition however of such high-embellished scenery, the relish becomes insensibly less poignant, till at length, satiated as it were with the luxuriance of his repast, he passes the richest assemblage of landschape

with little or slight observance – To him therefore as to the Voluptuary *"luxury is always repletion's cause."* [Greek]. How different however are his Sensations, who having long beheld, wheresoever his eye shall have happened to glance, nothing but a wild region, prolific only of naked Mountains and rugged rocks, shall at once light upon some close Vale, watered by a simple stream and shadowed by a Wood or a few trees – to his sight this common rural imagery, shall be embellished with beauties not its own, and be raised into a temporary importance to which on any other occasion it could have no pretensions. I will suppose therefore that the Scenery at New bridge, emerging as I was from a wild and drear Country, might, from recollected contrast appear in stronger beauty. Wherever yet it might be placed, or however it might be seen, it could not fail of having its claims allowed to picturesque beauty.

Nor had Holne Bridge to which, after having past an intervening Mile full of Sylvan and Romantic charms, lesser pretensions. – the whole of this fine region (where at every step a Painter and a Lover of wild Nature must be delighted) I have already gratified myself by pourtraying in a variety of drawings and descriptions – in regard therefore to the preceding one of Holne Bridge I shall only observe that I have taken it in a new and singular point of view. The Rocks, the Woods, the River, had in this part in particular been intimately known to me in my Younger days; and their association, whenever I have since paid them a visit, has given me inexpressible delight – for these sweet sensations I shall, as a tribute of Gratitude offer up a Sonnet –

View entitled 'From Holne Bridge', dated Jan. 1798 (DRO, 564M/F15/65)

To the River Dart

"Dart! whose swift stream still rolls itself along
Through heath-clad Mountains, and high-waving groves;
As when, thou conscious wer't of my rude song,
What time, A Youth! I roved thy scenes among;
Scenes! which my unchanged heart yet fondly loves!

Those rocks, that Wood, past hours to me renew
  Or lost in social sport, or better spent
Whilst that my artless hand their beauties drew,
  And thy wild Genius its bold pencil lent;

Still with thy Charms my Soul a union holds,
  And on its chords sweet Sympathy has twine'd
Her softest bands – ev'n now her Power unfolds
  The mazy lapse of Time; and bids the Mind
From thy love'd scenes the truest pleasure find.

Having treated myself with one other Sketch I pursued my ride towards Ashburton, at which place I arrived about an hour after noon. Here in my own house, now converted into one of the best and pleasantest Inns, in the West of England I took my dinner. The Gardens, the walks, and the Prospect here offer ample amusement for an hours idle lounge, from which the Other in the center of the Town is altogether debarred, – to supply this defect, I cannot forbear recording An ingenious device which the Landlady hit upon about forty years ago, to while away a few minutes of a Travellers suspense before his dinner could be prepared.

She had collected a few curiosities, and among them as a very singular one she exhibited a large Oyster Shell with two Mice dangling from it. The circumstances of the History were to this purport. In an underground Cellar, a dish of Oysters (from Wembury on the river Yealm) remarkable for their large size, was laid by way of coolness. At the time the tide flows it is well known Oysters open their shells to admit the Waters, and take their food. At this period a large Oyster had expanded his jaws, and at the same instant, two Mice, searching for prey, pounced at once on the Victim and seized it with their teeth; The Oyster shrinking at the wound that had been inflicted closed her Shell, collapsing with such force as to crush the Maroders to death.

An incident of so uncommon a Nature hath been generally considered as unique – with regard to the two mice it probably may be so, and its oddness

View entitled 'Holne bridge on the Dart', dated Jan. 1798 (DRO, 564M/F15/69)

is thereby considerably heightened. As to the Singularity however of the Event I shall produce an apposite instance epigrammatically recorded in the Greek Anthology.

[Seven lines of Greek] which I have thus paraphrased

"Crept from his hole, a taper-eating Mouse
Who I wont to range and nibble thro' the house
One night was led by 'his nose for prey
Where, in a cellar Oysters lay:
One, from the rest, He instant spied
With gaping jaws extended wide,
And, urg'ed by hunger, nought deterr'd
To seize the 'amphibious Creatures beard:
When sudden! on his startled Ear
Burst sounds that more than Mouse might scare;
The portals close! and with portending knell
Include the Caitiff in the crushing shell.

Ah! luckless thief! unheard my wond'rous doom
Spontaneous thus to meet a living tomb:
There where he seized the dread collapsing prize
There with the Victim rent, the Victor dies!

So that it may be verily said with another Poet

"The loser is wretched, but the winner is dead." [Greek]

Having taken my dinner, about five I quitted Ashburton, proceding homeward on the turnpike road, leading through Bickington to Bovey Heath field.

In one of my excursions to Dartmoor, I made my return through the little Town of South Bovey, and took a few sketches and observations from the Coal works which are contiguous to that place – these however I shall not introduce

View entitled 'New bridge on the Teign', dated Feb 1798 (DRO, 564M/F15/75)

here but shall reserve them till I shall have it in my power to make a more satisfactory investigation of the nature of this singular fossil, so as to have the opinion I entertain of it set aside, or confirmed.

At the Deuxs bridges, or as they are commonly termed Jews bridges (the chief of which is over the Bovey river) I turned from the turnpike road towards the right, and after a while came to New bridge, consisting of two Arches, raised over the Teign; thus again revisiting the River which in the outset of this Tour had afforded me so much delight; the Scenery however was not as that at Fingle bridge, magnificent and romantic, in consequence of the Mountains and Woods by which it was environed, but beautifull and Picturesque, as where, at Chagford or Rushford bridge the gentle River winded its less rapid waters through a tract of level and highly fertile meadows. The whole of this belongs to a fine farm, called Belle marsh, the property of James Templer Esq. A succession of lanes conducted me through the hamlet of Gappa, and between the Park of Ugbrook on the right, and the enchanting grounds of Lawell on the left, where (from hence as indeed from almost every other point of view) the grand rock of Chudleigh exhibiting, through its rich Accompanyments of Wood, its grey tints of marble constituted the chief feature and great object of attraction.

The town of Chudleigh soon after came in view, which, as well as a considerable extent of a fine diversified country was well seen, and discriminated from this ridgy Eminence. Not far from the Eastern Extremity of the Park the Ascent of Haldown commences – a Down as little productive as Dartmoor which having traversed I soon reached my own Home.

finished feb. 3d. 1798.
John Swete. Oxton House

The River Exe

Having in a former tour explored this beautiful River from the Walls of the City of Exeter to the Forest in the County of Somerset from whence it derives its Source: the Object now before me is to trace it from its mouth where it loses itself in the English Channel, upwards, to the Southern most part of the City, in the completion of which, nearly the whole description of the River will be effected.

And in this pursuit I feel myself more than common interested. The Scenes which I am about to delineate, are neither remote, nor those to which I have been a Stranger – the greater part of them are under my daily view, and the more intimate my research into their beauties! the more familiar my acquaintance! the more forcible I find their attraction, confirming a maxim of Classic notoriety "*Si propius stes, te capiat magis*"!

And besides, to this acquaintance with scenes in my immediate neighborhood I may not unfrequently add an Association with incidents, Persons, or thing. "*Quaque Egomet forsan non tantum vidi, sed quorum Pars magna fui*".

And this I have ever found to be one of the most impressive Sources of delight, whether it be excited by local accident as the Spot on which some eminent Character has signalized himself, where he was born, or resided – By the remains of Antiquity as the ruins of a Castle or an Abbey – or more particularly, (as what comes home to ones own feelings) by that Personal attachment to long known objects (perhaps indifferent in themselves) as the favorite seat, the tree, the ride – the walk – or the Spot endeared by the remembrance of past events.

"Objects of this kind (says One of the first taste in modern improvements of Landscape gardening) however trifling in themselves, are often preferr'd to the most beautiful scenes that Painting can represent. Such partialities should be respected and indulged, since true taste, which is generally attended by great Sensibility, ought to be the Guardian of it in Others."

In consequence of "Local Attachment" then I shall indulge myself in descriptions more than usual diffuse, and in delineations taken from a treasured stock of accumulated sketches. And not confining myself to the little Voyage which I am about to describe I shall expatiate as I see occasion to some little distance from either bank so as to take in whatever object I may find that has anything remarkable in it, or that may be possessed of Picturesque beauty. And of both of these there will be an ample display – for though

> "In these sequestered glades
> No antient Abbeys walls diffuse their shades
> With mouldering Windows pierced, and turrets crown'd
> And pinnacles with clinging ivy bound;
> Yet here the Ruin'd Castle rears its crest,
> And Seats and Villages by Beauty drest;
> And here may oft be seen the straw-roofed Cot
> (of painful Industry the humble lot)
> With spiry grass and mosses covered o'er,
> And honeysuckles climbing round the door;
> While mantling Vines along its walls are spread,
> And the bright Myrtle rears its fragrant head."

On the 7th of September 1798, having rode to Starcross I took boat at the quay by the Courtenay Arms, a most delightfully-situated Inn, erected by the late Lord Courtenay in the year [blank] for the reception of the principal Gentlemen resident in the vicinity who assembling here at dinner once a fortnight during the months of Summer, from the place of meeting have been denominated the Starcross Club. The number is restricted to thirty, among whom I have had the honor of being enrolled a Member above twenty years.

The tide being nearly at ebb, to gain the boat which lay in the natural Channel of the River I was obliged to walk over a sort of wooden bridge raised about four feet from the oozy bed that was now dry, and which for the better accommodation of those who wished to take boat at low water had been carried to a considerable extent outward from the quay.

Here with my Servant I joined My two Boatmen, and having laid in a large jug of Porter from the Inn to cheer them in their labours, we took in our anchor and gently glided down the stream towards the Rivers mouth. One of the Men whom I had chosen for my days excursion was old and had been all his life exercised on the River, – the Other, (Who was the Owner of the boat) had by the explosion of a gun lost an eye, and had one of his hands dreadfully shattered: perhaps it was as much upon this account, as from the Poor Mans general good character that I gave him the preference to the other Boatmen of the place: recollecting at the time that admirable trait of benevolence recorded of Sir Roger de Coverley, and willing to imitate it! "We were no sooner come to the Temple stairs but we were surrounded with a crowd of Watermen offering us their respective Services (Says the Spectator) – Sir Roger after having looked about him very attentively spied one with a Wooden leg, and immediately gave him orders to have his boat ready. As we were walking towards it "You must know (says Sir Roger) I never make use of any body to row me that has not either lost a leg or an Arm. I would rather bate him a few strokes of his oar than not employ an honest Man that has been wounded in the Queens service. If I was a Lord, or a Bishop and kept a Barge, I would not put a fellow in my livery that had not a wooden leg."

With these two honest Sailors, and my Servant (as Sir Rogers sober Coachman) for ballast we past away from the Starcross shore – At the Southern extremity of the Village we were gratified with the front view of several neat houses, among which Dr Stones was most conspicuous. These were situate at the outlet of a Valley called Staplake, consisting of a narrow track of green pasturage, screened by gentle acclivities of corn grounds among which cots and farm houses were rurally intermingled and backed at no

View entitled 'Cockwood Village and Mamhead from the sod', dated 1799 (DRO, 564M/F15/85)

remote distance by the hill of Warborough. The current winding with the shore soon wafted me in front of the sod – Here thro' a marshy valley slow pacing, the rivulet Coff gave its waters to the Exe – the Scenery here was picturesque and called forth the first exertion of my pencil. The Village of Cockwood, rising on the left up a steepish headland, where, (exclusive of a few that were seated on the shore beneath the Cliff) All the Cottages were embosomed in trees, exhibited itself in the most interesting manner, and on the right, just within the sod a group of Lime kilns pleasingly caught the eye. Between these a narrow marshy valley stretched itself to the West, and over (at the distance of about three miles), rose the verdant Lawns and House of Mamhead, diversified with all the varieties of Sylvan decoration; the clump, the grove, and the wide extended wood. Elevated above the side screens of Staplake and Cockwood This charming spot appear'd in high beauty and bating the want of minutely discriminating objects the consequence of distance, I never met with a station from whence it could be seen to more advantage.

The Lime kilns just noticed require more attention than a transient glance. Seated under a hill overhung by hedge-row trees, with the usual accompanyment of a road fringed with thorns and furze – They formed a group, highly picturesque; two buildings, similar to the round towers so frequently met with on the borders of Scotland stood contiguous to one another with their appendages of sheds and buttresses; and in front worked its winding way the River Coff, through the reedy valley, which swelling at Spring tides by a flood of water, and overflowing its low banks, is seen to spread itself nearly up to the kilns and to form a beautifull expanse, as a mirror reflecting them and the trees from its lucid bosom.

On the left of this fen, (for it scarcely deserves any other title) beneath the Cockwood Hill which rising to a very considerable height at the morning hour throws a breadth of shade over the subjacent flat, winds along a road, which partakes for near half a mile of the sinuous flexure of the stream, and then branching off towards the South, quickly reaches the hamlet of Coffton

consisting of a few cottages, a low mansion almost a ruin and a Chapel completely one.

This latter was the object of attraction, and (exclusive of the serious reflexions which a desolate Religious Edifice cannot well fail of producing), was, in a picturesque light, very well worth a digression. On a knoll nearly at the Western foot of the Cockwood hill had been erected this little Chapel, which from the peculiar appearance of its form and Architecture, however small it may now seem, must originally have been of much lesser dimensions. Occupying not one fourth of the at present inclosed Area, stands what I conceive to have been the first erection; This does not warrant a supposition that it could ever be intended for the reception of more than a single family – for the whole of its space is comprized within walls not more than 14 feet long

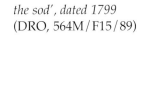

View entitled 'Lime kilns at the sod', dated 1799 (DRO, 564M/F15/89)

View entitled 'Interior of Cofton Chapel', dated 1799 (DRO, 564M/F15/93)

107

and 12 wide. In this small room are three windows, and two doors both of which latter appear to have been long walled up. This strikes me as having been the original Edifice for it may be considered perfect in itself, but when in consequence of an increasing congregation, it was found not sufficiently spacious, I imagine a large opening, resembling a door of Gothic cast, was broke out in the Western wall so as to communicate not unseemly with the additional building, and to form as it were a kind of Chancel. The width of this outer area is 16 feet and its length about 40. To what period to ascribe this Chapel I have no document; Tradition reports its Founder to have been a Doctor of Divinity of the name of Kendall, who residing in the Manor House contiguous, is said to have erected it for his own use and for the accommodation of his Neighbours, who were between three and four miles from the Parochial Church. The sacred offices of Religion were here performed by him, during his life; but whether (as no endowment was annexed) it continued to be thus appropriated to the use of the Established Church I can find no authority; certain however it is, that till within these last twenty years, it has been the resort of Sectaries of various denominations: but as Societies, and Pastors of such description are rarely in possession of revenues, it has happened (as a natural consequence, that the sacred Edifice in process of time, for want of necessary repairs fell to decay and became dilapidated. If this Tradition be well grounded the Edifice must have been erected about the beginning or middle of the last Century – for to the Memory of Doctor Kendall there yet remains a Mural Monument in the inner Chapel or Chancel which tells us that He died in the year 1663. From the gothic turn of the doors and windows I should however conclude that this Eastern end was of a more antient date, without it may be conceived that in the formation of these doors and windows, instead of the one in use, an earlier stile of Archiecture had been purposely adopted. The Inscription runs thus

View entitled 'Cofton Chapel',
dated 1799
(DRO, 564M/F15/97)

"In memoriam Viri eximie eruditi, Georgii Kendall S.Stæ Theologiæ
Doctoris, Filii Georgii Kendall de Cofton Armigeri Qui e vita decessit

*XIX Aug: MD.CLXIII. et juxta hic sepultus jacet. Nec non in memo-
riam Lectissimæ ejus conjugis Mariæ, Filiæ Periam Pole de Talliton
Armigeri Quce obiit X.mo die Aprilis MD.CLXXVI.*

The area of the Chapel, excepting the part at the Eastern end, is as the Antient
Temples, open to the heavens, and like the Abbies of the land becoming desecrated has never perhaps had within its walls a Worshipper to offer up his
orisons – sub dio. Where the roof remains, the whole of the surface has
become occupied by a mass of vegetating plants, among which ferns and
mosses were most predominant.

In the foregoing sketch, some idea may be formed both of the building and
of its situation. As thus seen from the road it is beheld in a very picturesque
light, and though it may be found deficient in the clustered pillar and the
ramified Window, (the peculiar and most beautiful parts of our Collegiate
Ruins), it has yet traits of Gothic Architecture and a degree of pleasing
Simplicity to recommend it to notice. The whole of this Hill, on Which Cofton
Chapel is situate, which from a wide base rises high, and in many points of
view appears conical, is a detachment from the parish of Dawlish, Whose
boundaries on three sides are the Æstuary of the Exe, Cofford brook and the
Water, which descending from Newhouse washes the hamlet of Wick on the
South. On the Eastern aspect of this Hill close on the shore is seated a House
belonging to Dr Drury Master of Harrow School, surrounded on all sides but
that in front by pleasure and improved grounds which are lain out with taste
and cultivated with judgment. A sketch taken from a vast sand-bank stretching itself on its eastern quarter, and shutting it from the Sea, will convey a
better notion of the place and of the Cockwood hill, which rises at its back than
any verbal description. I shall therefore here introduce it. On the apex of the
hill, (as seen in the view) has been erected a small rotunda pleasure house,
which has not only the command of a very extensive range of country, but in
the more contiguous parts (where the natural eye has the power of discrimination) of a beautiful and picturesque one. Around this elevated spot (prior to
its being purchased by Doctor Drury, A waste tract of land spread itself out to
a considerable distance, wholly unproductive of any thing but a stunted furze.
But this Gentleman animated by a most laudable spirit of enterprize not only

*View entitled 'Dr Drurys from
the Warren', dated 1799
(DRO, 564M/F15/101)*

reclaimed much of the Common from its state of barren Nature, but by his Example stimulated others to do the same. A Devonshire Farmer (and I conceive it may be the actuating principle of all other Farmers) has never been found blind to his own interest: He is in himself biassed by local usage, and being prejudiced in favor of the mode of Agriculture practised by his forefathers, is averse to Experiment. But when such experiment has been made by Another, and from its success an Argument demonstrative has been brought home to Him – No one perhaps is more ready to adopt a system, from which he is convinced He cannot fail of deriving Emolument. – Such has been the case in the present instance. Doctor Drury first set his hand to the plough, and the neighboring Farmers have followed him; insomuch that considerable advantage has not only accrued to the Individual but to the community, and at the same time the face of the Country has been converted from features that were rough and wild, into those of pleasure and fertility: I speak now as a rational member of Society, who prefers the utile to the dulce, – and not with the enthusiasm of a Painter, who beholds the incroachments of Art on Nature with a jealous eye – and who had rather cast that eye over tangled forests, gnarled Oaks, and deep-rutted lanes than over the richest pastures, the straitest and most luxuriant trees, and roads which for smoothness of surface might vie with a gravel walk.

But it is one thing to be a Farmer and another an Amateur of the Picturesque – to be a Member of an Agricultural Society, or of the Royal Academy. These indeed cannot well coalesce, but they are both excellent in their respective departments. The occupation of the One is an absolute necessity of the other an elegant amusement. However fond I may therefore be of Picturesque Nature, I will not quarrel with the Man, who by the aid of Art, tho subversive of many of its beauties, shall yet render it more subservient to the use and comfort of Mankind.

But to return from this digression! Wafted on by the reflux of the tide towards the mouth of the River I now approached the large Sand bank called the Warren which extending itself at right angles with the current of the River (and that nearly for the whole of its width,) at a little distance appeared to prohibit all egress of its waters. On this bank I shall make an excursion, as in

View entitled 'Mt Pleasant',
dated 1799
(DRO, 564M/F15/107)

View entitled 'Mt Pleasant'
no date given
(DRO, 564M/F15/108)

several of its parts the Scenery is not undeserving of the pencil. At its Westernmost end, the Country terminates in a headland, at some places bold and abrupt, and at others, dropping towards the plain by a shelving declivity, rendered not unpleasing to the eye by the thick growth of briars and low brushwood. On the verge of a precipitous part stands Mount Pleasant. An Inn this, much resorted to during the months of Summer by parties from Exeter and the circumjacent Country; In consequence of its elevation above the level that stretches itself out beneath it on every side but towards the West, it has the command of a diversified and extensive view. The nature of its situation may be ascertained by the preceding sketches which I took from the Warren below. The waters I have introduced on account of the additional beauty which it gives to the Scenery, though I understand it never reaches so far into the interior of the Sand bank except when at Spring tides, a more than ordinary volume of water is driven into the River by the accidental cooperation of a strong easterly wind. But the view from the Inn cannot be comprehended by the power of the pencil – The objects are too numerous, too extensive, and too remote. They are all comprized in a birds eye view from the crest of the Cliff, which however delightful it may be to the sight falls not within the scope of the Painter. On the right a wide expanse of Sea, in front a long waste of sand terminating apparently in the town of Exmouth: and on the left The River lengthening into indistinctness and at last, in remote distance, melting as it were into air; Such are the outlines of Natures picture: Which Art has contrived to fill up with great diversification and ingenuity.

When at Dawlish in 1795, As the distance was not above two miles, on the Cliff, or on the beach our walks were frequently directed to this favorite spot. And in a small poem describing one of these strolls I introduce the following lines

"Nor seldom do our footsteps stray
(When ebbing tides have left a way)
To where above the spreading sands
High on the Cliff Mount Pleasant stands;
Here on the green, or sheltering tent

Oft are the hours of Evening spent
And while we sip the fragrant tea
'Tis Ours to mark the Rivers way,
Or o'er the Oceans tranquil face
Some Vessel's lucid course to trace
Nor wants there Pastime to enhance
The hour of bliss: To sprightly dance
Some lively Fair by trippings light
The ever-ready Beau's incite.
Ah yet upon my Senses play
The blissful joys of Yesterday:
Still do I hear the mirthful sound
That drew the rustic train around,
Still do I mark - - - - - - s grace
- - - - - - - - - etc - - - - - - -
- - - - - etc
What rapture such a band to view
And every charm, and step pursue;
Where, at each pause the roving eye
Might Natures loveliest Scenes descry,
Dwell on the rifted rock, or mark
Far oer the wave the gilded bark " etc etc

From this spot as the approach is made towards the sea, the Cliffs become bolder and more precipitous, till at length terminating in an abrupt Promontory, All access to the Dawlish strand is precluded by the Surge (which here beats violently against the rock) unless it be at low water, or at half tide: when a communication is opened between the two shores by means of a hollow passage thro' the body of the Cliff sufficiently large for the admission of a Man on horseback. The nature of this headland with its caverned sides will be gathered best from the drawing: and from its appearance an inference will at once be drawn that the tide through a succession of Ages has advanced

View entitled 'Passage thro' the Cliffs at the Warren', no date given (DRO, 564M/F15/115)

on this part of the Coast, and that the waves in a storm from the East dash tremendously against it. Indeed the incroachment of the Sea, as well as the violence of its surge may generally be ascertained by the steepness of the Cliffs and the boldness of the Shore. In places where the force of the Sea is less violent, or its tides less rapid The Shores are commonly seen to descend with a more gradual declivity: here only are to be seen gentle Surges making calmly towards land, and lessening as they approach.

But the common Character of the Shores on almost the whole of this Western Coast is that of boldness, and a degree of grandeur. Here the progress of the Sea is checked on a sudden by the prominence of rocks, or an abrupt elevation of the Land; and dashing with all the force of its depth (when as I have just observed it is driven onwards by winds from the East) against the obstacle that opposes it, forms by its repeated violence those caverns, high and deep which are met with every where (especially in the Sandy stratum at the western extremity of Torbay) and that rugged abruptness of the Shore which proves a firm barrier to its impetuosity. We have very few strands throughout the whole extent of the Southern Coasts of Devon (the Northern may be said to be without any) and even these such as Budleigh, the Warren, Dawlish, Teignmouth, Paignton and Slapton are extremely narrow; All of which (excepting the latter) are wholly covered by high tides, and all spread at the mouth of rivers and streams.

As the Sea against the neighboring Cliffs is generally seen (in consequence of their greater prominence) to present prospects of tumult and uproar, so, on these little tracks of levelled sand, it more usually exhibits a scene of repose and tranquil beauty. Its waters which when surveyed from the precipice appeared to be tinged with a muddy greenish hue, arising perhaps from its depth and position to the eye, When regarded from these low and shelving shores wear the colour of the sky, and seem as it were rising to meet it. The deafening noise of the deep sea is here converted into gentle murmurs – instead of the Waters dashing against the face of the rock it advances and recedes – still going forward but with just force enough to push its weeds and shells by insensible approaches to the shore.

Close by the spot on which I stood when taking the preceding sketch, but a few days before was discovered the body of a fine athletic Young Man, which had been left on the strand by the receding tide. The Warren being in the parish of Kenton a Messenger was dispatched by the Master of the Inn to apprize me of the circumstance and to be informed what steps he was to take on the occasion. The Coroner of the district being sent for, I rode to Mt. Pleasant, and from the Cloaths being found neatly folded together in an Old Lime kiln under the Cliff, it appeared that the Person had there undrest himself; in bathing had gone beyond his depth, or had intentionally drowned himself. And this latter in all probability was the case: for it came out afterwards, (on the body being recognized by a Person from Exeter), that the deceased had laboured for a considerable time under a derangement of mind, and that escaping in the afternoon from his Keepers house, he had made his way direct to the Sea where, thus unfortunately, he had met his fate. By mere accident this Man got information of the catastrophe of an unknown Person; and on his arrival at Kenton (where I had ordered the corpse for interment) at once ascertained it to be Him of whom he was in search. In consequence of the light that was now thrown on the matter I wrote to Mr Tucker of Coryton, whose brother it proved to be: and in a few days after, the burial took place in the Church of Kenton, in a manner which testified respect to the memory of the deceased but with all the privacy which so distressful an occasion required.

It is very rare, that Events of this nature occur with Us, and it is the more extraordinary, as the Parish for a considerable extent has the River and the Sea for its boundaries. By a strange coincidence however it happened, that on the succeeding morning Another Person met with a similar fate in the river. My old Boatman gave me the detail to the following purport. The poor fellow Sir (said he) had weathered many a rough storm during a longish life, for he was past sixty: He had formerly known better days, and had initiated many of our young Captains of vessels at Topsham (where he lived) in naval matters, but He had of late become much reduced. At this time he had made an arrangement with the Captain of a Vessel, moored at Starcross for a voyage at £4 pr month: and having had his cloaths conveyed on board was on the eve of his departure, when he had a sub poena served on him by the Chamber of Exeter that he might appear at the ensuing sessions as Witness on some cause in litigation respecting their rights on the river, of which, as being an Old Seaman, He was supposed to be intimately acquainted: And to make him an adequate compensation for the loss he might sustain in foregoing his Voyage, The Chamber agreed to pay him the sum he would have received and half guinea pr week board wages. These stipulations having been adjusted, He had gone with a young Man from Topsham in a small boat to the Vessel for some of his cloaths, and on his return, (having taken as it is supposed, a little too much grog) notwithstanding the wind, which blew violently, he carried such a press of sail, as to run the head of the boat under water – in an instant it became full of water and sinking, left the Old Man and the lad to contend with the rough waves for their lives – the struggle on the part of the latter was attended with success, for having strength and dexterity enough to keep himself buoyant for twenty minutes he was rescued from the danger by ye coming up of a coal-lighter, not so the Veteran, he could sustain the conflict but for half the time, when yielding to his fate he sunk, and was probably carried out to sea as his body was not afterwards found.

As there are few rivers more safe than this of the Exe for the navigation of boats and small vessels, the sad incident which thus took place, can be attributed to nothing but to the want of precaution in the old Seaman who had become pot valiant and overlooked all danger. – rarely is it indeed that the craft on the river are deterred by Weather from their avocations either of business or pleasure – for the Winds are more constant here, than on most other rivers in the county (on the Dart and the upper part of the Tamar in particular) which are surrounded by high hills, and where they blow in gusts and eddies; of course not being obnoxious to instantaneous changes and sudden squalls, a boat is infinitely more manageable, and sailing a more safe amusement.

But to return to the Warren. At what period this vast Sand bank (which now extends itself two miles in full front of the River so as to compel it to take a circuitous track) began first to emerge from the waters falls not within the reach of Tradition, much less of written records.

Its formation may well be attributed to the effects occasioned by the waters of the Sea and river opposing one another: Islands are thus often produced by Rivers or Seas carrying mud, sand and similar substances along with their currents, and at last depositing them in some particular place. At the mouth of most great rivers there are to be seen Banks thus formed by the Sand and mud, carried down with the stream, which have rested at that place where the force of the current is diminished by the junction with the Sea. The Tamar, the Yealm, and the Dart, are the only Rivers which, on this Southern coast of Devon are found to be exceptions to this remark, and this peculiarity I conceive to arise from the steep rocky sides of the Rivers, which contracting their mouths into a narrow space encrease the depth of the Volume of waters, and give a force and rapidity to the current which counteracts the deposition and subsidence of sand that would otherwise naturally take place. At the mouths however of All the Other Rivers, whether large or small; (and on this coast we have abundance of both) as there is an expansion of Channel so there is a proportionate diminution of power – reisistance here produces its general effect, and Sand banks uniformly arise which At Sidmouth and Slapton block up altogether the Mouths of the two streams – which being thus absorbed are seen to percolate and filter through the side towards the Sea. Where the width also at the mouth of a River is considerable, there will be found the greatest

deposit of mud and Sand; which by accretion create in process of time dangerous shoals; and give quick and intricate windings to the natural current. Of
this we have a most striking instance in the Exe, which perhaps from Topsham
to its junction with the Sea exhibits at low water a more serpentizing channel
than almost any other of our Rivers, verifying an observation which I have
somewhere met with that "Rivers run in a more direct channel as they immediately leave their sources, and that their sinuosities, and turnings become
more numerous as they proceed: in confirmation of which it is further
remarked that among the Savages of North America it is held as a certain sign
that they are near the Sea when they find the Rivers winding and every now
and then changing their direction" – According to the Stratum of Country
through which the Rivers flow, whether it consists of Rock or soil of a looser
nature, so likewise will be a greater or less accumulation of mud or sand banks
at or near their mouths: The progress however is insensibly effected; and
seldom noticed till by their increase they become impediments to navigation;
Where however such an occurrence has been obvious to remark "the water in
such places has been found by mariners by slow degrees to grow more and
more shallow – at length the bank rises above the surface – for a while it is
considered as a track of useless and barren sand, but the seeds of vegetables,
chiefly of the maritime class, floating thither with high tides, or wafted by
winds take root, and thus binding the loose sandy surface the whole spot is in
time cloathed with verdure. – Such has exactly been the case with this great
Sandbank, which in many of its parts, and especially towards its Eastern
extremity, rises not seldom twenty feet above the waters that surround it; Here
where the tide never reaches, the surface is bound together by long grass
which effectually prevents that locomotion which from the gusts of high
winds would otherwise take place. But there is no plane Superficies to be
seen. All is a jumble of large banks or hillocks; and where by the effects of
Time and the matted rooting of the Grass, a part has been rendered more
dense and solid, excavations have been formed by Rabbits, which tho now
destroyed, till within a few years, overran the whole of the Bank and gave it
the denomination which it still bears of the Warren.

*View entitled 'Exmouth from the
Warren', no date given*
(DRO, 564M/F15/131)

Somewhat of the nature of these Banks may be collected from the drawing, which takes in part of Exmouth with the country beyond, and has for its foreground an old Boat which by an inversion, or turning upside down, not only supplies the pencil with a picturesque object, but what is of higher consideration affords a shelter from a storm to the Traveller, who having given a Signal for the passage boat (which is kept on the Exmouth shore) may be waiting its arrival.

From this Eminence a tolerably correct notion may be formed of the antient course of the River, and of the space over which the tide flowed before those usurpations had been made on it, by the Sandbanks; which have been productive of many inconveniences. For Here, as well as at most other outlets of Rivers, where there is naturally no large volume of water and a considerable expanse of channel, this bad consequence must arise that by the progressive increase of such Sandbanks the navigation up becomes every day more difficult, and the probability at least is, that at one time or other it will be totally obstructed. Thus from both the Shores the accretion of Sand and mud has been of vast extent, insomuch that the Western Cliffs at Mt. Pleasant, and the Eastern ones, on which the new buildings have been erected at Exmouth have not had a Wave dashing against their sides for some Centuries. No longer subject to the influence of the spray, so fatal to vegetation, The shelved Cliff has assumed a verdant garb; and instead of exposing its ruddy crumbling side has submitted to the great law of nature, and become cloathed with most of those adventitious productions, which originate from seeds, thither wafted in the winged state by a favoring breeze, or brought by the secondary interposition of birds. These patches of verdure in alternation with the red stratum of the perpendicular Cliff, which derives its sanguinary teinture from its impregnation with manganese, or the ore of iron, (pure globules of which adhering to one another, of the size of marbles, I have found detached from crumbling masses lying at its feet) form not an unpleasing interchange of colour, as it gives relief to the eye which by a continued survey of one uniform mass would otherwise become fatigued or dissatisfied. This is the general effect produced

View entitled 'Exmouth from the Warren', dated 1799 (DRO, 564M / F15 / 139)

by the perpendicular range of Cliff on the coast, which is as yet beat upon by the surge: but has long ceased to be the case with those which once rose as barriers to the tide but have now been deserted by it. In consequence of the protrusion of these tongues of land the River is compelled to make a quick flexure towards the East, bounded on the South by the Warren and on the North by ye Sand bank extending itself from Exmouth which is a shelter to a vast number of fishing boats, and has been lately decorated by a Windmill, (a very rare object in this county so prolific of rivulets) which while it serves as an ornament to the river, has proved an essential benefit to the town.

This winding, at first sight, appears to be an unnatural outlet of the Exe; and Tradition asserts that about 150 years ago, it exerted itself, and recovered its long lost right of pouring its stream by a direct channel into the sea. Plainly distinguishable does the course appear which it then effected; the side banks are even now rectilinear, and mark the boundaries which restrained the waters from inundating the sandy plain on either side. From the same cause however which originally diverted the current has this channel been filled up, and tho a temporary overflow about ten years ago again took place, yet the present bed of the River notwithstanding the disadvantage which in consequence of its winding, it labours under, is too deep ever to be dispossessed of the honour which it holds of contributing to the opulence of the City of Exeter.

The ride from Mt. Pleasant to the Ferry at Exmouth being for the most part over deep Sands, is in this respect extremely unpleasant: but at neap tides, when the Sea has far withdrawn itself from the level shore; from the Western Cliff to the pebbly beach opposite Exmouth, the Strand is firm and smooth, insomuch that a fleet horse may traverse it from one end to the other exciting but little sound and leaving scarce any impression: perfectly the reverse of the effects that may be conceived to have arisen from a race on the ground described in the fine line of Virgil

"Quadrupedante putrem sonitu quatitungula campum"

In the course of a ride on the strand at such a season, as an approach is made to the mouth of the river, another large Sandbank extending itself in a line parallel with the other is plainly discoverable further out in the Sea and forms what is termed the Bar, which cannot be passed by Vessels of burthen but nearly at high water. Between these two at the recess of the tide a large body of the Rivers water, conducted betwixt them to an outlet on the Western quarter is seen to flow; the depth however is too inconsiderable to admit at any time the navigation of ought but the smallest craft; and the main Channel (notwithstanding the circuitous track which the more interior current has been forced to take) is yet found to keep its course near the Eastern Cliffs, where the larger volume of waters lose themselves in the Sea.

On turning round the point the surge-compressed strand becomes at once loose and the horse sinks below his fetlock joint. But if there be a detraction from the pleasure of riding there is an accession to the Scenery; Exmouth, as in the opposite sketch is beheld in a pleasing point of view; and if the eye be directed Northward up the River, the whole of its expanse is descried as far as the town of Topsham and the principal objects on both shores (particularly that on the west) are without difficulty to be discriminated especially the little town of Starcross and the Castle and Belvidere at Powderham.

In the subsequent sketch I have endeavored to give some idea of this Scenery & of the entrance into the harbour between the Warren and the Exmouth sand bank. Little more however can be effected on a confined scale, (if the Scene to be delineated should happen as in the present case to be extensive and of wide compass) than a mere simple display of the disposition and locality of objects: Of these the Sight may be gratified even in their complication, variety or indistinctness, and in the reality there may be Beauty which the stroke of the Pencil may either be unable or unfit to express. There cannot be doubt but that there may be found innumerable Scenes in Nature to delight the Eye besides those which may be copied as Pictures: and indeed, One of the keenest and most intelligent Observers of Picturesque Scenery (Mr. Gilpin) has (as it is observed) often regretted that few are capable of being so represented without considerable licence and Alteration.

The "*Quidlibet audendi Pictoribus*" may be a good axiom for those, who have a bold hand and an excursive imagination and whose object is to compose a perfect Picture "*tota teres atque rotunda*" But as that which in the commencement of these tours I proposed to myself was a verity of description, and a similitude of portraiture, that the nature of the County, its diversified Scenery, its Architecture, its Buildings public and private, in short All that might attract curiosity, or be deserving notice might be collected together and placed as it were in one mass before the eye; So I have never thought myself at liberty to avail myself of the license which Horace has allowed the Painter, but have invariably restricted myself to the nature and disposition of the Objects as they lay before me, and adhered in all respects to a fidelity of representation.

Hence a value, trivial tho' it may be, will be annexed to these volumes; which possibly at some future day may be estimated not from any merit that they may possess in their delineations, or descriptions but from their truth. Conscious as I am of the insufficiency either of my sketches, or my remarks to exhibit a striking and satisfactory portrait of the County; yet, thus united and accurately drawn they serve to illustrate each other - and as it has been my endeavor not only to communicate my ideas of places but faithfully to exhibit their appearances to the eye; so the full Advantage of the plan, whatever it may be, has been obtained; and the descriptions and representations reciprocally heighten their effects.

"Alterius sic
"Altera poscit opem res, et conjurat amice"

"Indeed there are subjects, (and such a River as the Exe may be considered to be one of them) which to be completely illustrated require the combined aid of the pen and the pencil. Verbal description is inadequate to give a correct idea of a landschape; or of that combination of objects by which any particular prospect becomes beautiful – While views of rural Scenery, of Castles and

View entitled 'River Exe from the Warren', dated 1799 (DRO, 564M/F15/143)

Abbies, or of towns and cities are incompetent to instruct in the history of the inhabitants, or in recording the memorabilia of their Worthies.

By the union of these Arts the effect produced, is complete: individually exerted, every effort must be imperfect. By combination, the end is admirably gained, of explaining, and illustrating each other.

From these remarks and from the Warren on which I have thus long expatiated I make my return to the boat; and launching again into the stream, with the flowing tide pass rapidly over a deep part of the river, called the Bite towards the northern shore of Exmouth.

Where the River turns round the extremity of this extended Sand bank, an eddy is formed by the tide, and by it, has been effected this pool which probably has been termed the Bite, either from the deception into which Strangers are led from the quick turning of the channel of the River; or from the instant passage from shallow into deep water; for here at the recess of the tide the sounding is from two to three fathom; and at Spring tides the depth is found to be near six fathom. The waters rising at this period about 18 or 20 feet.

Steering in a gut between Exmouth and a vast Sand bank lying in mid river which was now beginning to be covered by the tide, We came in view of Marpool, the seat of Mr Hull, low-situated at but a small distance from the water. From hence in an oblique course we made our way to the Western bank, necessitated to confine our track to the Rivers bed in consequence of the slow advance of the tide; but surrounded as I now was by numerous objects of attraction, the line which I pursued, whether it were zigzag or Serpentine was incontestibly that of Beauty.

The intricacies of the Channel, at this early period of the tide would however have baffled the nautical skill of the most experienced Mariner previously unacquainted with it – to my Boatmen they were thoroughly known and we threaded them all without difficulty.

Starcross on our re-approach wore a neat and rural appearance: for though the greater part of its buildings ranged themselves on the bank of the River; Yet at their back, Orchards and hedge-row trees crowded in close; and not far behind the hill of Warburrow, crested with firs rose in picturesque beauty. As we left Starcross the Seat of Capt. Crichton, lowly tho pleasantly situate rose

View entitled 'Powderham Castle', dated 1799
(DRO, 564M/F15/158)

to our view, and in quick succession the house of Mr Marler at Starpoint nearer to the Shore; But over all these and indeed over every other object on the River (whatever be its Attraction) *"Quantum inter Stellas Luna minores"* towered the Castellated Grandeur of the seat of Lord Courtenay, which now presented itself at some distance to our notice. The assemblage of beauties, under the combination of Architectural variety and magnificence, and of Scenery most picturesque, as we made our approaches, or (in the Sailors phrase) neared them, became more striking. The Sketch will give the best idea of them; and as it takes in (with the Castle and Belvidere of Powderham) the tower erected to the memory of Genl. Lawrence by Sir Robert Palk on Pen hill, will Point their relative situation.

Too remote however for discrimination. This Water sketch will give but an inadequate notion of the Castle or the grounds: I shall therefore expatiate on them; and quitting my boat, shall take my first station before the Antient pile itself, and introduce that to notice.

On a near approach towards the front of the Edifice, the eye is at once arrested by the style of its Architecture, and by the multiplicity of parts, which at different periods, have been added to the original Mass, and now form one whole.

In a Gothic Pile, when the Character of the Antient Architecture has been scrupulously adhered to, no additional structure can well offend the sight: One of its component principles, is irregularity and if the peculiar cast predominates, in the pointed door and window, the pinnacle, and the battlement. The Antiquarian Architect will not admit that the Costume has been violated by any appendage how numerous soever they may be. And if in an Architectural light there Shall be no incongruity or disgust in this irregular mode of Building, in a picturesque one there cannot possibly be any: indeed no style whatever can be so adapted to the pencil, as one of these old Gothic Edifices: for the strongest and most beautiful play of light and shade must necessarily proceed from those bold projections either of towers or buttresses, that break the uniform surface of the front: and from the pinnacles turrets and battlements which destroy the Horizontal line of roof and constitute the principal (and I may add) characteristic enrichment of Gothic Architecture.

View entitled 'East front of Powderham Castle', dated 1799 (DRO, 564M/F15/162)

These are the features of the front of Powderham Castle towards the East, which is the chief one of entrance and that delineated in the foregoing page. The suite of apartments at the Northern end is the only one that has any pretensions to size or magnificence. Here was the Chapel: a compartment once deemed essential in a Baronial Mansion, wherein Religion (if not virtually) was at least ritually observed and venerated; In those days the Hall was presided over by Hospitality, and the Chapel by Devotion – but these old fashioned notions are now become obsolete: their remembrance is but barely retained; and as the hospitable board is no longer spread; and the Chapel, by its conversion into a Saloon, has been desecrated, even this will soon pass away and be forgotten. But the alterations which this range of the Building has undergone, have not been confined to the interior part: an excrescence has of late grown out of the northern angle, from the designs of Mr Wyatt, the Cynosure of Gothic Architecture, the plan of which has been conceived by many to be not less injudicious than the situation. In this opinion I can not bring myself to coincide, – The drawing room presented to the North a blank wall and a recess. Of course on this part there was wanting somewhat to arrest and satisfy the eye: the building that has been erected does both, – the vacant space is filled up and that with an object decidedly beautiful. If there be ought to find fault with, I conceive it is not in the structure or in the situation, except it be in its projection beyond the front of the drawing room, which possibly to render the whole plan compleat could not well be avoided.

The two following Views exhibit this Northern front, in a near and more remote distance. The Scenery around and beyond the Castle is most picturesque, but a very small part of what the eye can comprehend, is taken in by the sketches; from these however it will readily be admitted, that the Edifice in this point of view possesses a more than common grandeur, and the prospect greater variety and beauty than can be perhaps enjoyed from any other station. Part of the Western front is introduced into these two drawings; which, consisting of square towers of considerable height and simple undecorated Architecture, carries with it more of the antient style of Castellated structures;

View entitled 'North View of Powderham Castle', dated 1799 (DRO, 564M/F15/166)

Untitled view, no date given
(DRO, 564M/F15/168)

Untitled view, no date given
(DRO, 564M/F15/172)

Indeed there is little doubt that the original Building consisted altogether of these square towers; in their simplicity there is more grandeur conveyed to the mind, than what can be derived from the crowded ornaments of later times – and that the Edifice in such a state is most picturesque will in all probability be allowed on the inspection of the opposite sketch, which represents it chiefly

in this aspect. Where a lane, branching from Kenton opens into the marshes, between the terminating angles of hedges which afford most excellent side screens, these elevated Towers offer themselves to the view, as massy bulwarks; in earlier times impregnable to every assault. Embosomed, as it were in groves of Elms and Oaks, scarcely any part of the Castle is visible, excepting this the most antient; indeed but a few years have elapsed, since All Other was shrouded from the sight: the humbler parts of the Edifice, offices and Servants rooms were there concealed; The former Proprietors with due taste and judgement permitted the old Elms to spread out their branchy arms on every side; and thus luxuriant and unpruned *"nullo violata securi"* – they afforded protection, and instead of exposing a modern mean building to the eye of the Spectator they wrapt it in becoming obscurity, and suffered it not to detract from the venerable magnificence which rested on the other parts of the Castle.

But alas, on the Stewards parlour, and on the Servants hall few rays of a noontide Sun were in consequence of the thick tree-trunks and interwoven foliage allowed to play – The look of Cheerfulness, and the feel of comfort was of course denied! ! !

Hæ nugæ seria ducunt in mala"

To redress such intolerable evils, the shrubbery beneath these noble trees is hewn down and cast into the Hall fire – Many of the trees themselves coæval with the greater part of the Buildings, are rooted from their firm beds, and even the lateral branches of the few that were permitted to remain are deprived of their leafy honours and amputated to the bare trunk – insomuch that the shabby front which had for so long a period lain in concealment, now exhibited itself to open view; and the Sun at the hour of dinner smiles cheerily on the table in the Servants hall! !

Ast non Nostrûm est . I shall therefore betake myself to a distance from whence these minutiæ, too conspicuous in a near view, will be indiscernible,

Untitled view, no date given
(DRO, 564M/F15/176)

or at least lost amidst a confluence of objects, which so bewitch me, whenever I behold them with their transcendant beauty that I quickly forget my disgust and am apt to exclaim "where there is such a profusion of attraction, such an assemblage of the rare excellencies of Nature and Art *"Non ego paucis offendar maculis"*.

From the hill of Warburrow, this western front is seen in high perfection, but about midway, from the crest to the valley, in a point of view more picturesque and discriminated. From this station the preceding sketch was taken in which the Castle appears a conspicuous and most beautiful object – around it crowd noble groves of oak, elm and beech. Over them rises the tower of the parochial Church, beyond which in a wide expanse is spread out the River Exe, whose opposite bank is decorated with Nutwell the seat of Lord Heathfield and with the town of Lympstone seated within the recess of a creek, whilst to crown the rich Landschape a termination is given to it by the rising hill of Woodbury, marked on its summit by the Valla of an encampment. Such is the verbal description of this most enchanting view – but inadequate is the power of my pen or pencil to do it justice – and were it even equal to the task, but a circumscribed notion of the prospect at the utmost could be entertained – for the eye of the Spectator on the spot expatiates over a vast extent of Landschape, which no one delineation could comprehend – and which, if attempted by several, by being comprized within small and limited space, the objects in general would be confused by their number and approximation, or indistinct by their remote distance.

I must therefore rest satisfied with my endeavors to convey a general idea of the local situation of Powderham Castle, both with respect to the beauties of its environs, and to the Edifice itself; and more fully to effect this I shall accumulate my sketches of the contiguous scenery and not be sparing of my remarks.

But it may be proper before that I return to my descriptions of the picturesque to introduce somewhat of the History of the Building which for so many centuries has been the possession and residence of the Courtenay family. By whom the present Castle was erected does not appear to have been well ascertained. Antiquaries have different opinions, as will ever be the case where there are no records to identify facts. It seems generally to be allowed that there was a Castle here either before the Conquest, or that one was built by Willm de Ou, a Norman of rank who attended the Conqueror on his expedition, and to whom (for his good services Powderham and Whitestone were given, as appears from the book of Domesday. No vestige however of this original Edifice can be traced in the present one – that is on the supposition that the style of Architecture be allowed as a test – for all the Arches of the doors and windows are Gothic, and there is no one apparent circumstance that can refer us to a period prior to the reign of Henry the 3d. when the Gothic Architecture had, in All kinds of Buildings, Religious or civil, superseded the Norman. – I shall not stay to consider whether its erection may be attributed, (as Camden asserts) to Isabella de fortibus, Countess of Devon and Albermarle or to any of those Proprietors, who stiled themselves "de Powderham", but shall hasten to the period in which by a marriage with Margaret Daughter and Heiress of Humphrey de Bohun Earl of Hereford and Essex it became vested in the person of Hugh (second of that name of the Courtenays) Earl of Devon, whose Ancestor, Reginald came into England with Queen Elinor (Wife to Henry 2d.) in the year 1151) and who towards, or (more correctly perhaps) beyond the middle of the 14th century gave it to his fifth Son Sir Philip Courtenay who is said to be the first of the family who took up his residence at Powderham. What alterations have taken place in this Edifice during a space of 450 years, in which the Courtenays have been the sole Proprietors cannot now be ascertained. Throughout the whole period however there cannot be a doubt, but that it retained not only its Castellated form, but that in reality it was a place of Strength, and defensible against an Enemy. From an Engraving extant of it by Buck, we may form a correct notion of the fortified state in which it had perhaps remained for some Centuries – Superadded to the square towers which are yet in being there were battlemented walls which enclosed an area in the front; which at the entrance was strongly guarded by a gatehouse of similar structure – Whether these ever experienced an Assault before the commotions in the time of Charles 1st., I am at a loss to say. At that period it was converted into a garrison for the King, and was attacked by a detachment from Fairfax's Army; who fortifying themselves in the Church at Powderham, (after having made a fruitless attempt on the Castle), were therein in their turn besieged. Contriving to procure provisions from Nutwell which was then also a fortified House, they held out for some time, (in the course of which hand Grenades were thrown into the Church) and at length despairing of reinforcement, they made good their retreat over the river. – In consequence of the great preparations, which were making by the Parliament forces for the sieges of Exeter and Dartmouth (which last was taken by storm Jan.19th 1645–6) all further attempts on the Castle of Powderham, were protracted 'till Sunday 25th January; when Colonel Hammond having sat down before it with some force, it was the same night surrendered to him – notwithstanding that it had within it for its defence 300 Men under the command of Sir [blank] Meredith with 4 pieces of Ordnance, 5 barrels of gunpowder, and Match and bullet proportionable. – In 1715 the North wing, projecting in front of the Castle, was erected by Sir Wm the great Grand father of the present Lord Courtenay, which consisting of a suite of three rooms, had in its furthermost a Chapel, and over it a Library. Since his decease (which happened in 1735) all the buildings which were before the Castle have been demolished – the walls and Gatehouse which from the lower windows shut out the view of the Park and the River – and by the present Proprietor, as has been already observed – the Chapel has been desecrated by its conversion into a superb Drawing room. On this head there is rather a curious passage in Polwheles 2d. vol. of his Hist. of Devon – In page 170 He says "The present Lord Courtenay has greatly improved and ornamented the house. Among other alterations He has converted the Chapel into a very elegant Drawing room." From which, I think the only inference to be drawn is, that this alteration of the apartment, this conversion of a Chapel into a Drawing room, is by Mr P. considered as an improvement, and an ornamenting of the House! ! ! – In such a Mansion, as Powderham Castle, a considerable part of which, has beyond a doubt stood for four or five Centuries, We might have expected to find, Rooms capacious if not elegant or comfortable. In feudal times an immense Hall at least was not to be dispensed with. Such there must have been here tho' no vestige may be now apparent. Whether such an apartment existed on the spot where the North-wing has been erected I know not; but as the antient Chapel was a portion of this range of Building, it is more than probable that the Hall might have also formed a part. – All of the present rooms of any consequence that are used by the family are comparatively of modern erection. All the magnificence of the Castle consists in the suite of room which was built in 1717. And the additional one, united with it by the present Lord Courtenay. These are of handsome size and splendid in their decorations. – The pier glasses, the Chimney pieces and the furniture equipment – in the highest ton of prevailing taste, have been all lately introduced. The Music room, over which Lord Courtenays natural Genius in a more than common degree, has fitted him to preside, may be considered as the finest and most expensive room in the County: – And to it Taste seems to have been restricted; for I cannot find any of her handywork in the Alterations that have been made without doors.

The most prominent of these is that which relates to the Water. The late Lord in the formation of the Canal, committed in my opinion, and in the opinion of others of acknowledged taste a palpable error, – and I conceive a no less mistaken judgment has been evinced in the late embankments and rectangular ditches, the intention of which was to drain off the stagnant water without heeding what effect it would be productive of.

To lay out such grounds as these of Powderham, (those on the East and Southern aspects – for to the others but little improvement could be given, so beautiful are they by Nature) required no small degree of Genius for "Landschape Gardening" and a purse not easily exhausted:

> *"Ce noble emploi demande un Artiste qui pense;*
> *Prodigue de Genie, mais non pas de depense"*

but in the alterations which have taken place in the marsh at Powderham, the obtruding reflexion will be the inverse of (part at least of) this quotation.

Niggardly will be found the Genius that plann'd tho' great prodigality has been lavished in the expenditure. As there have been various opinions respecting the taste, ingenuity, and beauty of the plans which have at different times been carried into execution in this part of the Grounds, I shall occupy a page or two in the discussion.

In the formation of the piece of water, as well as what regards the later alterations on the Marsh nearer the Castle, I cannot think that sufficient attention has been paid to the situation, or to the Character of the place. A Master in the Art of Landschape gardening has asserted that "All rational improvement of grounds is necessarily founded on a due attention to the Character, and situation of the place to be improved". Let the question then be asked, whether when a Natural stream was found running in the lowest part of the marsh the design was judicious to fill up the original Channel and compel the waters to pursue their course in a new one and that on nearly the highest part of the ground or was there consistence (when the River Exe, widening into an Æstuary washed the eastern boundary of the plain) that there should be scooped out a broad Canal, whose waters in a sluggish current might empt themselves into it? When the Eye of the Spectator from any eminence, took both into view, it could not refrain from making a comparison 'not very flattering to the latter'. I am satisfied therefore that in the formation of this large sheet of Water the Character of the spot has been violated and that it would have been preserved, with credit to the taste of the Proprietor and without the disbursement of £5000, (which first and last has been expended on the Canal, and on the dams and ditches which have been found necessary since to carry off the overflowings of the water, stagnating in the low ground) had the River Kenn been permitted to run on its antient bed, broken perhaps by a rough wear, and here and there overhung by a few Alder trees and Willows. – If this Marsh had been freed from any conspicuous inæqualities, which by mishapen excrescence, or subsidence of water might obtrude themselves upon and offend the eye; it had been (especially when put into contrast with the bold prominencies of the contiguous Park, and its crowded treasures of trees and groves) an object of beauty from the house, instead of disgust. It certainly wanted not the variety which has been given it, by the round clumps of firs which dot its surface; or by the unnatural piece of water, which on the highest part, between equal banks, has been conducted through it.

J. Swete. May 1799.

JOURNAL EIGHTEEN

Devon Record Office, 564M/F16

In Journal Eighteen the Reverend Swete continues his description of the Exe estuary including Powderham, Nutwell, Lympstone, Topsham and Exminster.

PICTURESQUE SKETCHES
OF DEVON

John Swete, Oxton House
May 1799.

Continuation of a Sketch of the River Exe and its Environs

The cheerfulness of an extensive level plain, rich in its verdure, and well-stocked with cattle (especially when it is bounded, as is this of Powderham by a noble expanse of water on one side – on another by a Village here and there distinguished among tufts of trees and verdant inclosures – and backed by a gently rising hill diversified by glade, and woodland). Would have compensated for want of further diversification by water, or by petty circular clumps of plantations: indeed, I conceive, such an interchange from the more picturesque scenes of the Park to have been what would have been most wished for, as an alternation of the most desirable nature in forming one of the component parts of a place of grandeur and consequence. I have hinted that small circular plantations of firs, instead of contributing to the embellishment of grounds, most sensibly detract from their beauty and their consequence. In this (if I err not) I deliver the sentiments of those whose Taste in Landscape Gardening appears to be the criterion of truth; and by which the Fashion of the day, has regulated all its improvements.

In a poetic garb Mr Knight has denounced them by a repetition of anathemas; and especially when, having poured out his enthusiastic encomia on the wild unrestrained beauties of an antient forest.

> *"Where every shaggy shrub, and spreading tree*
> *Proclaimed the seat of native liberty;*
> *In loose and varied groups unheeded thrown*
> *And never taught the Planters care to own"*

He proceeds to place in contrast and to lament, the effects produced by the mistaken efforts of Art under the direction of a false Taste

> *"But ah! how different is the formal lump*
> *Which the Improver plants, and calls a Clump!*
> *Break, break, Ye Nymphs the fence that guards it round!*
> *With browsing Cattle all its forms confound"*

"Whatever singularities and capriciousness Mr Knights didactic Poem of the "Landscape" may possess, in these reflexions, I believe he will be found just, and supported by the opinion of All who have given their sentiments on the matter; "No Man of Sense (says Mr Repton) can hesitate betwixt the Natural group of trees composed of various growths and those formal patches of firs which too often disfigure a lawn under the name of a Clump. But the most certain method of producing a group of five or six trees is to plant fifty or sixty within the same fence; and this Mr Brown advised with a mixture of Firs to shelter the young trees during their infancy. Unfortunately the Neglect, or bad

129

taste of his Employers would occasionally suffer the Firs to remain long after they had completed their office as Nurses: Whilst Others have actually planted Firs only in such Clumps, totally misconceiving Mr Browns original intention." Amongst those by whom Mr Browns design appears to have been misunderstood Mr Knight may be classed – for he bids the Fiend of Deformity follow to the tomb his favorite Brown:

> "Brown whose innovating hand
> First dealt thy curses o'er this fertile land
> First taught the walk in formal spires to move
> And from their haunts the secret Dryads drove
> With Clumps bespotted o'er the mountains side
> "And bade the stream "twixt banks close–shaven glide"

From this censure Mr Brown is vindicated by Mr Repton who further observes "Clumps, like Mr Browns are to be considered in a less offensive light than a number of starving single trees surrounded by heavy cradle fences which are often dotted over the whole surface of a Park" – Besides, a Clump is never to be considered as an object of present beauty, but as a more certain expedient for producing future beauties than Young trees which seldom grow when exposed singly to the wind and Sun"

I am sorry to remark, that besides this instance in the Powderham Marsh, the taste of introducing circular Clumps of firs, intended to stand, has of late strangely prevailed in this neighborhood, and instead of becoming an Ornament have certainly proved a deformity to the lawns on which they have been placed. If "*Artis est celare Artem*" be an axiom religiously to be attended to, by all those whose wish it may be that the alteration of their grounds should make as near approaches as possible to Nature, then most assuredly circular clumps should never hold a place among them, for nothing more conspicuously will betray the interposition of Art – nothing will savour less of the picturesque; for nothing can be found less conformable to the free and ever-beautiful operations of Nature.

At a spot where the Lover of Picturesque Beauty finds much to disprove, and more to commend, how pleasant to pass from the Strictures of the former, to the approbation of the latter. Leaving therefore the unhappy Marsh I take my way through the Park to those high grounds, whose rounded summit has been crested with a triangular turreted Building called the Belvidere. – in the line to which the two following sketches occurr'd.

The view is towards the S. West, and the Scenery is of the most beautifull and rural nature. The Village of Kenton conspicuous in its tall tower of elegant Architecture and sober colouring; with the sweetly-situated House of Mrs Cookes tufted with Elms on the right compose the middle ground; whilst, in one of the drawings in particular, the more distant part is seen to terminate in the prominent grove of Oaks which surround my Cottage, and in the pine-clad eminence of Mamhead.

From various parts of this aspect of the Park the prospect is delicious – not so full and extensive as when it is commanded from the windows of the Belvidere, but perhaps, to the Painter more gratifying, as it is set off by a foreground of Old Oaks.

Under a hanging wood composed of an intermixture of firs and forest trees, hewn from the living rock, and separated from the Park by a high pale, is here to be seen a Grotto; not one of those damp subterranes, from whose dropping roof the pendulous Stalactites hangs, and over whose fretted floor the chrystalline rill gurgles: but a dry, cool Excavation, forming a delicious retreat from the Summer Sun. The shelly decorations intermingled with spar and moss, owe their arrangement to the taste of the fair Sisters of Lord Courtenay, by whose hands also have the Roses been planted, and the Woodbines trained which o'er canopy the entrance of the grot, and fill it with perfume.

This is indeed a spot of attraction and not unworthy the strain of some such Muse, as heretofore celebrated a Grotto composed by the united labours of

View entitled 'Kenton and High house', no date given (DRO, 564M/F16/7)

View entitled 'Kenton', no date given (DRO, 564M/F16/9)

nine Sisters than these perchance, not more fair, or ingenious? The situation of this Grot is at the commencement of a walk or drive, extending upwards of a mile round the Southern acclivity of the hill on whose elevate summit stands the Belvidere; This winds most charmingly, gradually ascending through some of the fine Plantations of firs, and forest trees in the County whose beauty and luxuriance arrest every ones admiration.

Below these, on a glade, in part open to the Sun are the pleasure gardens, formed within the last ten years by the direction of Lord Courtenay; These are much visited; and consisting of Pastures of the most beautifull flowers, interchanged by close shaven lawns, shrubberies, and a Summer building forming at once an elegant room and a conservatory for curious plants certainly deserve the attention of every Visitor of Powderham.

I shall now bend my Steps to the Belvidere itself, but as when beheld on the open hill it has far less of the Picturesque in its appearance than when viewed from the lower grounds, where, over trees and woods it is seen to tower in a more pleasing distance, I shall here introduce two sketches of it, taken from two opposite points by which a tolerably clear notion may be gathered of the nature of the Building and of its local circumstances.

Beyond the Mill and somewhat westward of the pleasure gardens, where a lane leads to Kenton, rises an old foot bridge, consisting of a single Arch, over a branch of the River Kenn (or perhaps rather over the antient course of its waters, before the chief volume was diverted from its natural channel to subserve the use of the Mill) – From hence, was taken the opposite sketch, which exclusive of the object I have in view of giving an idea of the Edifice itself, would in a picturesque light from beauty and variety of its accompaniments have been recommended to my notice. Indeed had there been a greater degree of magnitude, in the bridge, and a more important swell of water, the objects in the foreground of themselves would have constituted a Scenery, that could not have failed of arresting every Painters admiration; the turn of the arch, in a state of dilapidated beauty fringed with weeds and brambles, overhung by old Alders, was in the highest stile of picturesque excellence, and the tout ensemble composed a scene which I have never passed by, without stopping to gaze at and admire.

On the Eastern side of the Hill, where the public road conducts from the Village and Castle of Powderham to Exeter, I took the other sketch to which I have alluded. A Gate here gives admission into the Park contiguous to a vast Walnut tree and to a small thatched building, used as a stable, both of these are picturesque objects, especially the latter whose roof and walls are in a great degree overspread with ivy. The whole of the ground on this part is as naturally diversified by the undulations of hill and Valley, and wood, thicket and groups of trees, as that which lies more towards the South, and which (to speak more correctly as being the place where the Deer are kept) is properly the Park.

Ascending from the ivy-clad building, a glen rises between two hills, towards the summit of the ridge on which appears the Belvidere. This glen is rendered more than commonly beautiful by successive groups of Oaks, which in the sketch raise their heads over the rounded glade of greensward, and which rising towards the turreted Edifice give it the appearance of emerging from a grove:

Having expatiated thus much on the scenery in the immediate environs of the Belvidere, "*et quorum Pars magna fuit*" I come to the Building itself: In the year 1770 it was begun under the auspices of the late Lord Courtenay, who conceiving that this eminence was happily adapted for the erection of a Pleasure building, which might serve for an ornamental object to the circumjacent Country, and from, whence the beauties of that country might at leisure and with convenience be desired: hit upon a tower [later notes in pencil interpolated].

With some trivial alterations, upon this plan did the Edifice rise, and in the space of three years, came to its completion: It consists, (as may have been already collected from the drawings) of a triangular Body, with a turret of a hexagonal form at each of its corners – the height of this latter is near 62 feet, and exceeds the tower itself by about 12. The ground floor is an area into which open three iron gates; from thence a Staircase winding within one of the turrets, conducts into a room of the same dimensions as the area, which has a large semi-circular crowned window corresponding to each of the gates beneath. The interior beauty of this room is considerable: but by it, the attention is for a short time engaged, if the eye of the Spectator has glanced towards the prospect offerr'd to it by either of the windows. The superior excellence of all these, to the views commonly enjoyed from an eminence, is distinctness, and discrimination:

The whole of a most beautifully-diversified Country lies around, spread out as it were, a Map, where every object has its place without confusion, and can

most easily be ascertained. Was I to dilate on this, I should have it in my power to introduce into my description almost every object of consequence within twenty circumjacent Parishes. But as a plan of this nature would occupy too great a number of pages, I shall compress it within a few.

Pursuing the course of the Sun, from the S. East Window, the eye ranges over the Church and Parsonage of Powderham, crosses the fine expanse of water formed by the Aestury of the Exe and resting awhile upon the cove and close-compacted town of Lympstone, follows the line of the River, studded with Villa's and enriched by Elmy hedgerows, towards its embouchure where is most pleasantly seated the bathing town of Exmouth. Beyond extends an horizon of sea, elevated above the Warren sands, and continuing Westward, till it is excluded from the sight by the hills at Mt Pleasant. Nearer is the

View entitled 'Belvidere S. W. aspect', no date given
(DRO, 564M/F16/15)

View entitled 'Belvidere N. E. view', no date given
(DRO, 564M/F16/19)

crested height of Warburrow, beneath whose plantations of fir, the town of Kenton, stretching itself for a mile in the most picturesque manner, houses, fields, and orchards most rurally intermingled at length, on reaching the River, collects itself into a larger mass of Buildings at Starcross; here the features are of a maritime cast: an extent of shore being visible and the surface of the water covered over by boats, barges, and Vessels chiefly in the coal trade, of too large a tonnage to pass up the river to Topsham or Exeter.

Nearer yet appear the grounds of Powderham: whose marshy level, intersected by the canal, loses by distance all its deformities, and gives an agreable variety to the more unequal and delightfully wooded Scenes of the Park; Shrouded by trees, little of the Castle itself is seen but the summits of its Western towers – these however tell us where the Mansion is situated, to which these grounds belong, and heighten the embellishment.

Much of this delicious Scenery is taken in by the S. West window, from whence in particular that fine specimen of Gothic Architecture, the Church and tower of Kenton, is seen to high advantage: contiguous is a pleasingly seated house belonging to Mrs Cooke, while in the remotest distance Mamhead, the seat of the Earl of Lisburne, noted from afar by its pine woods, and obelisk marks the extreme point visible of Haldown to the South: – Full in front if the view be taken early in the Morning, appears the Valley of Oxton, Situate amongst woods unless the Sunbeam rests on the Eastern face of the House, the Building is but faintly distinguished; Let the light be introduced between its hills, and it at once becomes an object of consequence and beauty: – beyond to the West, little is there to be descried in the Edifice line but Haldown House, the fine seat of Sir Lawrence Palk and the tower which caps the the cone of Pen hill. There are several other seats which lie in the intermediate Country, such as Bickham and Trehill in particular but these are situate in dips which descend from Haldown, and (different from the Valley of Oxton) the eye passes towards them in a transverse line and of course is intercepted by the hills which decline parallel with the Vallies.

Turning now to the N. East window, and taking in the view at Lympstone, which was the commencement of the prospect towards the S. East, the first object that arrests the attention is Nutwell, the newly-erected Seat of Lord Heathfield – this with its inclosing woods, which seem to open themselves only for the reception of the Edifice, is certainly the most beautiful spot on the opposite side of the River – from thence the waters begin to widen, and the tide at flood, fills up a bason of considerable expanse, which however contracts itself into a much narrower space before it washes the town of Topsham, which is seen pleasantly seated on a level strand, at whose projecting point the Waters of the Exe and Clyst form a confluence. The Scenery here is too charming to be passed away from lightly; the rural appearance of the town hitherward houses blended with trees, with the numerous Vessels that have reached thus far up the River to unlade their cargoes, not withstanding the shoals of sand in which it abounds, afford a singularly-motley picture to the sight from which no detraction can be made but in the Church, which is a heavy unmeaning Pile!

The light reflected from the surface of the water, now only points out the course of the River, which winds through pastures of the most fertile nature, whose contiguous uplands, gently rising, are adorned, with a greater number of Villa's of consequence than any other part of the county, among which may be enumerated.

The Retreat of Sir Alexer Hamiltons, Wear, Mr Spicers, Newcourt, Mr Shapleighs, Mt Radford Mr Barings! These with the towers of the Churches of Exminster and Alphington, conduct the eye onwards to the City of Exeter and its Cathedral which, proudly supereminent, stands aloft, exhibiting its southern front, in majesty and beauty most conspicuous. The greyish brown tint of this stately Edifice, on the supposition that it had not been situate in the center of the City, would have kept it in its true place of Perspective – Not withstanding therefore its magnitude there is no deception in regard to its distance;

as there visibly is respecting the White towers before noticed; A Stranger unacquainted with the Country, should the bright Sun shine on these towers, would conceive them to be situate much nearer the sight than they are in reality. This however is the case only at times and is altogether dependant on the Sun, operating on the atmosphere; A Master of the laws of Perspective, has offer'd some ingenious observations on the subject. He says, "We observe that Objects, not only diminish in their size but in their distinctness in proportion to the body of air betwixt the eye and the Objects. Those nearest are strongly represented, while other parts, as they recede become less distinct, till at last the outline of a distant Hill seems melting into the air itself"

Such are the laws of Aerial Perspective on all Objects but not on All alike, since it is the peculiar property of Light, and the other reflection of light unmixed by Colour to suffer much less by comparison than any other object – and it is for this reason that we are so much deceived in the distance of perfectly white objects – the light reflected from a white-washed House makes it appear out of place. And effects of similar nature are produced by snow, and the placid face of water shining as a Mirror. But to return from this digression to the Belevidere, which from the bold considerations of Prospect beauty, detailed in the foregoing descriptions, may well be conceived in those essentials for such a Building to possess a supereminence over every other spot of the kind in the county. Indeed, according to my own ideas on the subject, it does possess that supereminence; for I know of no Prospect Station, that can be brought into comparison with it.

Descending from this point of elevation, into the Park again, it cannot but be remarked that what the prospect loses in extent it gains in picturesque beauty; the alternation of swell and depression in the ground, the grove, the avenue, the wood, of old venerable forest trees, the deer sporting among them in numerous herds, and the gleams of light and shade shot athwart the green pasture, in narrow checquered lines, or in a broad mass; All together, with every now and then catches of the Castle, of the river, and the sea constituted what in every sense of the Word might be termed Picturesque.

I am now to direct my steps to the Boat-house, in my way to which I cross the great Avenue, which in former days led from Exeter, through the Village of Powderham to the Gateway of the Castle. The avenue indeed, correctly speaking, in the general acceptance of the word, has long ceased to be such – the regular uniformity of the trees, by rooting them up here and there, has been destroyed and tho' perhaps much of the stiffness and heaviness of the avenue has by this means been overcome, still however a certain portion of the Effect remains, and which no art of Man, in a less period than half a century can efface. From this part of the Park, a few houses of the Village are seen – they are within the pale, and would in continuity with the remainder, was it not for the gate which excludes them. Well is it indeed that they are thus excluded, for a more miserable and offensive Village is scarcely elsewhere to be found. It may be said that when discoursing of the Castle and the Park all observations relative to the Village (which no Visiter in the routine Tour is conducted to see) are extraneous!

In regard to what concerns the Visiter they may be so considered, otherwise however, when the grounds are taken as a Whole, or when the taste, or the comforts of the Owner (speaking to feelings which the Owner of such domains should possess) are regarded. "In former days (says Mr Repton) the dignity of a house was supposed to increase in proportion to the quantity of walls and buildings with which it was surrounded – to these were sometimes added tall ranks of trees where shade contributed to the gloom at that time held essential to magnificence. Modern taste has discovered that Greatness and cheerfulness are not incompatible. It has thrown down the antient palisade and lofty walls because it is aware that Liberty is the true portal of happiness – Yet while it encourages more cheerful freedom, it must not lay aside becoming dignity.

When we formerly approached the Mansion through a Village of its poor dependants, we were not offended at their proximity, because the massy gates and numerous Courts sufficiently mark'd the distance between the Castle and the Cottage. These being removed, other expedients must be adopted, which if they do not restore the dignity, may at least be not uncharacteristic with the general cast of Scenery nor detract from its beauty.

Was I the Owner of the Castle of Powderham I should conceive, nay I am sure I should feel, that a Village ought to be an indispensible appendage to it. Instead of guarding a Visitor from exploring habitations (as is now done and with propriety) deformed and loathsome from filth and penury, it would be my pride and my delight, to lead him to my Village, instead of putrid exhalations from stagnant waters, pools and ditches, heaped up with a mass of offensive matter, He should be gratified with the combined fragrance of the rose and honeysuckle, breathing their sweets from every garden – instead of ruinous, discolored mud walls, without doors, and damp, dirty rooms within, demonstrating from their effects on the countenances of those who made them their abode, variety of wretchedness – He should see cleanliness pervading every part, if he did not find regularity and a trim uniform neatness, (as may often be met with in a row of brick Houses at a watering place. He should be pleased with thatched Cottages surrounded by beds of flowers and culinary herbs; detached from each other) sheltered at their backs by clumps of Elms, and enlivened by a little green in front, where under a wide spreading tree in the center, the rustic seat might be placed for the repose of Age, from whence might well be observed the gambols of playful Youth.

When such objects had been brought before his sight, instead of exclaiming, this is out of place; this harmonizes not with the stately Castle! would he not have whispered blessings on my head; And his prayers would they not be, that the comfort and happiness which it had been my study thus to accumulate, on my poor dependants, might in the most ample retribution, return into my own bosom!

Nor do I see the difficulty of rendering such a Village Picturesque! tho' it has been questioned by one at least of the great Masters who have discuss'd the point – with all the convenience which Mr Gilpin met with at the Village of Nuneham, which Lord Harcourt had benevolently raised for his Cottagers, I would avoid its regularity. If places are not to be laid out with a view to their appearance in a picture, but to their Uses and the enjoyment of them in real life; and if their conformity to those purposes be that which constitutes their true beauty; If this assertion be well grounded! Yet I can see no reason, why, when a combination of what is picturesque, shall fortunately conspire, with convenience and use, why (I say) it should not be taken advantage of – Mr Gilpins idea of a winding road a spire, as concomitant parts of a Village, would be too grand for me! and from local circumstances would not be accommodated to that of Powderham; the Picture which I have already drawn might without difficulty here be fixed; and it would give me more delight, was I the Lord of Powderham to see it realized, than to have it in my power to boast that the taste and expence which I had lavished on a gala fete, were equal to those of Lucullus; or that my Gardens, might have been produced as rivals to those far-famed of the *Phaeacian Aleinous.*

Having such impressions on my mind, and being in the act of passing from the domains of Lord Courtenay, I cannot take my leave without an additional reflection.

At a spot dignified by local circumstance, by Antiquity of family, and by the venerable magnificence of the Mansion, its place of uninterrupted residence for upwards of four Centuries; The lover of Harmony, whether resulting from the sweet touches of order, and consistency on the mind; or from those of the Picturesque of Nature on the eye, will expect a Unison pervading every part, actuating, and connecting the Whole. In the Possessor of all these objects of estimation, He will look for the dignity and the Worth accumulating throughout a series of honorable Ancestry; which would stimulate him to emulate the worthiest of their deeds not by – but by an establishment uniform through the several allotments of Equipage, Servants, and furniture; regardful of antient

Usage appropriate to family – observant of genuine magnificence resulting from Antient honour, acknowleged wealth, true taste, and Hospitality – conformable in decorations to Modern fashion yet not devoid of Essentials, so long warranted by time and reason. And He would look also for something beyond this. That a congruity of taste and Unity of Character should extend themselves to All that He might be connected with, that the Buildings should as much as possible, be accordant in stile, and that the Grounds should have All the Grandeur which their Situation and Character would admit of!!!

"*Sed Hae nugae –* " I therefore shall have done. It has been my aim in these remarks to point out

"*Quid deceat, quid non; quo Virtus, quo ferat Error*"

and whether I have succeeded or not

"*Verbum non amplius addam.*"

I now make my retour from the Park by means of a large gate (the chief entrance to the Castle) which, under the spreading Arms of a most stately oak opened into the public road contiguous to the River. At but a short distance from thence, was the Boat house, where was a repository also of sails, cordage and all the other accessories and implements required for the equipment of Lord Courtenays yatcht cutter, and boats, which were generally moored in front of the Building, and of a battery consisting of a few old cannon. The Yatch has a very elegant and splendid appearance, and possesses every sort of accommodation which the nature of such a Vessel will admit of. The Cutter was at this time on Shore, and as an object of picturesque beauty is introduced in the opposite sketch of the Boathouse: Little description will be required to explain the other parts of which the View consists. The whole is simple, and on the first glance easy to be comprehended. In the stile of the Castle, the front of the Edifice appears of Gothic Architecture, it has its battlements, and towers

View entitled 'Boat House at Powderham', no date given (DRO, 564M/F16/39)

at the angles. the wooden building on the left is for the reception of Masts, and was it not for its convenience might as well be away. In itself however it is not an unpicturesque appendage, and overshadowed by the old Oaks in the Park, contributes its share in the formation of a Scene, which when beheld from the Water must be allowed to have its particular attraction.

From hence floating with the tide less than the space of a quarter of a mile brought me before the Parsonage House of Powderham and its adjacent Church; In his passage to Starcross, whether by Land, or by water this spot must be the subject of every Persons admiration! The most incurious Stranger cannot fail of having this attention irresistibly arrested by the snugness and beauty of its situation! It carries with it, externally a prepossession that all within must be peace and comfort; And what the Stranger presumes from its appearance, the Friend and the Neighbour is satisfied of by experience! In a few words to speak of its Possessor and his charming family would not do them justice, and to expatiate on them to all who have the pleasure of their acquaintance would be superfluous, and to those who have not that pleasure would appear but an exaggerated encomium of partial Friendship. I shall therefore pass from an eulogium of Persons to that of the Place, which without a doubt is to be esteemed as one of the prettiest spots on either bank of the River. The locality of its situation, as far as it has respect to the fine expanse of water before it, and to the delightful grounds of Lord Courtenay, is doubtless its first recommendation, but beyond these, it has excellencies in itself which fall to the lot of few Parsonage Houses in the County, for many of which it is indebted to Mr Andrew, the present Incumbent, who has added not inconsiderably to the Building, and very much improved the gardens and the glebe;

Unconnected with the Lord of the Castle, to me, its contiguity would be considered as a drawback of no little weight; I speak as a Clergyman, who would be solicitous for the welfare of his flock; and who is fully satisfied that his most earnest exhortations to the poor dependants, to be zealous after God and to attend their Church, would have but a momentary effect, when He, who should set them an Example was –

View entitled 'Powderham Parsonage House', no date given (DRO, 564M/F16/43)

"Parcus Deorum Cultor, et infrequens"

Reflexions of this sort, have at times rendered the situation of my Friend irksome to him: but considerations of gratitude and consanguinity have enforced their suppression: –

"*At nunc non erat his locus!* –

By the Garden only is the House separated from the Church; which may be collected from the preceding View – and as the Edifice is in itself an object of some consequence I shall reintroduce it, as it is seen from the public road: Its form is neither Greek nor Latin; for it has no cross aisle, and consists only of nave and Chancel. These are divided from each other, nearly in the midst by a screen; and the latter, (excepting the pew of the Rector), is appropriated solely to the Family of the Castle. Contiguous to the Altar are two large massy tombs; and on the South wall is a mural monument and a Bust to the memory of Lady Mary Bertie Daughter of James Earl of Abingdon 1718. The only Remains of this nature, savouring of Antiquity, is a procumbent Statue in one of the North windows in the Nave; it appears to represent a female, but as there is no inscription to ascertain Who she might have been, Tradition has supplied the information that was wanted, by declaring her to be Isabella de fortibus!! On the consideration that this was the Church of the Parish of Powderham in which the Castle was situate, it would naturally occur to the Visiter, where are the memoranda of the Courtenays? have they for Centuries past been laid in the silent tomb without one record to bear a testimonial to their worth? Are there no Effigies, no Inscriptions, to hand down to Posterity their personal merits, their renown, or their names? In vain would such inquiries be made in the Church of Powderham; and the Antiquary would find his researches baffled by disappointment; – There are few such instances, I conceive to be met with in the kingdom! In the Parochial Church of a great and antient House, Where the heads of the Family in particular, for a succession of Centuries, have in their turns occupied the same vault, one would have

View entitled 'Powderham Church', no date given (DRO, 564M / F16 / 47)

View entitled 'Cottage at Powderham', no date given (DRO, 564M/F16/53)

expected to have seen Statues, busts and various sorts of Monuments to their Memory; for thousand instances of the kind must occur to the Traveller whereso'ver He may take his way!

But here every token of former existence is indiscoverable and not a single M : S is to be met with to gratify curiosity! A few funeral banners are suspended from the coved cieling of the Chancel, which give us to understand, that the celebration of the last rites of some Individuals of the Family may have been attended by Pomp but they minister to Us no further information.

> *"The boast of Heraldry, the pomp of Power*
> *And All that Beauty, All that Wealth e'er gave*
> *Await alike the inevitable hour*
> *And meet Oblivion in the silent grave."*

Untitled sketch, no date given (DRO, 564M/F16/57)

In the Environs there is many a Scene of Picturesque beauty, And as these have often occurred to me in my rides, I shall curiously describe, and delineate them, confining myself within the limits of the Parish.

Following then the Course of the road, and having past the Antient way which led through the Village and Avenue to the Castle, a Cottage presently offers itself to the view situate on a little eminence to the right: Above the road from the opposite grounds, it, and the Scenery around it, is beheld in the greatest perfection – for being lifted higher, the Eye is enabled to comprehend the more distant Valley, through which the Waters of the Exe pursue their way.

The sketch will shew the local circumstances, and perhaps confirm the eulogium which I pass upon the Cottage, for shelter, snugness, and rural simplicity. The Wood which forms the background, is part of a plantation, ascending a hill rising towards the North, and consists chiefly of firs, there are however a number of forest trees scattered about, and with the little Orchard contribute to its embellishment. From hence the Public road passes on for a considerable way through the demesnes of Lord Courtenay, and in traversing it, I have often thought, how much better it would have been, had the way to the Castle deviated from it into the beautiful grounds on the right. It is generally allowed that the first Essential of Greatness in a place is the appearance of united and uninterrupted Property; Now if an Approach towards a Mansion House, should avoid skirting the boundary of a Park or ornamented grounds on the consideration that the want of extent, and the unity of Property may thereby be betrayed; with still greater reason should it be conducted as little as possible on the Public road! for surely no one circumstance can detract more from consequence than this!

To the Park Gate the Visiter is now led over the Parish road to within less than half a mile of the Castle; part of which is of the narrowness of a lane, subject to interruptions, and blending into quick successive flexures, and (what is more injurious to the beauty of Powderham) opening below the Church on the finest prospects of the River; These most assuredly should be so managed, as to seem to constitute one of the admirable features of the Park and to be, as it were appropriated to it. We are now conversant with them before we enter the grounds and of course the zest is impaired. On the supposition then that my idea of the matter is just, the entré into the grounds should commence not far from the sixth mile stone from Exeter – and leaving the Village on the left, should wind according the undulations which it would meet with, naturally to the Castle. I pass on now to the extent of the Parish, where from the road the opposite view is seen of a Farm House, which from situation and accompanyments I hold in a light exceedingly picturesque; The buildings under the shelter of the wooded hill, are of the most rural cast, and these, with the verdant meadow are thrown into high contrast by the ruggedness of the Quarry in the foreground, and the richness of its colouring. I have often considered this as one of the most pleasing pictures of the kind in the neighborhood, and it is singularly in this respect, since it derives none of its beauties from the River prospects, which of almost all others is the greatest embellishment.

Returning part of the road I now turn from it into a large field on the left, which about mid part rising into a knoll affords a most charming view of the River and in particular of the town of Topsham; – from this field a gate opens into a wood and plantation, where a rivulet is cross'd, which emptying itself just below in a marsh, feeds a piece of water, where a decoy for Wild fowl has been formed; In the winter season abundance of Duck, widgeon and teal are taken here for which purpose A Man experienced in the art is kept in a neighboring Cottage by Lord Courtenay.

The Plantations at this place chiefly consist of Larch and serve to ornament part of a farm which the late Lord C. kept in hand, where he fitted up a few rooms and established a little menagerie. The situation is extremely agreable, as may be collected from the opposite sketch; indeed, just beyond the House the ground rises high into a conical knoll, which exhibits itself as a fine object

View entitled 'Exwell Farm House', no date given (DRO, 564M/F16/61)

to many parts of the neighborhood, and especially to the River, which of course is commanded from its summit in great perfection. On the eastern bottom of this Hill skirting a wide extent of marsh land, the farm-road passes; and entering a hollow rendered gloomy by overhanging woods, leads to a Quarry of the red grit so prevalent in these parts, which though but of a small size when compared with those of Peamore and Exminster, is yet from local circumstances exceedingly picturesque.

There is much less of the trimness and regularity here, than is met with in most other of those excavations: The accompanyments which surround it are all wild and natural, and they are the consequence of Disuse; it does not appear that any Stone has been taken from it for many years, and of course it is rendered shaggy by thicket and briars, in short it is the very picture drawn by the Poet

> *"The Quarry long neglected, and o'ergrown*
> *With thorns, that hang o'er mouldering beds of Stone"*

From hence, passing through another field the track-way, conducts by a Dove house with a cupola by a shorter route into the public road or, if continued, over another field or two, gives an opportunity of rejoining it by the side of the Cottage, a description and sketch of which has been already introduced:

It is inconceivable what diversification the same Scenery undergoes in rising from the Valley to the knoll or alternately descending; Exclusive also of objects that were permanent; in my repeated rides, I have met with a most entertaining variety, arising from incidental circumstances, particularly from Vessels sailing on the river, or from fogs, and the effect of the sunbeam, on their rise, or on their breaking off. When on the neighboring hills, or even at the distance of those at Oxton, I have beheld the whole Valley watered by the Exe, often times filled up by a thick mist, now forming a level sweep with the contiguous eminences, and now assuming shapes of the most fantastic and diversified nature.

"Before me thick and sheety vapours spread
Seem, like a lake, to level all the Vale.
While drives the drizzling fog, and o'er my head
The bending Clouds in pillowy darkness sail,
These are the Scenes in which (howe'er I rove)
In doubtful paths my fancy loves to rise
Ideal buildings people every prove
And fairy forests bound the approaching skies;
Clad in the grey obscurity, I view
More beauteous Scenes than Nature ever knew"

View entitled 'Powderham
Castle', no date given
(DRO, 564M/F16/65)

From the eminence We again descend into the Valley and have on the left of
the road, a wide track of level ground, the greater part of which appertains to
the Glebe: the Marsh doubtless at one time constituted the whole of this plain.
It is however now restricted to narrow limits; and the Inclosures westward of
the Church are cultivated as arable lands. In the lowermost field many years
ago; long ere the demolition of the old Edifice of Nutwell I took the opposite
sketch. The Northern windows of the Church of Powderham, overshadowed
by Elms form a singularly pleasing foreground; and heighten the effect
produced by the milder scenery of the river and the Gothic building embosomed in woods on the opposite bank. To this I now bend my course (Having
expatiated with a free rein over the wide and beautiful domain of
Powderham).

In the approach to Nutwell, the new Mansion erected by the present
Proprietor Lord Heathfield, tho' yet unfinished exhibits itself most charmingly
to the View: From a description of this however I shall at present desist; And
taking a retrospect of what it was a few years ago, before the demise of Sir
Francis Drake its then Possessor, I shall have recourse to sketches which I at
that time made. Unwilling that so antient and repectable a Structure, so soon
sharing the fate of its Master, should be lost to the River which it once embellished without a memorandum, or a vestige of what it was. Fuit Ilium! is a

*View entitled 'Powderham
Church and Nutwell', no date
given
(DRO, 564M/F16/69)*

melancholy and an unsatisfactory reflexion! To the Antiquarian Scholar of the present day, what a morceau of inestimable worth would a discovery of but a bare outline of this celebrated city be, or a mere ichnographic scrawl: – In addition to the local arguments of Messrs Chevalier and Morritt, how delighted would they be, possessing a weapon so irresistible to be enabled to overthrow in the field of controversy their sceptical tho' venerable combatant Jacob Bryant!!

To prevent therefore all possible disputation that might in after ages arise about the situation or the stile of Architecture in the Edifice of Nutwell, I shall enter into a discussion of them, and illustrate both by a variety of delineations.

Historical Annals record the name of Dinham as Proprietors of Nutwell as far back as the time of Ed. 3d; This was a family which came from Normandy

*View entitled 'Old Nutwell –
Seat of late Sir Francis Drake',
no date given
(DRO, 564M/F16/72)*

with the Conqueror, and at the first had their possession at Hartland in the North of the County. At Nutwell it continued untill the latter end of the reign of Ed. 4th when in consequence of a failure of issue male, it was alienated by one of Lord Dinhams Sisters, a Coheiress, to a Prideaux; from this family, it pas't to the Fords, the Pollexphens into that of the Drakes, and at the period in which these sketches were taken, it belonged to, and was the occasional residence of Sir Francis Drake, (the lineal Descendant of the great circum navigator) Who also as I have before shewn (was the Proprietor of Buckland Monachorum, the original Mansion House of the Family). In the cursory notice which has been taken of this place by Mr Polwhele, He observed that Sir F. Drake "has made considerable alterations in the House, Among other improvements he has converted the Chapel into a very handsome library."

In the conversion of the Chapel at Powderham Castle into a Drawing room, it was by inference only from Mr Ps expressions, that we conceived him to have deem'd such an alteration an improvement – but here his words cannot bear a doubtful meaning; – and they too palpably convey to Us his Sense of an act: which from a Divine one should rather have supposed, instead of praise would have received reprobation!! Of this Chapel, which has undergone (in my opinion) unwarrantable desecration A sketch of the Eastern window, with the highly decorated niches, that had been Statues in them, will demonstrate the magnificence of the antient building, which in Ed. 4ths time was castellated, and shew the stile of Architecture.

In the alteration made by Sir Francis Drake on this part of the Edifice, if (with impressions of veneration on my mind for a place consecrated to religious uses) I cannot persuade myself to call it improvement; so neither can I adopt the term when I consider it with the eye of an Architect, which feels a disgust at the want of consistency, and when the several parts, not accommodated to each other, do not constitute, an uniform and accordant whole.

This is the case with the Library at Nutwell, where, when the end Window is of a Gothic cast, All the others are plain and in a modern stile: of such ingenuity, what Man of taste can speak with approbation? What Man of scientific information can call it improvement?

View entitled 'Nutwell Chapel', no date given
(DRO, 564M/F16/76)

*View entitled 'Nutwell –
W. View', no date given
(DRO, 564M / F16 / 80)*

This, and the preceding View taken from two opposite points in the lawn will give a full idea of the front of the House; whose Architecture cannot be referr'd so far back as the time of Edward 4th; when in the words of Risdon "of a Castle Lord Denham made it a fair Mansion House Its erection I should conceive would be more correctly appropriated to a period in the 16th Century, for it does not appear to me to be of a more antient date than the reign of Elizabeth.

At the back, and on the Northern side of the House, a most picturesque appearance is given to it by means of its old and venerable trees; the groves of oak here stand inviolate, and thick spreading protect the Mansion from the buffeting of every wind but the S. West. It was impossible passing from the almost denuded front of Powderham Castle not to draw a contrast between it and the snug comfortable appearance of Nutwell; I could not help thinking but that the Sylvan Genius had flown from the one to the other – There –

> "The Venerable Trees by Grandsires reared,
> "From storms their shelter, and from heat their shade"
> With branchy foliage from the Stewards room
> Exclude the garish Sun! – aloud is bade
> Art and her ruthless Myrmidons, to rear
> The sacrilegious axe – see, it descends;
> Too late the Venerable Genius mourns;
> Exiled, he flees the once loved spot, and seeks
> In glades more hallowed, where true Taste abides
> Secure protection" –

And not withstanding what I have said in regard to the Windows of the Chapel I yet think that "True Taste" has presided over and directed the improvements of the grounds. The open groves of antient trees; the interwoven thicket of plantations; the neat gravel walk, winding through them, or at intervals traversing the verdant lawn, All together were in harmony, and were accommodated to the Building, and to the character of the place.

"The Environs of a House (says Mr Gilpin) should partake of the Elegance or grandeur of the Mansion they adorn, because, Harmony, and propriety require it"

View entitled 'Nutwell – East View', no date given (DRO, 564M/F16/84)

A remark, which in these matters, I conceive, ought to held as an axiom, founded on truth; and to be a complete answer to Messrs Price and Knights Hypothesis: which would bring Picturesque scenery, such as stunted trees, lanes of ruts, shaggy rocks, thistles and nettles home to the very doors and windows of a Gentlemans house: – In passing from the Lodge through the plantations, and shrubberies, which consist of a variety of trees and plants, amongst which are several fine Magnolia's; it struck me, that a vast accession might easily be made to the scenery by introducing where the walk skirts a wall of a court yard into which the Eastern window of the Chapel opens, a catch of it: The grove is at this place thick and gloomy, and by the removal of the high wall, which now intercepts it, the fine Gothic window would offer itself to the view, and under such circumstances it may readily be conceived that the effect would be of consequence. The Grounds are of no great extent and there is little inequality in them; their pleasing nature however and the beautifull views which they command compensate for the want of boldness, or grandeur.

In lying opposite to Powderham it has in view from every park of those most beautiful grounds; All those defects on which I have commented, are from hence overlooked; whilst the charming variety of ground, the woods, the Hill, the Castle, the Belvidere and the sheltered Parsonage with its contiguous Church, form, as it were a constellation of Landscape beauties, and are the chief ornament, of every spot on this side of the water.

With one other sketch, I shall close my descriptions of the antient House; It was taken from an entrance road on the East and from a kind of avenue of forest trees of different sorts, the Mansion is seen in a most picturesque point of view, guarded by its woods; and beyond, at the most distant reach of the River, the City of Exeter with its Cathedral, finishes the prospect in a stile of excellence rarely to be met with.

View entitled 'Nutwell',
no date given
(DRO, 564M/F16/88)

Twice in my life I have had an opportunity of traversing the grounds of Nutwell; once by a scalade of the barrier walls at the River, at another time, by the intervention of a Friend in the neighborhood, in the absence of the present owner – But the day of admittance is past by; – the place is guarded, by the walls and chevaux de frise on every side; and no Personal interest can seduce the Dragon Porteress at the Lodge, there placed to guard the Hesperian fruit! The late Sir Francis Drake was a strange compound of absurdity & of excellent sense! Though refined in his manners, and from his appointment at Court, versed in the fashionable world, He was yet one of the shyest men! – Very few of the principal Gentlemen of the County had any acquaintance with him, and not many knew him personally; When his attendance at Court was dispensed with, He past his solitary hours, at his seat of Buckland, or at Nutwell. Report has classed him among the "*Ancillarioli*," and there is no difficulty in conceiv-

View entitled 'Nutwell. Seat of
Lord Heathfield', no date given
(DRO, 564M/F16/94)

ing that a Man thus shutting himself up from the world, would at times want other "amusements" than his books and ornamenting his grounds.

"*Je m'amuse a faire les petites tournebroches –*" said a Monk, who having little other occupation, without this one, would have been ennuyé; Report however does not say that Sir Francis did absolutely make any "*petites tournbroches*" but that he endeavored to make them:

By his will, he bequeathed nearly the whole of his fortune, consisting of a large personal and landed property to his Nephew, the Son (by his Sister) of the gallant Veteran who so nobly defended the Rock of Gibraltar Lord Heathfield! – By this Gentleman the Antient Mansion has been in a great degree taken down, and another, in the modern stile of Architecture erected; The front exhibited towards the River is perfectly regular and handsome; to me however it does not seem in the same unison with the Character of the place as was the last. It is probable that this remark of mine may appear fastidious! be it so, – Taste is not to be accounted for, and mine may be derived from associations which perchance was I to make the attempt I might not be able to express; or if express'd, might be disallowed!

The face of the Building, is covered with a tile imitating in colour the Portland Stone, which at the same time that it serves to give it protection contributes to its decoration. The opposite is a sketch which I now took from the River, having been precluded since its completion from setting foot within its pale.

If Sir Francis Drake was tenacious of the privilege which his ground afforded him of sequestering himself from his neighbors; he is followed by his Nephew. I may say more than "*passibus aequis*" That the solitude of his woods and lawns might not be violated, All ingress to them from every quarter is denied; No Spanish Don could be more jealous of his fair Spouse or contrive more sedulously to keep her from the contaminating eye of Man, than has been done by Lord Heathfield in regard to his grounds! – And that which renders this his conduct more extraordinary is, that his visits to Nutwell are but seldom and but of short duration. On the supposition that a Man has a right to do what seemeth to him best in regard to his property, does it follow that He should always exercise that right? Singularity, (except in goodness) in a state of Society where mutual wants create mutual kindness, and courteous offices (is always reprehensible – I know not of what disposition that Person must be. Who (as in the present case) possessing a spot of beauty and attraction, shall yet shut it up from the view, and selfishly keep it for himself! In the course of my excursions in different parts of the kingdom I have not unfrequently experienced such illiberality and I am sorry that I have it in my power to make the remark, that too much of this narrow sentiment is prevalent in my own neighborhood! In my conception the Proprietor of a beautiful place is flattered by the visits of Strangers, and to those who think otherwise I would wish to propose the example of the Duke of Argyle; who on my apologizing to him at his place of Inverary for my intrusion, replied, "that every visit paid to his House and grounds He considered as a compliment and with the greatest courtesy gave orders that I should be shewn every thing that was worth my observation! – These were the feelings of a liberal mind; they were those of a Gentleman! And in consequence at Inverary I found no barrier, no gate locked, nor a single Servant gaping for a douceur, or who, on its being offered, could by any intreaty be prevailed on to accept it!!!

Almost contiguous to Nutwell is Lympstone to which tho' there is a pleasant walk by land, I shall pay my visit to it by means of my boat and that in consequence of the superior attraction which the Scenery possesses when beheld from the water; I had but barely pas't the S. Eastern point of the demesnes of Nutwell when the Parsonage House of Lympstone offerr'd itself to my view. Placed on a gentle acclivity at a short distance from the river, its local circumstances were in perfect contrast with that of Powderham which it commanded on the opposite shore; In beauty indeed they were nearly alike;

View entitled 'Lympstone Parsonage', no date given (DRO, 564M/F16/98)

but there was a distinction of Character which made an essential difference;

Of this indeed I need only to refer to the preceding sketch; which exhibits it in a most picturesque point of view, with a romantic wildness of shore and Clift which the western strand does not possess except it be towards the mouth of the River – the Stratum of rock is of the same species with that on the other side of Water, such as the Quarry at Powderham and its tint the same. This tho' I acknowlege to be beautiful I cannot hold it in the same estimation as that of the rocks at Chudleigh; the red cast must certainly be considered as inferior to the grey if it be only from the greater contrast which it forms with the ivy or the brushwood which hangs over its surface. There may be an exception however to this general observation; and I conceive that it may be found in my Quarry at Oxton, where the ruddiness of the stone is most beautifully checquered and variegated by the innumerable Lichens, mosses and ferns, which creeping over the greater part of its surface, have given a softness to the red colouring which otherwise would too abundantly have prevailed. As the shore at the Parsonage is on one side, so the cove in which Lympstone is seated is on the other side of a Promontory, which protruding itself somewhat further into the water ends abruptly in a Cliff as has been represented in the two foregoing sketches. The Appearance which it exhibits in the end towards Lympstone, declares it at once to have undergone an alteration in its strata in a very short space. The rock nearest the Parsonage seem'd to have been a more compact and indurated Mass, it had been operated on indeed visibly by the spray and dashing of the Waves, but the effect had been in a great degree uniform – the whole superficies had mouldered away and fallen together; Here however its change and decomposition had been partial; and by its hollows and prominences betrayed an alternation of friable and solid strata.

The fractured appearance of this Cliff was more curious in the eye of the Naturalist than the other, but it was certainly less picturesque. Yet as a foreground to the delineation of the cove of Lympstone, in conjunction with a detached mass called "Darlings rock" it was productive of no inconsiderable

View entitled 'Lympstone',
no date given
(DRO, 564M / F16 / 102)

effect. Lympstone and the contiguous Cliffs are in the Parish of the same name, but this Darlings rock, which (as may be seen in the sketch) is but a few yards removed from the Cliff, forms a portion of the parish and royalty of Kenton, whose extent is such, as to take in nearly the whole of the River from hence to the warren; nor indeed is this the boundary of its prerogative for it is said to stretch itself so far into the sea as an "Humber barrel" can be discerned from the land by the natural eye.

Among the fishing huts on the strand there are two Lime Kilns, which with the hedge-rows of Elms close behind, as seen from the water form a picture of the most agreable Nature; Higher up on the Cliffs on both sides the Cove are a number of handsome modern built Houses, and these with the Church embosomed in trees, from the mid channel of the River, are beheld in the highest perfection, and when combined into a whole may be considered as one of the many embellishments of the River; – Of such a character indeed, are most of the views which will engage the attention of a Spectator from the Exe.

Here, there are no varieties of Scenery which can excite astonishment from their boldness and sublimity (as are to be met with, where up the Tamar or the Dart the flux of the tide rolls itself) but the River Exe has claims to beauties of a milder and more gentle nature, which waken sensations of pleasure and may fairly if not technically (for in this light Mr Gilpin would probably enter a caveat) be termed, Picturesque;

The ride on the higher lands where the public road leads from Exeter to Exmouth at the back of this charming Village, commands views of the most extensive and beautiful nature. The whole of the Country lying between the River and Haldown appears spread out before the eye, and that the most discriminated manner; There are few if any parts of the country which can vie with this tract in picturesque and diversified beauty; and amidst all this loveliness Powderham stands conspicuous, as

"Fairest of the Fair"

View entitled 'Distant View of Exmouth', no date given (DRO, 564M/F16/108)

Towards the North the most prominent objects are Topsham and the Cathedral and city of Exeter; and towards the South, a long extent of a fine expanded River terminating its course in the Sea, the town of Exmouth rising in its more elevated parts, and Torbay just discovering itself in the remotest point between its two Promontories. I introduce a birds Eye sketch of this latter Prospect, as in a Geographical light it shews the relative bearings of those places to the River, and the nature of its Embouchure quick turning in a strait between the Sands of Exmouth and the Warren. Embarking, we made our "*retour*" to the mid channel by means of our oars; but there a light breeze crisping the waters, by way of interchange and relief to the Rowers, we set up our sail

> "*Aurae*
> *Vela vocant, tumidoq inflatur Carbasus Austro*"

Thus most pleasurably we scudded away before a Southerly gale, steering up the River with an inclination rather to the N. West. I had hitherto objected to the Sail, as it would too much have expedited my voyage, and precluded me the enjoyment at my leisure of dwelling on the enchanting Scenery by which on both sides the River, I was surrounded. But these were now left behind, and my eye had little now to expatiate over, but a vast mudbank on my right, barely covered by the coming tide, and the wide champain of Powderham and Exminster marshes on my left. The line of Navigation was here in some degree mark'd to the Stranger by perches or poles, which erected at every turning or angle of incidence, served as Beacons to guard the Vessel from grounding. As Cockswain however I was not unfrequently under the necessity of referring myself to my Boatmen and profiting by their experience – for as the mudbanks were now become invisible & the flexures of the Channel quick and intricate, it required more nautical adroitness than I possessed to avoid the "disagremens" which would have attended our running aground;

In the width and flatness of the Channel have originated these immense subsidences, which by their accretion prognosticate in some future day an interruption in the navigation of the River; It may truly be remarked of this County, (as it has been of some other) that its Rivers assume almost every Character incident to their Nature; Associated with the leading traits of the tract through which they pass As that is roughened with rocks and hills, or smooth'd with level pastures, so are the Streams broken and tumultuous, or unruffled and gentle; Its Aesturies from a similar cause are marked by Characteristic features – they are either contracted, deep, and obnoxious to rolling tides in consequence of their being environed by rocky Cliffs, as the Sound of Plymouth, and the entré into Dartmouth harbour, or they are expanded, more shallow, and less liable to the effects of high and boisterous tides, As the Aestury of the Rivers Taw and Torridge at Barnstaple, and this of the Exe. The Waters at this place (in consequence of the width of the Channel) spread themselves freely over the whole surface; and not withstanding the flatness of the Country West of the River, they are rarely known to effect an irruption over the low dams raised for their protection, without there has been a land flood, and (coincident with it) a full tide has been driven upwards by the violence of an Easterly wind; Such a Coalition No banks have power to withstand; – An inundation then covers over the wide and long expanse of Marsh, and without due care is taken, Many a Farmer has to lament the tardiness which has occasioned the destruction of his Flock. For as most of the dikes have communication with the River, it sometimes happens, that by the cooperation of the Causes afore mentioned, the Waters rise suddenly, and expand themselves forthwith over a plain where there is no Superficial irregularity: Of late years this tract of land, which by human industry has been reclaimed from the constant usurpations of the tide, in the points of value and salubrity has obtained the greatest melioration. Some years ago, the agues and intermitting fevers, with which the resident Inhabitants of the Lands contiguous to these marshes were afflicted, sufficiently evinced that miasmata of a most noxious nature were produced by the waters which these stagnated during the greater part of the year. In the philosophical and Physical view it has been asserted that "Water Plants are remarkably vigorous in their faculty of yielding pure air to correct the inflammable air which is bred by the Soil in low marshy grounds" and if so, it may be brought as corroboration of a remark often made "that the best remedies are produced in every region for its native Evils, and that all things (by the dispensations of a most kind Providence work together for the general good"

However this may be, as I conceive that the Water Plants were as abundant in these marshy grounds, when the Agues were prevalent, as they are at present I must look out for some other cause to which the good effects of a more salubrious air may be ascribed; and that most clearly is at hand in the draining which of late years has taken place by which the Land has not only become more salubrious in that it is discharged of the watery particles with which it was saturated, but has generally increased in value, in so much that the acre which 20 years ago let for one pound pr ann is now (for the greater part of this valuable tract (consisting of at least 1000 acres) productive of three;

But to hazard an opinion on the Hypothesis of Water Plants correcting the inflammable air which is bred in fens and marshes, may it not be answered by another? The Physical idea (if I read aright), is, that pure air is only drawn from Plants when the light is cast on them, and in particular when they receive the influence of the Sunbeams – but that on the contrary, when Darkness is spred over them they exhale from their flowers and leaves effluvia in the highest degree injurious to life. On this supposition the gain and the loss would nearly counterbalance one another, or at least if any benefit accrued the one by inhaling the salubrious particles and avoiding the other, by getting without the reach of their noxious Atmosphere. By way of enlivening and at the same time closing this digression I shall introduce a Sonnet on the Subject which I wrote some years ago,

Sonnet

"Ah stay thee Delia! nor in cautious range
To yonder Bower enwrapt in gloomy shade;
The fragrant Plants which the close Arbour braid
Now undergo a deleterious change,
Those odorous Flowers, which, to thy ravished Sense
So late did yield a pure and rich perfume;
Now, by the touch of Night fell death dispense,
And what thy treasures were, would be thy doom!

From every shrub, or flower with golden dies,
(You Myrtles green, which live but by thy care)
Ev'n now the deadliest exhalations rise
And with their poisonous breath infect the air;

Then stay thee, Delia, at the Morning hour
The Sun shall lead thee harmless to thy Bower.

We had now just past the Decoy, close sequester'd amongst willows, and had left behind Us the conical Hill and Farm of Exwell when up a narrow Valley a most pleasing and extensive view of the interior Country opened upon Us, in whose background I could clearly discriminate the Woods, Cottage, and encampment of Oxton, and the Obelisk rising over the pine-crested height of Haldown. The Wind had now died away, and the tranquilled Waters had assumed the smoothness and transparency of a Mirror; A trading Vessel, awaiting the flood of the tide, lay before Us aground midway in the channel, its sails, (expanded to dry) were productive of the most beautiful Effect, and the whole was reiterated in the lucid bosom of the Water to a degree of picturesque excellence that almost bordered on Enchantments. Other adventitious circumstances of less Value in themselves, but in Union very attractive, gave additional life and beauty to so still a Scene; Though

"Laeta Boum passim campis Armenta videmus"

Yet many were the groups of Cattle driven by the heats of noon along the oozy shore of the River nor were there wanting to give yet further variety fishing boats, extending their nets in dotted circles. On the right also, stretching itself far towards the opposite shore, was a vast Mud-bank, a great part of which being uncovered was almost liberally whitened by immense flocks of Aquatic Birds. At Powderham I had lately seen

"campum
"Pascentem niveos herboso flumine Cycnos"

But these were of a wilder cast, and when, by a shout they whirled aloft in the air, were then objects of greater picturesque beauty. Of these the Sea gull were most numerous, and most attractive! but to view them in the highest stile, it must not be in a clear sky, but amidst dark clouds; when haply a gleam of Sunshine, bursting from the gloom shall "light up the storm" then (in the brilliant description of Mr Gilpin) "If the Seagull wheeling along the storm shall turn its silvery side strongly illumined against the bosom of some lurid cloud, by this single touch of opposition it gives double darkness to the Tempest" and admirably heightens the effect.

The Marsh now extending itself far into the River, gave it a circuitous track which brought Us nearer to the Eastern shore; Here however (exclusive of a well-cultivated inclosed Country rendered rich to the eye by its Elmy hedgerows) there was not an object to arrest attention but Ebford, the seat of Mr Lee. The Mass of this building gives it consequence and arrests the

Spectators eye from almost every part of the surrounding country; but it can never be fixed on it with pleasure, for its apparent figure at a distance is that of a cube, and its colour the deepest brick red. The fashion of the day may be to decry the light tint for Edifices, and in the language of Landschape Masters to say 'that it throws the object out of place, and does not harmonize with any thing around it; In the chaste eye of the Painter, who wishes to dispose of every object in his sketch in that just arrangement which their relative situations demand, this may be an argument of weight; but what has this to do with the conceptions of the Many? how few are there of those even who delight in picturesque Scenery, and diversified Landschape prospects, who understand the slightest rule of perspective? – And I can see no reason why Taste (on such points at least) except in a possess'd dissertation on the subject, should be fettered or regulated by scientific System: To discuss the merits or demerits of a Painting, I own that there ought to be a portion of Connoiseurship a certain degree of technical and professional knowlege; I am yet further of an opinion, that the Landschape Painter has more exquisite enjoyment of a picturesque Scene, discriminates an object more correctly, and with a quicker glance catches them in all their fluctuating tints and positions, than the Person who has no practical information, and is merely an Admirer of the beauties of Nature.

But tho' this be allowed, I cannot see why if I derive greater pleasure from the aspect of a white building, than from that of a red, It should be hinted to me, that this is a want of taste and knowlege; When I say red, I merely meant to put it in contradiction to White, for I conceive that no Landschape Painter would ever introduce a red building into his piece! – To me No whitened Object is unpleasing, or unpicturesque without I have it near and before me; then if the Sunbeams are reflected from it, it becomes without doubt disagreable and unharmonious; but when remotely seen the transition from disgust to pleasure is instantaneous; how beautiful is that white Church tower embosomed in the grove of old Elms have I often exclaimed? And in Wales (where such objects are for ever occurring) how charming is that group of white washed cottages, peeping midway up the side of a mountain from the thicket of an opening copse, or relieved by a dark wood overhanging it from behind? – With such sentiments I should say (returning to the cause of this digression) how handsome Would Mr Lees House appear were it of a light cast! but Red, deep red as it at present is how disgusting! how unpicturesque!! – But in a discussion of the tints of Buildings, I have an opinion (whimsical perhaps) that there should be a distinction appropriate to the use of the Building! Thus I should have a predilection for a cottage being spruced up by the lightest; there is a simplicity and neatness in a common white-wash; it is generally at hand and in particular in S. Wales in the shires of Glamorgan, Pembroke &c it is in such general adoption among the poorer Classes in the Country, that if a Cottage be not thus trimmed, its occupier will be commonly found to be a sloven and an idler – On glades diversified by gentle and steep acclivities, and cloathed with woods, when Cottages are thus discovered it is hardly possible to conceive (me judice!) Objects of greater rural and picturesque beauty. In the same cast, or rather perhaps in that of a light grey I would have the Village Church and its tower drest, this is agreable to the eye when it is without accompanyment, but, if set off and relieved by rows or a grove of Elm trees the effect is beautiful.

In the Gentlemans Villa nothing carries a degree of Elegance equal to the Portland stone, and that stucco, or composition whatsoever it may be, which shall the nearest approach to that happy tint, I conclude to be the most perfect. the front of the New House at Nutwell is the work of art. It is altogether formed of a patent tile, intended in its colouring to resemble the Stone of Portland; but I think it has failed in this point, its cast being much too deep and Yellow. The invention however was an ingenious one, for it had for its object not only to render the Edifice which it covered beautiful, but (what by most would be considered of higher consequence) to secure it most effectually from the beatings of the severest Storm.

There remains but one other sort of Building for me to advert to, and that is the Antient Gothic Mansion; this we generally find garb'd in a simple plain dress: the rough-cast or slap-dash of the Country, and I conceive it to be well in unison with the Character of the Edifice; of these however, (dependant on the colouring of the gravelly stratum of the neighborhood) there are a great variety of tints; but I am then most pleased when the predominant cast is grey, variegated with innumerous shades, which have been communicated to it by the effects of time, weather, smoke not forgetting amongst them all the inter-mixture of green, yellow and orange-tinted Lichens. Such was the colouring of Old Nutwell and such was that of the Castle at Powderham. I know not however how it happened but some years ago a disgust was taken at the appearance of this latter Edifice; its teinture was considered as dirty; and all at once to the admiration of the Country around it exhibited the whole of its fronts, nay' even the huge square towers on the West, as nice and as white as lime and the Art of Man could make it: Though it had thus become the subject (as I have observed) of general admiration. Whenever in my walks through my woods, my Eye glanced on it, it became at once associated with a comical Epigram which I had somewhere met with and appeared instantaneously in a most ridiculous light. I know not that I should introduce Verse in themselves somewhat indecorous; but as there is nothing highly offensive, I trust the little indelicacy which they may be thought to possess will be compensated by their wit. The lines are supposed to be an impromptu effusion of an old Waterman on saving the back front of Lord Pembrokes villa towards the Thames brushed up by a spruce whitewash.

> *By Pembroke Earl's backside Ive roed*
> *Of years at least full thirty*
> *And all that time its walls I've viewed*
> *Black, yellow, brown & dirty*
> *But now how changed! amazed I cry'd*
> *To spruce and white it made is*
> *It cannot be my Lord's backside*
> *It merely is my Lady's*

From this digression occasioned by the glaring ruddy tint of the house at Ebford I return to the more beautiful Scenery of the River. By the flexures of the channel, We were now making a quick approach to the town of Topsham, and began to have an opening into the mouth of the Clyst which here unites its waters with the Exe. The junction of these two streams is not without its beauty! – arising not more from the singularity of the circumstance, than from the contrast which from one point of view is exhibited by the two rivers, for on the banks of the Clyst, whilst every trait is of a rural, and tranquil cast, the grounds rising from its sedgy brink being of some acclivity and richly wooded; and on the surface of the waters, nothing being to be seen but a soli-tary barge unlading her cargo of marble at a kiln where it was to be calcined; at the same instant the eye being on the western side of the projecting rock cast up the Exe, the whole of the rural scenery is lost, but a compensation is found in the pleasing appearance of the town, and in the multitude and the variety of the Vessels moored before it. As in one of my former tours, when crossing a ferry from the Exminster Marsh, I have introduced a sketch of the lower part of Topsham which I considered from that station to be very picturesque. So, I forbear a repetition, as from every point in which I now moved the Church was a prominent object, and having since my former visit been enlarged and undergone other alterations, possibly very accommodating to the Inhabitants but by no means gratifying to the eye; so great was the detraction from its picturesque beauty as to destroy all inclination for using my pencil.

Gliding on with the tide I had the pleasure of passing in front of the chief buildings, the quay and the Shipwrights yard, and reaped much amusement from the bustle, which animated every part: At one spot Vessels were on the

Stocks; at another, unlading their cargoes, Wharfs full of timber obtruded themselves on my notice, Storehouses, for sails and cordage were also in view, but the manufactory of cable and rope requiring more space, were established in the narrow inclosures at the back of the town. Almost all the supplies for the craft resorting to, and navigating the river being drawn from hence; and Vessels, which by their tonnage are precluded from passing through the canal to Exeter here dispossessing themselves of their cargoes; it may well be conceived that the trade of the place must be of consideration. – indeed in such light it has been generally esteemed; and even tho' Vessels of lesser burthen proceed through the works to the quay at Exeter; it may perhaps be a matter of doubt when the expence of passing the locks, and of conveying the goods by drays and carts from thence to their places of destination in the city, be computed whether it may not be as much for the interest of the Proprietors to have them unshipped at Topsham) as is done necessarily in the case of the larger Vessels) and transmitted at once by land carriage!

There was a period, when the river being free from obstructions the tide conveyed all the craft which navigated it home to the very walls of the City; – This however in consequence of a misunderstanding, with the Chamber of Exeter, (as it is reported) but perhaps more with a view of benefiting his town of Topsham was wholly destroyed by Hugh Courtenay first Earl of Devon; who in the 4th of Edward the second, (1311) raised a mound so effectually across the river as to bar the farther progress of the tide. This was carried into execution at a place called Countess wear about a mile higher up the river: Near a Century before Isabella de Rivariis Countess of Devon, having her manors of Topsham and Exminster, one lying on the east, the other on the west side of the Exe erected a wear for the benefit of her mills across the river, which from this circumstance was denominated, and has ever since retained the appellation of "Countess Wear". A remonstrance reaching her from the citizens of Exeter, and testimony being given of the prejudice such a dam was to the trade of the place; she ordered an aperture to be formed in the middle to the extent of thirty feet through which Vessels were permitted to pass on to the city as they had been wont to do time immemorial; By Mary de Rivariis Robert de Courtenay (Whose Grandson this Hugh Was) acquired a vast property amongst which were the aforesaid manors of Topsham and Exminster resuming therefore the original plans of the Countess and that with additional instigations, Hugh again filled up the opening in the wear, fixing therein great trees, timber and stones so as present an invincible barrier to all future navigation to Exeter by the channel of the Exe.

I shall take leave of this Noble Earl (whose name we may conceive was never dear to the Citizens whose trade he had thus subverted) with the observation, that He was the first of the Courtenays who possessed the Castle and domain of Powderham, acquiring it by his marriage with Margaret, Daughter of Humphrey de Bohun Earl of Hereford and Essex, and that dying about seven years after this memorable exploit, He was buried in the priory of Cowicke, which appertained to the Abbey of Tavystoke.

The tide having now wafted me beyond the northernmost house of the town of Topsham I found myself at leisure to reconnoitre the Country lying to the West of the river. The beauty of the scenery indeed on this quarter was of too much attraction to be overlooked; along the gently-rising acclivity of a range of hill, running parallel with the river and beyond the expanse of marsh; peeping from the tufted hedgerows of Elms, appeared the Village and the Church of Exminster, amongst these Mr Lardners house the Vicarage and the tower were most conspicuous; The landschape was completely rural, and it had no accompanyment that did not harmonize; From a little dip beyond the gardens of the Vicarage the grounds began to swell into a more elevated mass, and being overspred with woods exhibited themselves as objects of importance. Embosomed in those woods are the Quarries of red-grit stone which have contributed more perhaps to the antient buildings in its vicinity than any other. This and that at Peamore in the same parish may vie with each other in

*View entitled 'Exminster
Quarry', no date given
(DRO, 564M/F16/137)*

their magnificence and picturesque beauties. Possibly the shape of the latter, could it be well defined by the eye, would be found to possess superior excellence, and I think that it would also rise above its rival, in sublimity, was it not crouded by trees of considerable height, and by thickets of laurel, which throwing into concealment the greater part of the rock unfortunately detract from the grandeur, and consequence which it would otherwise possess; but of this more in a future page; at present I shall enter only into a description of the Quarry on the farm of Millbury.

Bordering on the Marsh, as the approach is made to it from thence, the contrast is striking and perhaps gives it additional magnitude; the entrance is

*View entitled 'Quarry –
Exminster', no date given
(DRO, 564M/F16/141)*

through a grove of trees, which from the road precludes all view of the quarry, emerging from this it at once bursts on the sight, which though of considerable extent is easily comprehended. When stationed about midway its vast bulk excites unusual admiration which is in no small degree increased by the singular prominence of the upper part of the rock on the right which overhangs its base several yards. It would be impossible for a person unaccustomed to the scene to stand beneath the superincumbent mass without shuddering; for it seems to threaten momentarily to be dislodged from its hold in consequence of its enormous bulk and weight, which gives the idea of want of balance and of consequent support; and were it so to do, no other effect could be produced but instant and absolute annihilation of every thing that might be in its way below, I can account for this deviation from the perpendicular in no other way than by conceiving that the extreme parts of the several layers or floors (as they are locally denominated by the laborer in the quarry) must have terminated in longitudinal irregularity. These strata have their breadths and lengths well-defined; and tho' not of uniform dimensions, are easily distinguishable on the face of the rock; and in a very considerable degree by their ready separation from each other expedite the labors of the Workman; In general those vertical fissures run direct, so that most of the Quarries in the neighborhood exhibit their fronts smooth and even; this deviation therefore from a rule renders this of Exminster an object of singularity and admiration. In consequence of its narrowness and great depth it would possess but little of the picturesque was it not for the contributory aid of the groups of Oak and ash which at successive periods have arisen from amongst the waste of the Quarry – the happy disposition and light elegance of some of these relieve the cumbrous mass of rock; and at a variety of stations present to the delighted eye of the Spectator scenes of the highest beauty; and subjects admirably adapted to the pencil.

The first of the sketches exhibits the innermost part, and that which falls under the unremitted attacks of the Laborer and these he either makes silently by the insinuations of the wedge and the lever, or effects, by the mine, which in its explosion bursts with the force of thunder amid the hollow recess, and

Untitled sketch, no date given (DRO, 564M / F16 / 145)

reverberates its echoes from rock to rock in successive peals which insensibly die away among the trees. About a mile further North and contiguous to the road is another Quarry of a similar nature; The diversity here (occasioned by the stratum of rock being in several parts exhausted by its ledges, and fractured surface) afforded traits of the picturesque, very different to those which had offer'd themselves to my view in the other Quarry. The Scenery was indeed exceedingly pleasing, and the Public have to regret in more respects than one, that the liege way is not conducted through it; At the gate which leads to this rock the turnpike road commences an ascent of no inconsiderable acclivity and at its summit has risen to a level with the upper part of the Quarry. A hedge, excepting at one spot is a barrier to the precipice, and there by the slipping away of a loose mass, which possibly had been undermined, an aperture has been effected – even to the verge of the road, thro the rails of which (placed there for the security of the traveller) a glimpse is caught of an abyss which can scarcely be viewed without apprehension; From this point of elevation the ground begins to dip as suddenly as it rose, and by and by arrives at a hollow, which (avoiding all this danger and superfluous fatigue) with the utmost facility might be gained, by passing nearly on a level way in front of the Quarry.

The rich expanse of Pasture land skirts also the border of this rock over which the view to the north, taking in the city of Exeter and its towering Cathedral is unobstructed and is equally capable of exciting in the bosom of the Grazier or the Painter the most interesting reflexions. Such views are taken in by the window of 'the Cot" an adjoining Villa, in high perfection by which I pass, and that but a little way farther to the extremity N. W. of the Parish with the intent of sketching "Matford Mill" in former days an appendage Matford Dinham which stands bordering on a green valley of irrigated meadow just above; This, an antient seat of the Dinhams, and Northleighs, and a century ago of respectability among the mansions in the neighborhood, is now on the verge of ruin and desolation, by an anticlimax it has pass'd from the hands of the Gentleman, to those of the Farmer, and is now become the habitation of a

View entitled 'Matford Mill', no date given
(DRO, 564M/F16/148)

family or two of Laborers; dilapidated, and overspred with huge volumes of ivy, it will perhaps soon become untenantable. By a marriage with an heiress of the Tothills, the Northleighs acquired the property of Peamore and relinquishing Matford assumed the former as their place of residence.

The Mill of which I have given a sketch, in several of its parts retains vestiges of its antient architecture, sufficiently to demonstrate its connexion with the Villa of its quondam Lord; it has a good deal of the picturesque in its appearance in common with most mills, and is the principal Grist one in the neighborhood.

Thus having explored the parish of Exminster to its extreme limits, I have little more to remark on it, without (whilst I am in these parts) I take notice of a remarkable handsome Oak growing on the roadside near the farm of Matford possessed and occupied by Mr Trood the most substantial Yeoman perhaps in the County; as also of an Apple tree in an orchard contiguous to his house, which is of a vast size, in so much that, I was credibly informed, it produced from the pound last year not less than seven hogsheads of Cyder

Returning now to the River from which I have this far deviated, and having past the town of Topsham We begin to skirt the shrubberies and pleasure walks of the Retreat, the seat of Sir Alexander Hamilton. These for the space of half a mile trend on very pleasingly by the side of the River from which they are separated only by a rail, and possess beautiful and extensive views, taking in much of the intermediate country, from Lawrence Castle on Pen hill the extremest part of Haldown to the N. W. even to the Belvidere of Powderham of both which objects they and the house have a full command.

On this place I have already descanted in a former volume, and having also there introduced two sketches, I have nothing farther to observe, than that is is a good though not a picturesque object from the River in which its western front was at this time charmingly reflected: –

The level space on the Western bank to some extent was now covered with the waters of the flood, but at the recess of the tide bore all the Characters and all the productions of a fen.

"Namque illic Canna palustris
Et steriles Ulvae, et acuta cuspide junci"

At this spot commences the Canal, which (in consequence of the stop put to the navigation of the river by the erection of Countess Wear) has been formed by the Corporation of the City of Exeter to renew the antient communications which subsisted between it and the Exe. To a sluice or lock erected a short way up this Canal the tide flows and with its flood wafts Vessels of not more than [blank] tons burthen; Here a house stands, in which a Person resides whose business it is to facilitate the ingress of these Vessels into the interior of the

View entitled 'Mr Troods lime-kiln', no date given (DRO, 564M/F16/153)

*View entitled 'Lime kiln near Countess Wear S. View',
no date given
(DRO, 564M/F16/157)*

Canal; – It is called the lower sluice and taking advantage of local circumstances, offers the refreshment of good ale to the tars navigating the barges &c to which being rarely loth, of course a pretty profitable trade is carried on by mine Host of the [blank]. On the bank raised by the materials which had been dug in forming the canal, a trackway extends itself up nearly to the quay of Exeter where a junction is again effected between the artificial stream and the River: on this causeway by means of ropes, Vessels are towed both up and down either by the exertions of Men or horses; so narrow however is the path (in common not more than five feet) that a good deal of circumspection is required to guard against the danger which threatens either from the deep waters of the Canal on one side, or of a muddy ditch on the other. At near the distance of half a mile from the mouth of the Canal, a lime kiln has been erected by Mr Trood, whose form, and situation were much too picturesque to be past by unheeded.

The foregoing sketch exhibits it in some of its parts; chiefly those which were permanent, for the adventitious ones of the Scene, composed by congregations of Vessels, Men, horses and Carts, were much too numerous and diversified to be taken into the representation; The foreground is well formed by an old Kiln in disuse and dilapidated; and the remoter part of the prospect beautifully terminated by the Cathedral at Exeter.

Nearly opposite to this (the marsh only interposing) on the Eastern bank of the Exe are other Kilns appropriated to the same purpose of calcining marble for the uses of building and manure; These are the property of a Mr Davis who, having carried them on for a considerable time on an extensive scale, has, by their means, amassed a pretty good fortune; – The first that offer'd itself to my notice, exhibiting its Southern front of a single arch, in consequence of its contiguity to a cottage was exceedingly picturesque – the sketch is not sufficiently comprehensive to include many objects which give additional embellishment to the Scene – the glimpse of the Exe is but small, as is that also of a creek into which the barges laden with stone and culm insinuate themselves. Altogether, beheld at a station near a public road, they formed a landscape of more than common beauty.

I have called this the first Kiln, but I mean it in a picturesque sense; another which I had before past, had not enough of this character to detain me: In consequence of the ruins of a Glass-house and others of a worn out Kiln there appeared a confusion of masses, which distracted the Eye: – This second therefore in local order, having more attraction, fixed me for a time; and induced me to exercise my pencil by sketching its Western front, or rather part of it for its extent is much more considerable: – The arches and the rude masonry of this structure, were most beautifully decorated by Vines of an old growth, which spread their lateral branches over the higher parts of the Walls; where, open to the influence of the Sun and to the artificial warmth communicated by the unremitting fires of the kiln, they became unusually productive; and brought their fruit to that maturity and perfection to which in the cold and humid atmosphere of this Northern clime, it is rarely known to attain.

To these Kilns of Mr Davis the resort of farmers with their carts waggons and pack Horses, was astonishing – and the demand for lime as manure far exceeded the supplies of his kilns.

As well as I can recollect the nearest strata of calcareous rock in a circuit round Exeter, are on the Western quarter to be found at Chudleigh, on the N. West at South Tawton on the N. East at [blank] and on the East at Beer and Branscombe. These latter are of a soft arenaceous quality called free stone, but the three other Quarries are of Marble. More or less than twenty miles, are kilns in which these rocks are calcined, from Exeter, except that in the vicinity of Chudleigh; of course, to near within midway of these places the lime that is used in the intermediate tract of country is sought after at the Kilns on the river between Exeter and Topsham. Lower down also towards the mouth of the Exe as I have before noticed are frequent kilns, and in the marsh of Exminster just beneath the parochial Church, is a very capacious one erected by Sir Lawrence Palk for the use chiefly of his tenantry which in this and the adjoining parishes is numerous; Seated however not like Mr Trood's on the banks of the Canal, and being at a distance from the river it was found expedient through the marshy flat to cut a duct by which barges laden with culm

View entitled 'Lime kiln near Countess Wear', no date given (DRO, 564M/F16/161)

and stone might communicate with the kiln. In these works nothing but marble is reduced to a calx, and the whole of it is brought by water from the vast quarries belonging to Sir L. Palk at Babicombe near Torbay: –

The lands where Mr Daviss kilns are erected and those inland to a considerable extent, are the property of Mr Spicer. The father of this Gentm, who was a tradesman at Exeter, having had bequeathed to him by an Uncle a Broker in London a very large fortune, purchased this possession and fixed his residence at a seat on it called Wear. To the buildings he made additions, and by other improvements rendered the place of consequence: – Views of the River towards Powderham and a very rich scenery of verdant pastures and Elmy hedgerows are commanded well from the upper windows of the Southern front – but the flatness of the grounds, and their insulation by public roads, detract from their importance and render it a place of but little estimation: – Annual advertisements offer it for sale, but whether it be from ineligibility of situation, or from demands exceeding its worth, it is as yet undisposed of.

Bordering upon Wear Eastward appears another Villa called Newcourt which of less account as a building than its neighbour, far exceeds it in local circumstances. The roads around it are less public and not more than convenience would require; it stands on more elevated ground and has consequently the advantage of enjoying the beautiful prospects around it to a greater degree of extent and perfection: This Seat was the possession and place of residence of Mr Shapleigh Son of a Gentm who with reputation long practised as a Counsellor at Exeter: Possessing a liberal mind and having expended a good deal of money on his house and grounds, it was found necessary for Mr S to withdraw himself from Newcourt for a time accompanied by his wife and Son, in the hope that by distance from a too numerous acquaintance and a more aeconomical establishment he might be enabled so to recruit his finances as to have it in his power at no very distant period to return with honour to himself:

Ast spes vanae! He died before the accomplishment of this plan in some remote part of the kingdom and Newcourt continues to the present day in the occupancy of a Tenant, Mrs Sainsbury, Widow of the Lord Mayor of London in 1787.

From this short digression I again make my 'retour' to the Exe, and en passant observe from the road near to Mr Davis' lime kilns, the skeleton of a Vessel of very considerable size, which was there on the stocks and intended for the West-India trade; To questions which I put to one of the Shipwrights respecting its burthen and the safety of launching her in so narrow a channel and at such a distance from the main river, I was answered, that it would be about 400 tons, and that tho' it was the largest Vessel ever built on the Exe, there would be but little hazard in committing her to the water.

But a little above was the Wear raised by Isabella de Rivariis Countess of Devon of which I have already spoken – there are no remains of this dam now extant, but near, or over it, a bridge has been raised, consisting of [blank] arches: the object of which was to open a communication between the Country on either side the river, which heretofore had not been effected, but by the inconvenient and long circuit of the bridge at Exeter.

The result of this undertaking has not been equal to the expectations which had been formed of it; for, 'communibus annis' the tolls have not been found answerable to the expenditure on its repairs and the road leading to it, and to the payment of the interest of the sums which were subscribed chiefly by the Gentm of the neighborhood for its erection:

But a short way westward of this bridge, running in a line parallel with the river, is the canal, which here passeth athwart the highway, to obviate which difficulty, a draw-bridge has been placed, which being in common stayed at one end by a lock, when a Vessel is about to pass, is set loose, and turning on a pivot is swung back to the opposite bank thereby affording a free and easy communication with the upper water.

From the middle of the Stone bridge, that arch being more elevated than the rest, the Views both above and below, of the river and the circumjacent scenery, are such as would engage the attention of the most curious Traveller: – for he would see himself surrounded by the most luxuriant pastures, fed on by innumerous herds – through these he would behold the Canal keeping a course nearly direct, and trace it in its more distant way by the sail of some Vessel light-gleaming among the trees, and then again by the slightest transition of the Eye, He would dwell with all the heightening of Contrast on the River, winding unrestricted by rule, in all the wild and beautiful maeandrings of Nature. Rising from the verge of this verdant expanse in all the diversities, of steep hill and gentle acclivity, of close wood and open glade, He would successively mark a picturesque and well cultured country, and he would moreover find it embellished with almost every sort of Building that could decorate a landschape from the village to the town, from the rustic cottage to the elegant mansion from the tree-embosomed parochial Church, to the high-towering mass of a Gothic Cathedral!! -

From the toll-gate the ground rises by a quick ascent, thus enabling the Traveller to mount on a terrace, which for some little space both to the North and South, is carried on the margin of a cliff, in some parts of considerable depth and precipitous to the river. Here two houses of respectability are seated, enjoying distinct views. One having its front towards Exeter with a northern aspect, the other looking down the river having its exposure to the South:

Here I finish my voyage (as my return by the boat would be but a repetition of Scenes which I have already described) and shall make my further progress towards Exeter, either by the public road, or by the Canal and rivers side, using each in alternation, as I make my advances, so that nothing of consequence may be left unexplored.

I had but just past on from these houses, and from a row of trees which had been planted on the verge of the Cliff when a prospect opened of the whole of the Valley which reached up to Exeter, except where it was shut out from the view by the intervening groves and hedgerows conspicuous in the center of this most beautiful scenery, overtopping a wood of Elms rose the Cathedral with its double tower; Nothing at the distance could be productive of an effect more magnificent or picturesque; nor was there a deficiency of the latter in

View entitled 'Paper Mills from Mt. Wear', no date given (DRO, 564M/F16/173)

those objects which were nearer to the sight, consisting of a Paper-mill, a large branch of the River diverted from the present Stream for the use of these mills and a grove of Oaks. Dipping from hence into the Valley, I turned from the road towards the shore, and the tide being out was enabled to pass under a low Cliff so as to reach a little quay belonging to the uppermost lime-kiln of Mr Davis – this I found to be a structure of very considerable extent, and though the area in front was spacious, it was so crouded by Carriers, by horses and Carts that I had no small difficulty in forcing a passage through them; at the extreme part of this area where it was contracted by the Cliff on the right and by the stream on the left appeared a neat but plain house which had been lately erected by this great Lime Manufacturer, who by spirited enterprize had contributed essentially to the promotion of the Agricultural interests of his Neighborhood; and at the same time secured to himself an independent fortune, of which as *"quaesitum meritis"* may he reap a full enjoyment. Just beyond, raised over the current of water are the Paper mills, which form a picturesque object in the foregoing sketch. The Manufactory is carried on here by Messrs Oxenham and Pym of Exeter in its several branches and upon an extensive scale: In the inspection of some parts of the process I was very much amused, nor was I aware (having taken no previous examination of the business) through what a variety of operations, the linen rags pass, untill they are reduced to that fine impalpable state, which completing the manufacture forms according to its purity and thickness the several articles of fine, or coarser paper, pasteboard, or that of which cards are made. The powers of the Mill which is set in motion by water are applied to raising immense hammers which falling into troughs or mortars of thick oak beat the mass of rags, before duly cleaned and macerated, into a pulp which is then laded into boxes and undergoes a pressure. Three times having passed through these operations, the appearance of the matter is not unlike a mixture of flour and water, either in colour or consistence. When in a state of due preparation it is finally thrown into a vat and the mould,)which is a sieve about the depth of an inch, the bottom of which is fabricated of a brass-wire cloth, permeable by water and sufficiently close to retain the pulp of the required thickness being dipped into it, takes up just so much of the body as will spread itself out when dry into a sheet of paper! Many other departments has it however to pass through, such as drying, sizing smoothing and pressing, untill it passes into the shop of the Stationer for sale: Most of these operations fell within my inspection, but with no one of them was I so much entertained, as with that which first gave to the pulpy matter the appearance and consistence of Paper. The ingenuity of the contrivance, was not less a subject for my admiration, than the adroitness of the Manufacturer: – An inquiry into the progressive advance to improvement from the earliest period when a simple leaf or flag was in use, to the present time when this invaluable article has been brought to a very high degree of perfection would perhaps be productive of much curious information. From the Greek word *"Papyrus"* [Greek] We derive the appellation of paper, tho' it is most probable that as this flag was indigenous only on the banks of the Nile, and as it was originally applied to the purpose of letter inscription by the Egyptians that the Greeks among the multifarious mass of scientific knowlege which they borrowed from this people derived the name and the use of the plant. It would be a vain attempt to enumerate the almost endless variety of materials which at different periods have been converted to the fabrication of paper; almost every vegetable that has a fibre has had the experiment made on it; and even that most curious and brittle fossil the Asbestos, has been worked into sheets of incombustible paper.

A paragraph in a London Newspaper has just announced to the Public the conversion of Straw into paper, it runs thus "Yesterday was presented to his Majesty at the Levee by the Marquis of Salisbury, a book printed on the first paper which has been ever made from Straw alone, containing a succinct but general historical account of the substances which have been used to describe events, and to convey ideas from the earliest date to the invention of paper – together with some loose sheets of Straw-paper, of an elegant transparent texture, which possess all the qualities of the finest writing paper fabricated from rags. The loose sheets indubitably demonstrate that Paper may be made from straw alone in the highest state of perfection. It is regarded as a valuable discovery, and of great national importance, and the ingenious Inventor highly deserves the public esteem and support."

In the degree of excellence to which this Artist may have brought his straw-paper He may claim, and will doubtless obtain considerable praise and emolument: but He presumes too far when he arrogates to himself the merit of applying the article Straw to the manufacture and that on the assumption of priority of invention: – For to the Chinese it has long been known and in use; With that people it is fabricated of different articles in different provinces, and in that of Chekyang it is made altogether of wheat or rice Straw.

Linen Paper, which appears to have superseded all other sorts in Europe, was first introduced among Us towards the beginning of the fourteenth Century; and the first Mill established for carrying on the Manufacture was erected at Dartford in Kent by Sir John Spilman in the year 1588, under a Patent and a pension from the King of £200 pr ann.

With this discussion of the manufacture of Paper I take leave of the Mill, as also of the River for a short space, here however bidding farewell to the tide which had wafted me thus far most pleasurably on. By the fall at the Mill it has a stop put to its further progress, and having contributed thus much to the furtherance of Commerce, leaves the remainder of the supplies to be administered by the supplementary aid of the Canal.

The road from hence turning quick towards the right, soon joins the great public road leading from Topsham to Exeter. These together in a manner insulate the grounds of Major Hamilton called Northbrook, derived perhaps from a small stream which winding through the lawn on the western side empts itself into the Mill leat – the site of the House is extremely pleasant, commanding much of the expanding Valley of the Exe, and of the woodland hills beyond. Nearly contiguous to these are the inclosures of the farm commonly called the Old Abbey which are in the possession of a Mr Templer under lease from Kings-College Cambridge. Here was a Religious house, of which I have been able to obtain no other information, than that its appellation was the 'Priory of St James' and that the building or the lands which appertain to it, form portions of the respective Parishes, of Heavitree, Alphington, and St Leonards.

Loth however to quit the place with such a meagre account, no other being to be found in any historical collections professedly belonging to the County – it occurred that it might possibly be an Alien Priory, and that it might be noticed in Warburton and Ducarels enumeration of them; In this supposition I was not disappointed for I there found memoranda, of which the Substance is as follows:

> "Baldwin de Redveriis, or Rivariis – (Whose descendant Isabella Countess of Devon has been lately noticed) gave the Chapel of St James without Exeter, with the tithes and other estates to the Head Monastery of St Peter at Clugny and to the Abbey of St Martin de Campis in Paris, by the permission of the Empress Maud; sometime before A.D. 1146 – Stipulating that a Prior and some monks of that Order might be settled here which was accordingly done, and the Priory became subordinate to this last-mentioned House. After its suppression by Henry 5th the lands and their revenues were given by H. 6th and by his Successor Edward 4th to Kings-College which has enjoyed them ever since." Lit. Pat. Hen VI et Edw. IV penes Praepositum et Scholares Coll. Regal Cant. –

The Act for suppressing these Alien Priories being a curious document I shall make an extract of the part where the chief reason is alledged by the Parliament for such suppression.

> "E Rotulis Parliamenti anno secundo Henrici V apud Leicestriam. Stem prient les Communes que en cas que final pees soit pris parentre

vous nostre Sovereine Seigneur, et vostre Adversarie de France en temps
a venir, et sur ceo toutz les possessions de Priories Aliens en Engleterre
esteantz as chiefs maisons de Religeouses de par dela, as queux tielx
possessions sont regardantz, seroient restituz, damage et perde avien-
droient a vostre dit roialme et a vostre people de mesme le roialme par
les grandes fermes et apportz de monoye quel d'an en an toutz jours
apres seroient renduz de mesmes les possessions a les chiefs maisons
avaunt ditz a tres graunde empoverissement de mesme vostre roialme en
cel partie, que Dieu defende"

In consequence of this petition a Suppression of those Priories took place by
the order of Henry 5th, and in the 19th of the following reign A.D. 1440 An act
past for granting them in fee to the Archbishop of Canterbury and to other
Prelates Lords and Gentlemen:

ob grandem fiduciam quam penes praedictas personas gerimus et
habemus. Dedimus et concessimus eis omnia et omnimoda illa priora-
tus, maneria, terras, tenementa, redditus servitia, pensiones, portiones,
apportus et possessiones infra regnum nostrum Angliae ac Walliae et
marchias Walliae praedictae (quae nuper prioratus et possessiones
alienigenarum nuncupantur) alicui domui religiosae seu aliquibus
domibus religiosis in partibus transmarinis nuper pertinentia sive
spectantia, in manibus nostris existentia: Habenda et tenenda sibi,
Haeredibus et assignatis suis &&c" Rymer.

Whilst I was traversing the open ground around the House with the view of
discovering (if there were Any) vestiges of the antient Edifice. Mrs Templer
(Widow I understood of the late Proprietor) civilly accosted me offering to
shew me what she held to be the only curious Relique on the place, which she
said was a stone Coffin of one of the Monks who formerly lived in the Abbey.
This she carried me to see in a corner of her Garden behind the house, and I
found it to be, as she had reported, the shell of a coffin excavated in a single
stone of great apparent hardness for it was not mutilated; – It was now
converted to a use of a very different nature; for what had been the repository
of a substance that had ceased to exist, now teemed with life, – the dead body
of the Monk had been supplanted by a little parterre of flowers which gave it a
decoration, beautiful at least, if not appropriate. Let it but be supposed that the
Remains of one of the brotherhood were still there reposing – and in the allusion to an antient rite, there would be not greater beauty than appropriation –
I might appeal in support of this assertion to the usage prevalent in S. Wales,
on which I have expatiated, and to a remark of a Traveller on the funeral rites
of the Turks which latter, as being apposite to the present case I quote. "They
are buried in their gardens in Sepulchres without covers, filled within above
the cover with earth, and set with varieties of flowers according to the custom
of the Pythagoreans and universal wishes of the Ethnics. Thus Persius

"Dii majorum umbris tenuem, et sine pondere terram
Spirantesque crocos, et in urnâ perpetuum ver"

The Spirits of the departed being (as it was conceived) sensible of burthens, and
delighted with sweet savours or with the honor and affection shewn to them.
　Of this appropriation however I cannot flatter myself that Mrs Templer ever
heard: and I rather believe that she had not the most distant allusion to these
"spirits of affection" [Greek] of the Antients when she filled the sepulchral cell
with her hyacinths and Polyanthuses! – As the corpse of the Monk *'non erat*
inventus she thought she might take the liberty of turning the Kist-vaen to
another use

Where the dead Monk intumulated lay,
Sweet flow'rs arise to scent the breath of May.

JOURNAL TWENTY

Devon Record Office, 564M/F17

The final tour which Swete recorded for his Picturesque Sketches took place in 1800. He left Oxton on 12 June and returned home after visiting Exminster, the Retreat, Clyst St Mary, Bishop's Court, Sowton, Farringdon House, Aylesbeare, Talaton, Grange, Cullompton, Bradfield House, Uffculme, Holcombe Rogus, Hockworthy, Huntsham, Bampton, Tiverton, Bickleigh, Killerton, Poltimore and Polsloe.

PICTURESQUE SKETCHES
OF DEVON

John Swete, Oxton House.
Decm. 1st. 1801.

A Tour To the North Eastern parts of the County of Devon

On Thursday the 12th of June AD. 1800 I set out on horseback with the view of exploring the North Eastern parts of the County. I shall forbear to recapitulate any of the Scenery for the first ten miles, as it has been more than once described.

Noticing then that I pass'd through the Village of Exminster – over Countess–wear bridge, and that I skirted the town of Topsham on its eastern side, I shall begin my descriptions with a tribute to the River Clyst, which has the honour of lending its name as an adjunct to more places and parishes than any other river in the County, or perhaps, in the kingdom: Having maeandered through many a rich and verdant valley It has now nearly finished its course – its waters hasten to lose themselves in the vortex of the Exe; but though thus partially lost, still from its copious urn successive waters flow

"Et labitur, et labetur in omne volubilis aevum"

From the bridge over the Clyst, the road now passes on a low and level tract bordered on each side by an expanse of Marsh, which (I have no doubt) at some former period was floated (not partially as it now is) by the tide.

To reclaim a large space of meagre pasture land, now covered with scant herbage and burrowed into pools, would be attended by considerable emolument to the Proprietor! – the Speculation could not be abortive! for where the mouth of the Valley is but narrow, and where the power of the tide is but feeble (as must be the case here at such a distance from the sea) there could be no difficulty in raising a bank to withstand its inroads, and the expenditure, I

View entitled 'Lime Kiln. Clyst St George', dated 1801 (DRO, 564M/F17/3)

should conceive, would be very inadequate to the profit that must ensue. At the end of this marsh, and contiguous to the road is that picturesque lime-kiln which, tho' in a former volume delineated, cannot fail of soliciting the repetition of a sketch whenever an Explorer of the beauties of picturesque Scenery, like myself, shall happen to pass it.

This kiln forms a portion of that farm which has indisputably been in the possession of the family of Sucbitch, Sucpich, or as Sr Wm Pole denominates it "*Sokespich*" from the Saxon period to the present day:

I have before intimated that I imagined such a tenure was without its parallel in the Kingdom, but I have since found that I labored under a mistake similar to one into which Mr Boydell has lately fallen in his description of places which accompanies his celebrated illustration of the Rivers of Great Brittain; where is to be found this passage "in the neighborhood of Chertsey on the Surry side of the Thames is a very remarkable and perhaps solitary example of an uninterrupted continuance of hereditary possession in a small Farm occupied by a person of the name of Wapshote whose [word missing] appear from the most satisfactory documents to have successively lived on the spot ever since the reign of Alfred when this individual little property was granted to Reginald de Wapshote, the Progenitor of the present family".

In the present instance of the Sokespiches it may not be possible to produce authentic testimonials, that as the Wapshotes they were possessed of this their property as far back as the ninth Century, but it is generally understood that they have in their custody certain writings on parchment, connected with the holding of their Farm, which as being in the Saxon Character are clearly ascribed to a period prior to the Conquest; but whether they may be carried back to so early a period as that of Alfred, (as they have no date nor the appendage of a seal) cannot now be ascertained. In the recorded Annals of the County, (notwithstanding their residence has been in it for so very extended a space of time) we seek in vain for the name of Sokespich; neither of the 'deed of glory' or by that of dishonour has it been drawn from its oblivious secrecy. For ten centuries it has here probably merely existed, here in succession pass'd its "*inglorious aevum*" nor to it will an opportunity be now offerr'd of giving celebrity to a name of which it has nothing but its Antiquity to boast – by insensible gradations its right to this patrimony has been of late years by an accumulation of debt, diminishing, and that, which a thousand years has been unable to deprive it of, the undermining chicanery of the Law (if I read aright) has now effected.

The Mansion House of this Saxon family, (whatever may be the boast of its Proprietors) has certainly no claim to Antiquity; it is mean, and ruinous, and is situate on a low spot contiguous to the Marsh – there are spots however on the grounds, which command much beautiful scenery and have, of their own, rich woodland accompanyments. This Farm forms a portion of the parish of Clyst St George, the Church of which lies a little to the East of the road; – This road, (at the turnpike gate [word missing] turned to the left) soon brought me to the Parish of Clyst St Mary. Winslade, a house formerly of some consequence, but now in decay, is skirted just before a view is obtained of a large square Mansion, lately erected, the seat of Mr Cotsford, a Gentleman, who having acquired a large fortune in the E. Indies, has here fixed his residence; the local circumstances, (exclusive of some good beech and Elms) of the grounds, certainly gave no scope for picturesque embellishment; little therefore was to be attained; and I do not conceive, that in the canal, supplied by a scanty stream; and fir clumps, encircled by protecting mounds of earth, that little was to be found; if there be a deficiency however in taste for the picturesque, Mr Cotsford may be in possession of more valuable qualifications; for he is acknowleged to be an enterprising Agriculturist, and a most excellent Neighbor. Passing by a Lodge, and across the street of a mean Village, rendered of late more miserable by the devastations of fire, I soon after came to a grist Mill which probably, if it be not at present, was an appendage to the castellated Mansion high-seated on the brow of an eminence above it, in the day, when it was the possession and the Palace of the Bishops of Exeter. As most of the Water mills of the County it has many traits of the Picturesque:

there is not only a singularity in the style of the building, but it is accompanied by an air of antiquity, which renders it much more interesting: the landscape on its western side consists of a marshy pasture, through which the River Clyst, is seen winding its slow stream towards a bridge of an antient cast, which extends its arches, pointed and circular, (now and then separated from each other by a length of dead wall,) over the whole width of the flat, measuring perhaps a furlong; –

Detained here merely in taking the foregoing sketch I ascended the gentle acclivity which was to conduct me to the House – an object of curiosity to me on two accounts, both as it was a Remain of one of the most antient inhabited Edifices in the County, and as it had (for two centuries) been a possession of the Family of Beavis, with whom by intermarriage the Martyns had been allied. From the present Proprietor Mrs Beavis (a maiden Lady now verging on, if not arrived to, her grand climacteric,) as being through my paternal Grandmother Martyn, the Representative of that Family, inheriting their antient and chief Mansion, I had been presented with a curious genealogical, MS, written by Sir Nicholas Martyn (whose Sister an Ancestor of Mrs Beavis, had married) having much curious matter relative to himself intermingled; and, with equal liberality, she had further promised me a Painting of antient date, a family piece of the Martyns; which I have since become possessed of, and now hangs in my Hall at Oxton. Urged on by such motives I soon came in sight of the House, which at a distance, including the barn (a Structure of vast dimensions, and possibly coaeval with the Mansion), appeared a Pile of consequence. Seated also on the brow (as I have already noticed) of an eminence; on the verge of whose declivity were ranged a grove of high and venerable trees it carried with it an air unusually picturesque; From the road side I took the preceding sketch, and then hastened through the gloomy and long-drawn Avenue, to the House.

Emerging from the shade of the gothic arches formed by the top branches of the Limes intertwisting with each other, I had presented to my sight the front whose aspect was to the East. Here however there was nothing in the

View entitled 'Mill at Bishops Clyst', dated 1801 (DRO, 564M/F17/9)

View entitled 'South view of Bishops Clyst House', dated 1801 (DRO, 564M/F17/13)

cast of Architecture that savoured much of Antiquity – there was not a trait, (exclusive of the Chapel window which might be of an earlier date) that could throw the Building farther back than the sixteenth Century! – nor after a more minute inspection of the whole Pile, could I find any portion of it, excepting the round tower at the North west angle, which could satisfy me as having belonged to the antient Edifice that had been erected by Walter Bronscombe Bishop of Exeter in the reign of Edward the first; – At the entré of this outer court, I understood there had been a Gateway, which, as there was no prospect on this side to be acquired by its removal, had it not been in a state of dilapidation, ought on many accounts to have been preserved; Of the back fronts of irregular Gothic Mansions, little can be effected after the manner of modern improvement – to stop them of their appendages, offices, and walls, jumbled together without an attention to uniformity, and to lay them bare to the view

View entitled 'Bishops Clyst House', dated 1801 (DRO, 564M/F17/17)

by introducing the nicely shaven lawn or the gravel walk, would be a sole-cism, in my opinion in alterations that fell under the jurisdiction of true Taste; an approach to such an antient House as this, to be made only on this back front, could never therefore have been so consistently managed, as when it was effected through an old ivy mantled Gateway; the irregular Buildings were now too much exposed (as may be conceived from the sketch) and far too open to the glaring eye of Day – the Chapel will at once be discovered by its large ramified window, pointed with a Gothic Arch, and stone mullions; and the summit of the antient tower may be distinguished over the roof of the more modern Mansion. Over the door of entrance, I observed an inscription in large characters, which could not fail of being grateful to the feelings of the Stranger who sought for the hospitality of the Master – "*Patet janua! cor magis!* expresses the very soul of Courtesy and beneficence – such were the propen-sities of the Great Man in days of yore now termed uncivilized; but such sensa-tions, and such usage have long become obsolete, for, modern Refinement adopting too generally the reverse of this liberal Inscription; has "contracted the heart, and shut to the Gate" – In the old style however, (the antient custom I presume, of the House and long established habits are not easily laid aside) was I received at the door by Mrs Beavis, who expressed much satisfaction at the visit which I was making her: Having sat with her some short time, she gratified my curiosity by shewing me a part of the House, from the chief stair-case, full charged with Paintings she introduced me to the grand Drawing room, the dimensions of which were 29ft by 40. Here also the Walls were covered with Pictures, all of them, excepting a fine half length of Oliver Cromwell and a few family Portraits, of indifferent merit – of these latter, I had pointed out to me, the Miss Martyn Sister to Sir Nicholas who by her marriage with Mr Beavis, first connected the two families, her Arms also with those of her Husband exhibited themselves united in the Windows; and most conspic-uously in a large compartment in the center of the great Window, (seen in the sketch) where they were blazoned by themselves: As a corroborating testi-mony of the Alliance, the good Old Lady, unrolled a parchment in which on the genealogical tree, therein nicely traced and illumined, the name of Susanna Martyn held a [word missing] of high honour, as from her had sprung all the succeeding branches of the Beavis family, which appeared to have been numerous and flourishing! – they had now however nearly seen their last day – the Parent Stock had decayed, and the branch, which appeared before me, leafless and withered was hastening to the same state; verifying most truly the allusion to the process in the vegetable world, that both the tree and Man have the same appointed end:

"*as the race of leaves, so that of men.*" [Greek]

Previous to my visit I had been apprised of the melancholy situation of this old Lady, who from affluence, by the imposition of Scoundrels, and the gradual usurpations of the Law was hastening to a state, which to her (who had been used to the superfluities of life) was penury – the effects were visible in her countenance; and tho' to me she suppressed her grief, yet I too clearly discov-ered, that the parting with her carriage, the daily view of her dilapidated Walls, and the announcing to the Public that the Mansion of the Beavises was to be disposed of by sale; had together united in fixing deep a poisoned shaft, whose venom was preying rapidly on her Heart. *

With her permission, passing through a room or two, whose ruins, a glim-mering through the crevice of blocked up windows, brought to my observa-tion, I ascended, over a series of time-worn steps, winding up the height of a narrow turret, to the top of the Tower which I have before noticed. From this exalted situation the View, (excepting where the eye was precluded from ranging by the intervention of a grove of high and venerable trees) was exten-sive and beautiful; On the verdant pastures spread out below the tower on the West, watered by the river Clyst, and on the picturesque Village of Sowton, gently rising from its banks, it dwelt with most delight; nor did I longer wonder thus contemplating its rich appearance, that the artful [word missing]

---

who by a crafty device, had gotten possession of this Mansion, should adopt measures of the like oppressive nature to make himself Master of a portion of the goodly domain which he had daily before his sight; the Story is thus recorded;

"Walter Bronscombe, Bishop of Exeter, (who had here seated himself) had a Friar his Chaplain and confessor, who died in this his house of Clyst, and should have been buried at the Parish Church of Faringdon, because the said House was, and is in that parish: but because the parish Church was somewhat far off, the ways foul, and the weather rainy – or for some other causes – the Bishop willed, and commanded the Copse to be carried to the Parish Church of Sowton, then called Clyst Fomison, which is very near, and bordereth upon the Bishop's Lordship – the two Parishes there being divided by the little lake called Clyst. At this time, one Fomison a Gentleman was Lord and Patron of Clyst Fomeson; and He being advertised of such a burial towards in his parish and a Leech way to be made over his Land without his leave or consent required therein, calleth his Tenants together [words missing] to the bridge over the lake between the Bishops land and his; and there meeteth the Bishops Men bringing the said Corpse; and forbiddeth them to come over the water. But the Bishops men, nothing regarding the same, do press forwards to come over the water; and the others do withstand, and fall at strife about the matter, so long, that in the end, my Lords Friar is fallen into the water. The Bishop taketh this matter in such grief, that the holy Friar, a religious man, and his own Chaplain and Confessor should so unreverently be cast into the water, that He falleth out with the Gentleman; and sueth him in the law, and so vexeth and tormenteth him, that in the end he was fain to yield himself to the Bishops devotion, and seeketh all ways he could to curry the Bishop's good-will; which he could not obtain, untill for his redemption he had surrendered up his Patronage of Sowton with a Piece of Land, all which the said Bishop annexeth to his new Lordship. Having thus narrated in detail from the pen of John Hooker, in what manner a portion of Sowton was added to the abundant possessions of the See of Exeter.

[words missing] of Walter Bronscombe the then Bishop, I shall make another extract from the M.S. of Westcote, shewing how He acquired the Lordship of Clyst, since denominated from him Bishops-Clyst. "In the time of H. 3d, it was called Clyst Sachville of the then Possessor: but this Gentleman was ousted of this Manor and seat by Wr Bronscombe Lord B'p of this Diocese by soe cunning and facele a trick as I think it well worth the relating; excelling in subtlety and wittiness his getting of Sowton Patronage &c from Fromison by far. When St Lewis the King of France invited Prince Edward to a holy Pilgrimage for the rescue of Acon or Acre, or Ptolemais (then beleaguered by the Saracens) and for the recovery of Jerusalem, which by the permission of the King his father (with Eleanor his most famous and loving wife) Edmond King of Sicilie his Brother, foure Earles, more Barons, Knights, Esquires, and Gentlemen, Hee royally performed and underwent with great danger. This Esquire Sachville put himself with a noble and zealous spirit to serve his Prince in these holy Wars; and to bee the better furnished, engaged this Manor in mortgage to this B'p Bronscombe. In the deed amongst other Covenants and conditions, was this proviso inserted by Walr Bronscombe that if Mr Sachville redeemed it again, He should not only repay the principal, but also all such charges, as should be bestowed (in his absence, about the mayntenance, and improvement of his house and demesnes. Soe Mr Sachville was noe sooner set forward in his voyage, but the B.p travelled as earnestly in building an extraordinary fair and spacious house, rather to be accounted a Palace than a Seat for an ordinarie Esquire – repairing alsoe all the fences about the whole farm in exquisite manner, and there inhabited. After some three, or four yeares Sachville returns and viewing his old seat thus metamorphosed both in beauty and amplitude, was overjoyed with the Lord Bishops kindness; and with all possible speed provided the money, tendered it to his Lordship desiring restitution of his land; which the Bishop was almost ready to have granted but Walter Bronscombe denied it; taking a book out of his pocket wherein was sett down all the charges, wages, and expences (in full and large manner) that had been disbursed building the House and manuring of the land (reckoning very truly, not leaving out one pennie I warrant you) and earnestly required all that alsoe, or my Lord was not to return itt; which Mr Sachville perceiving to be very large and far exceeding his ability to pay, did not, (as some perchance woulde) appeale to the King his Master, or bring him into the Chancerie, but patiently yielded; having, no doubt, understood how he dealt with the Cannons for the Cornish wood; and being a Wise man had learned of Jhesus-Ben-Syrac, who counselled him not to strive with his mightier lest he fall into his hands; and againe "not to make variance with a rich Man lest hee bow down his weight" and here was both – the Bishop was his mightier and Bronscombe his richer, and therefore noe encountering, but what became of all his land at last, soe gotten? – it is a lesson for all men! for this Bishop was more griping and greedy to gain than some (especially One) of his Successors have been a wasting, reducing the Episcopal patrimonie to a far less portion than Leofricus found it at his first installment here:" In support of the [word missing] of which assertion; (availing myself once more of the M.S.) I make the following extract.

"In the second year of King Henry 5th A.D. 1414 at a Parliament holden at Leicester a Bill or supplication was presented which had relation to a former put into the Parl't holden at Westm in the 11th of Hen. 4th (which by reason the King was then troubled with civil discord took noe effect – both of them tended to this effect – "that the temporal landes devoutly given and disordinately spent by Religious, and other Spiritual Persons should be seized into the Kings hands sith the same might suffice to mayntain the honour of the King and defence of the Realm – 15 Earles – 1500 Knights – 6000 Esquires and 100 Almes-houses) for relief only of poore and impotent persons) and the King to have clearly into his coffers £20,000. At which time it was found by an extent thereof made that "the Church of Exeter could then dispend yearly £7,000, which according to the value of money now * current is to be tripled and so £21,000; and according to the new improvement [words missing] say, tripled againe, for it had then 17 Manors in this County – 8 in Cornewall, and 7 in other Shires – in all 32, and 14 faire Houses, furnished severally with all necessaries) but Plate and Linen: – Of all this trouble Bishop Voysey eased his Successors – I will forbeare to name them! – the account is cast up, and brought to this period "that All is gone; and the now Diocesan (Bishop Hall) hath only one house to rest in, and as Bishop Grandison foretold "*ubi caput reclinat*".

Thus, (observes Sir Wm Pole) speaking of Bishops Clyst (as Bronscombe cunningly gott ill, soe did Bishop Voisey wastefully loose it" – for after having continued upwards of 300 years a faire and predilected Palace of the See of Exeter Bishop Voisey returned it back to the Laity and gave it to John Earl of Bedford. Francis Erle of Bedford was Possessor of Bishops Clyst, when Sr Wm Pole made his "Collections" – the Knight died in 1635, and from the memoranda added to the M.S. of Sir Nicholas Martyn, I find that "Peter Beavis of Clyst House Esqr died A.D.1656. It may therefore be concluded that, as Peter Beavis, was the first of the Family who was Proprietor of this place, that he became possess'd of it soon after 1635. His Portrait and that of his Wife Miss Martyn, have the place of honour in the great room; and their Arms separate and conjoined, (as I have already noted) occupy the compartments of the chief window.

The appearance of the House externally is still in some points indicative of the original design – it shews it to have been a place of defence; a castellated Mansion! – in addition to the Tower, there yet remains the Moat encompassing three of its fronts, over which, on the aspect towards the West, there is a bridge communicating by a door with the House, here there is a terrace, overshadowed by a range of most magnificent Oak and Beech, through the huge trunks of which, the view which I had before seen from the battlements of the Tower, taking in the verdant pastures and the village of Sowton was beheld in a much more picturesque a light, as it had advantage of those noble trees which constituted the foreground.

Nothing now was left for me to explore but the Chapel and the antient Kitchin, which had now become detached and had been converted into a most spacious brewhouse. A compliance with my request as to visiting the Chapel, I thought was granted with reluctance; and the reason was soon developed, for on the door being opened, I found the ground floor full of Hogsheads – it had long become the Cellar of the Family – some degree of decency, had however been observed, (possibly on its first conversion to this use) – for it had been divided into two rooms, half had been desecrated, and the other half, having been appropriated to no secular use, might still be considered as retaining that Holiness which it had derived from its original application to the sacred offices of Religion! – Of the several Chapels (incidentally noticed in these Volumes) which (in the day when the tenets of the Roman Catholic were those established by the Government of the Land) were considered as appendages, (almost indispensible) to every House of consequence in the Country, I recollect but One now vested in a Protestant Family which has not suffered desecration, or been permitted thro' a successive lapse of years, gradually to moulder into a "Ruin". Whilst this at Clyst has been partially degraded into a Cellar, that at Nutwell been converted into a Library, and the spacious one at Powderham (in violation of the character of the castellated Edifice) not to use a reflection more harsh. (the seats, the desk, the altar being removed!) has assumed the appearance and been applied to the uses of a Drawing Room, the Chapel alone at Great Fulford has retained its original form, and is even now in possession of all its appropriated furniture, which is not only decorous, but elegant.

Through a broken part of what constituted the cieling of this Cellar at Clyst, thus mutilated (as the upper Chamber door is kept locked) by the hand of curiosity, I was enabled to peep into the room, which having been stripped to its bare walls, had nothing to denote a difference between it, and any other apartment but the coved cieling and the Gothic windows illumined with painted glass, of which the larger one at the Eastern end, was, as usual in a superior style of beauty and workmanship.

Taking my leave of Mrs Beavis, with acknowlegements for her courtesies, at the end of the Avenue of Limes, I took a road which I was told was the nearest to the Parsonage of Faringdon by a mile; – But I should not only have made more speed, but have labored under lesser Apprehensions for my safety, had

View entitled 'Faringdon Parsonage', no date given (DRO, 564M/F17/35)

I followed the old adage "*via trita, via tuta*! and have made my way to the house of my Friend by the turnpike road rather than by the lane, which is at present fully entitled to the epithet of "foul" & which (as we have seen in the case of the Friar), it possessed six Centuries ago – the Stratum of this part of the Country being clay, and the lane never having been conscious of the superinduction of a harder material, the natural consequence to be expected, was a mire, at times, so deep and adhesive that with difficulty my horse was able to extricate himself from it. At length having got into a better road, I passed on the left, Benbow, once a seat of the Martyns, but now a Farm belonging to the revd Mr Rous Rector of George's Clyst, and after a tedious ride of three miles, rendered more wearisome by the oppressive heat of the day, I reached the Parsonage house of Faringdon; Here I found my friend the Rector, Mr Hole, who, when I have distinguished him from the other numerous families of the name in the County by saying 'that he is the Author of the Epic Poem of Arthur and of the fine Odes to Terror and Melancholy, needs from me no additional trait or encomium to make him known to the Literary World; – In possession of a most comfortable House and establishment, which, with the lawn and shrubberies around from a union of Taste subsisting between Mrs Hole and himself have received every embellishment of which the nature of the Place will admit, Here He surrenders himself to the Muses not however, without that discretion which the Duties of his sacred function demand from him. Associated with Mr Hole in a Society at Exeter which not unjustly perhaps has been termed "literary" for the space of nine years we have participated together those rational Amusements which Minds, prepared to contribute and to receive information were capable of enjoying; Not indeficient in those accompanyments of the table which have a tendency to the gratification of the Natural Sense; Our Meetings may yet more strictly be said to have been productive of "The Feast of Reason, and the flow of Soul"

According to the prediction of Dr Downman our first President, it may truly be asserted that from this institution We have reaped not only "entertainment but advantage – In the conversations which have taken place after dinner "Wit has been joined with hilarity, learning with humour, information with decent gaiety" nor has that "bond of Politeness" been violated "which consecrates the intercourse of Scholars and Gentlemen". We have indeed to lament that from Mr P[olwhele]. the Historian of the County (since he ceased to be a Member of the Society) not only that, but several of the Individuals which compose it have (in consequence of the publication of a Volume of their "Essays" been hurried before the Public with aspersions, most indecorously and undeservedly inflicted. Suspicions of injustice, unsubstantiated by facts should never have led away a mind so well informed as that of Mr Ps to the commission of an injury which may be deprecated and repented of, but which is of such a nature as not to admit of reparation"

To me, satisfied of the impropriety of his conduct Mr P, "*quantum potest*" has made the "*amende honorable*" but many of the other Members of the Society, and I fear Mr Hole among the rest, he has offended beyond forgiveness: But of this "*satis, superque forsan*! –

After tea, taking advantage of the refreshing coolness of the Evening, we took a stroll to Faringdon House, the seat of John Burridge Cholwich Esq, the way to which conducting us over two fields of the Glebe to the Church, I stopt a while to reconnoitre the Edifice; – In the structure itself which was small and of common Architecture there was little for praise or censure – the Monument of the Cholwich family was handsome; and the Inscription to the memory of Fransisca the wife of the Rev'd John Lethbridge was an elegant effusion of conjugal affection. At the close of it are four Elegiac lines, from which (so similar is the leading thought, and in some parts even the Verbal expression,) I should almost have imagined Dr Lowth took the hint for his beautiful apostrophe to his deceased Daughter"

The lines are these –

"*Quem cum optata dies, cum sors extrema, peremptum*
Reddet in amplexus, Umbra beata, tuos;

Una maritatos cineres sociale Sepulchrum
Misceat, atque idem contegat ossa lapis"

With the *"optata dies"* how analogous would have been the *"felicius aevum"* of the Doctors; had not the expression of Mr Lethbridge, by its connexion with the tomb in the two latter lines fallen far short of it, both in beauty and propriety – the reference of *"Amplexus"* to the grave is cold, if not incongruous! – not so, on the supposition that they were to take place in the region of the blest, – where the Parent meeting again the beloved Child which had long been separated from him

– *"laeto tum dicat voce"* paternos
Eja age in aplexus! cara Maria"

Inferior however as this at Faringdon may be to Dr Lowth's in truth of thought, it still must be acknowleged to have much elegance of expression, and that if the reference to place had been the same, the coincident similarity would have been singularly striking; –

From the Church ascending to an Eminence encompast with noble Oaks, we had a very beautiful and extensive prospect, whose boundary on the West was the heights of Haldown – from hence, we had the first view of Faringdon House, the Mount indeed was in the grounds of Mr Cholwich, and being found a space of level ground, had been converted for the recreation of the Family into a bowling green, and if the estimation of a spot so applied, is to be appreciated from the excellence of Situation, where, when the Dogstar rages a Zephyr is to be found, and where the beauty of Prospect is without a rival in the neighborhood, then most judicious was the conversion of Windmill hill into a bowling green;

As there are mounds of earth yet visible on this eminence, it is more than probable that they have been Valla of some entrenchment; Mr Polwhele has intimated that they were Roman; but for such an assertion He must have other documents, than those which may be drawn from local appearances – the Spot is admirably adapted for an antient Encampment, – the nature of the ground has rendered it easily defencible on every quarter, and it is distinguishable from other *"Castra"* on the heights at a distance; but to decide that it was Roman, should rest upon somewhat more authenticated than conjecture! – contiguous to this green, nearly on an equal elevation, is the Garden rather I should conceive, (if not too much exposed) at least too remote from the

View entitled 'Faringdon House – seat of J. B. Cholwich Esq', no date given
(DRO, 564M/F17/41)

180

Mansion, but the fashion of the present day is in more points than one at variance with that which prevailed in the times of our Ancestors – the Antient Castle of the Baron, during the feudal period, was commonly erected on a craggy prominence or detached Hill, and the comfort of such situations must have resulted not from the commodiousness or convenience of the place but from the consciousness of being secure from the attack of an Enemy, which in those days (when it was not unfrequent for a Chieftain to derive the principal means of subsistence for himself and his Vassals from predatory incursions) was both sudden and attended by the most violent excesses; but when to this barbarous warfare, and confusion, Peace and Order had succeeded – "When this Necessity no longer operated, Houses were almost universally erected in the lowest situations with a probable design to avoid the inconveniencies to which the lofty positions had been subject. Hence (in the words of a late judicious Writer) the frequent sites of many large Mansions and particularly Abbies and Monasteries – the residence of Persons who were willing to sacrifice the beauty of Prospect for the more solid, and permanent advantages of habitable convenience; amongst which shelter from wind and a supply of water were predominant considerations."

Without losing sight of comforts to domestic aeconomy so indispensible a Revolution has taken place, which being effected by Taste in conformity to the systematical arrangements of Nature cannot fail of becoming permanent and of being regarded as a just criterion for every future attempt of the kind; – the spot selected for the Mansion House on an estate, is neither that which is offer'd by the high eminence which overlooks the whole of the circumjacent Country nor by the low Valley, where the View is restricted to the narrowest limits – a deep gloomy grove of Elms, or an elevated garden wall – but the choice has fallen on a knoll, or a gently sloping declivity; here the Edifice rises, with a wood, or thick plantations at its back to protect it from the more prevailing and violent winds – in front and on either side, according to the natural advantages of the place, the Lawn expands itself losing its artificial decorations, of shrubberies, and mown grass as it recedes from the House, and becoming as it were the single landscape of Nature, drest it is true, but without appearing so to have been; – Where the spot is naturally grand, a mark'd difference should appear in all accompanyments that may be introduced, so as to distinguish it from a Place of a humbler Nature, where an elegant simplicity should preside, for contiguity of Style, and unity of Character are (by all the best Judges) allowed to be amongst the first principles of good Taste. To the inspection of grounds where any glaring deviation from such a System shall be found where the Poplar shall be planted on the hill and the mountain Ash spread its branches o'er the canal; where the battled offices rendered antique by the Gothic Arch shall form a portion as it were of the Mansion of Grecian Architecture; where in rudest guise the Druidical Monument, shall circle the shaven grass-plot under the terrific projection of cannon resting on the crenellated top of a nicely whitewashed fort; * – when we behold such violation of the Costume, such aberrations from propriety and consistency of character, (et quaeque Egomet Ipse vidi), can we refrain from the contemptuous smile

"admissi! – risum teneatis Amici?!

But this is no reflexion on a System, beautiful in itself, – it is merely an abuse of it, and such also I cannot help considering that principle of picturesque Gardening which would introduce in the immediate environs of an elegant Seat, Docks, thistles, burrs and a road of ruts; in answer to which position of Messrs Price and Knight, I think the following observations may be deemed satisfactory, that "Places are not principally to be laid out with a view to their appearance in a Picture, but to their Uses, and the enjoyment of them in real life and their conformity to those Purposes, is that which constitutes their true beauty"

But to return to Faringdon Garden, – if no spot not obvious to the Eye is to be met with in the vicinity of the House, then as right angled Walls can never

---

* as it to be seen on an island belonging to Mr Pocklington on the Lake of Keswick or Derwentwater.

be made Picturesque, the Garden is to be placed at a remoter distance. Such we will conceive to be the case in the present instance; and therefore quitting it together with this digression We will pass through the fine young plantation along a gently-descending walk to a communicating road of the Farm in front of the House from whence, as may be seen in the preceding sketch, it is well-commanded. I shall not expatiate on the style of Architecture, as that will be best collected from the delineation nor will the interior of the Building detain us long; a degree of comfort appears to be attached to the suite of apartments – to the drawing room, library &c but the whole of its magnificence (at least that which results from space) will be found to be centered in the Eating room, but the dimensions of this not being in the rule of proportion with the others, in a comparative view will be productive of bad effect, for it will even, apparently at least, contribute to the diminution of those rooms, whose size (particularly height) will not well bear a reduction; We lounged a while among a large collection of books, many of which, from their titles have I doubt not lent their aid to give that legal knowlege and judgment to their owner which he is so generally known to possess, and which in the estimation of the Magistracy of the County, have so well fitted him to be their chairman at their Quarter sessions. Mr Cholwich being a Widower, without a family, has of late not resided much at Faringdon, which, tho kept in trim array, yet wore an aspect that could not fail of intimating the absence of its Master – the View from the Eating room had much extent, and no inconsiderable share of beauty, of which (tho' in a remote ground) the knoll of Killerton so conspicuously crested with trees, had most attraction; our return to the Parsonage would have been by a lane leading from the House, but the bogginess of the Stratum, not having been overcome by the Pebbles, historically memorized as a "Faringdon foundation", we were necessitated to submit to the lesser evil of pacing our way over the grass now charged with the Evenings dew; to this field the glebe lay contiguous, commodiously circumstanced for the House which it nearly surrounded:

The sketch I took the next morning before breakfast from the margin of a pond connected with a road leading to the farm Yard, a copy of which, being requested by my friend, I sent it to him, with the following lines: here introduced as being descriptive of the kind reception and entertainment that I met with from him, and Mrs Hole, who with her youngest daughter; the Eldest being unfortunately absent (delighted me by the performance of some excellent music on the Piano-forté and Tambourin, the latter of which instruments the young Lady handled in all the exquisiteness of touch and the grace of attitude –

> "To thee, beneath whose hospitable roof
> A few short hours on lightsome pinnions flew
> What time, my ear, in witching trance absorbed
> Drank the full melodies of sense and song
> This sketch I send – simple howe'er it be
> (By Friendships willing fingers kindly traced)
> Still let it hold some lowly station there
> Where Elegance, and Tastes refinements dwell"

Escorted by Mr Hole, the breakfast being over, I rode on the road for a mile or two which led to Sidmouth but about the 8 mile from Exeter, we turned to the left over a private lane, which, being no exception to the rule of the neighborhood, was rather more than indifferent. The Country through which we passed, was in common culture, and the hedges tolerably stock'd with oaks of moderate size – scarcely a house however in view untill, having travelled three miles we reached the Village of Aylesbeare, where there was nothing in the few buildings which I saw, of consequence enough to invite a second look. Being now put into a road free from intricacy Mr Hole took his leave, and as for several miles (, journeying over a barren comfortless Moor) nothing of the interesting productions of Nature or of Art offerr'd themselves to my notice, I had the more to regret the deprivation I had sustained; Arriving at length on a more large and open common, I made towards an Eminence on my left, from whence, in consequence of the peeps which I had taken, I conceived that I should be gratified with prospects that might repay my trouble: and in this I had the pleasure of not finding myself mistaken. In the wide-extended circle which my eye was able to comprehend on the West; I could well distinguish the Churches of Whimple, Rockbear and Broad clyst, the latter of which was of preeminent size and beauty, and ranging over the tufted heights of the Park at Killerton, with a glimpse of the river Exe it at last finds a boundary in the purple ridge of Haldown; – but the View towards the East, being more limited in extent, possess'd a greater discrimination of objects, and therefore engaged more of my attention – on the common below me, rose from the plain Belsbury Castle, an encampment discernible from afar, in consequence of its deep fosse and high Valla; beyond this, was spred out that delicious Valley, where among the richest pastures, decorated in the most picturesque manner with hedgerows of trees, the Otter, in many a mazy winding played with his silver stream; Here, in the center of this charming landscape, with its fretted turrets rose the Collegiate Church of Ottery surrounded by the buildings of the Town; which thus emerging as it were from the encompassing groves, and set off by the bare and elevated Common behind, was an object of Beauty, not often to be parallel'd! – the closing point towards the East of this admirable View was the Sea, seen where the mountainous Hill terminating in an abrupt Cliff, has the denomination of "Sidmouth gap" – Pursuing my ride still over a long track of moor-ground, which however I was pleased to see, had here and there begun to be inclosed within strong fences thick-planted with willow; I now gained an Eminence, burrowed by gravel pits, called straitway head, or more properly, Street-way, being part of the Strata via or Roman road, which led from Moridunum to the Isca Dunmoniorum, from Seaton to Exeter; In earlier times, when this eminence was covered with thicket, which offerr'd means of concealment, It was rendered infamous for harbouring Robbers and "in the words of an old Historiographer" – "for that it had as notable name as Shooters Hill in Kent; untill Industry and exemplary punishment enlarged the one, and reformed the other" the Vestiges of this work of the Romans having been obliterated by the modern turnpike road leading from Exeter to Honiton I cross'd it, taking a more private one which soon brought me to Larkbeer, a neat Edifice of brick, which having been a possession of the family of Stone, by the marriage of an Heiress had become the property of the Rev'd Thos Clack Rector of Kenn and Moretonhampstead; the Scenery in front is perfectly rural, but at the back of the House skirting the gardens, and affording them shelter from the North winds rows of Pine trees rear high their verdant heads, contiguous to which and supporting a very different character, are most stately avenues of wide spreading beech; – from the brow of a hill rising from Larkbeer, a view presented itself of the Park of Escott, enriched by Plantations, but rendered more picturesque by its antient groves. Escott having been already visited by one and described, I have now only to observe that the brick fronts of the House, (much to its improvement in the beauty of its appearance, embosomed as it is in woods) have been stucco'd since that time; and that Sir George Yonge having been reduced to the necessity of parting with it, it has fallen into the hands of Sir John Kennaway, a Gentleman who deriving his birth and education from the city of Exeter; went early in life as a Cadet to the East Indies; where for his meritorious services in the Army during a space of [blank] years, He obtained the mark'd approbation of the King and of the Honourable Company – by the Former he was rewarded with a Baronetcy by the latter with a Pension! – I must not here forget to observe, what I omitted to record in my notice of Faringdon, that both this Gentm and Mr Cholwich are members of our Literary Society at Exeter.

The road now conducting me over a small common, brought me to the Village of Tallaton, near which on the left, stood the Parsonage House pleasantly situated. From a ridge, as I pursued my way, I had a rich prospect of the fertile Valley of Pea, or petit Hembury, in contradiction to Broad Hembury, backed by the wild eminence of Blackdown, which eastward was seen to terminate in the precipitous declivity at Hembury fort, the earthworks of

View entitled 'Grange Mill',
no date given
(DRO, 564M/F17/57)

which encampment were very visible. I now made my approach to Grange, over roads which had exchanged the pebble for the sand stone mixed with flint, and soon after I had cross'd the turnpike road to Honiton, I came to the Mill a sketch of which on account of its uncommonly picturesque appearance I have introduced, the Building in itself is singular, composed in its lower parts of stone work, and in its upper of uprights and transverse layers of wood, whose interstitial compartments were covered over with a ruddy-tinted plaster: By its figure, irregular in itself and much in the Cottage style it is in particular recommended to the notice of the Painter, especially when it is set off by the very beautiful Sylvan accompaniments, which render this one of the prettiest scenes of the kind that I have at any time met with.

The head above, by which the Mill is supplied expands itself into a large sheet of water, which is very agreably overshadowed by a grove of tall firs and other trees. At this spot I enjoyed for a while the cooling breeze not unde-lighted at the same time, nor unemployed in making a drawing of the House of Grange, a venerable Mansion, which for the space of two Centuries had been the seat of the family of Drewe, the front that offerr'd itself to my view, though irregular did not carry with it an antique look, and was by no means to be referr'd to the period of the original erection of the Building by Mr Drewes Ancestor who, the first of his family here took up his residence; the cast however of this Western front was perhaps of a more picturesque nature, than if it had been raised according to the uniform principles of modern Architecture, and the varied accompanyments, which the Prospect from this spot brought together, harmonized as well with the Mansion as to form a land-schape of more than common beauty. Finding Mr Drewe at home, I was easily prevailed on to stay dinner, and as we had yet an hour or two before us, He was so good as to satisfy my curiosity by shewing to me his House and the immediate environs; In these latter there was not much to gratify the Taste of an Amateur of the present Style of laying out grounds; Nature had been here divested of her freedom and artless Simplicity. Her every look and production was under constraint; the Ponds were scooped into parallelograms, the walks

were raised on terraces, and the trees were planted in military files, *secundum artem*; – Still however as the general tenor of the Edifice was Gothic, or at least nothing that approximated to the Grecian style, so I was not displeased in seeing there its appendages associating with it – there was a consistency not only in the general outline, but also in the several inferior and subordinate parts. I saw before me the Villa of a Country Gentleman of family and fortune, such as it might be supposed to have been at the beginning of the 17th Century, and as it was a specimen of an antient mode now become obsolete, I had no inconsiderable gratification in tracing it through all its departments; receiving a pleasure not unlike to what I now and then participate, when I peruse an interesting tale of Spensers, which perhaps imparts a zest not very dissimilar, from the antiquity and uncommoness of its dress.

Whilst escorted around the Premisses by Mr Drewe, who at the pond fed his carp, and in the Poultry yard his Pheasants (which latter followed him as far as their range allowed, eagerly pecking the grain which he drew from the pockets of an old great coat that he wore) – whilst he shewed to me his high-bred mares, his Cocks that were staunch game, his sheeted Cows, and the gable end of his barn overspread by the exuviae of Vermin which had been destroyed by the Squire, Kites, hawks, Herons fitchets, Weasils Polecats, otters, and innumerate brushes of foxes, which he had hunted down with his own dogs, and at the same time whilst I beheld a thin meagre form with a keen eye and animated countenance, lovely fitted to the shell of an old tye perriwig, and a Surtout somewhat the worse for wear, I could not persuade myself that the Proprietor was of a different cast of character with his Mansion and his Grounds, nor look upon him in any other light than as a curious Original of a date not less antique.

Much of the interior of the House had been modernized particularly in the front exhibited in the sketch; the Eating room and the drawing room were the only ones of size; the latter was curious in consequence, of the Historical figures that were sculptured in the wainscot, which according to a date over the Chimney piece were placed there in the time of James 1st which probably was on the fitting up of the House on its first erection – through the mullions of the window of this room, I had a very beautiful view of a valley rising towards the East, at the extremity of which the Church and Tower of Broad Hembury arose, in fine perspective, tinted of a brownish grey, and fixing the eye, not more on account of the beauty of its situation than of the elegance of its architecture. In the eating room one only object drew my attention; this was a fine painting, a copy from Vandyke by Old Stone, representing the Earl of Strafford dictating to his Secretary a letter to the King (Charles 1st) as it is generally conceived) after Sentence of Death had been past on him. The Original by Vandyke I well remember to have seen and admired at Wentworth Castle in Yorkshire the seat of the late Lord Strafford. In the picture before me I recognised the expression in the features of the Nobleman and of his Amanuensis – and became again fully satisfied that the Painter had entertained a just conception of what was at the time passing in the mind of this illustrious Character. In the opinion of the late Earl of Orford, this was esteemed the "finest Picture of this Master" I can forgive him (says the Earl) at that time indeed Horace Walpole (any insipid Portraits of perhaps insipid people, when He shewed himself capable of conceiving, and transmitting the idea of the greatest Man of the Age". He adds "there is another of these pictures at Blenheim but infinitely inferior". Thomas Wentworth Earl of Strafford was but in his 49th year when He thus fell a Victim to the implacable rage of his Puritanical Enemies; The delineations of his Character by Hume and by Whitlocke appear to have been drawn by the pen of impartiality – and I transcribe them from the pleasure I have ever received in their perusal, and from the wish of impressing the eulogium of so great a Man as strong as possible on my mind. Hume observes "An accusation carried on by the united effort of three Kingdoms against one Man, unprotected by power, unassisted by counsel, discountenanced by authority, was likely to prove a very unequal contest; Yet, such were the capacity, Genius, presence of mind, displayed by this magnanimous Statesman, that while Argument and reason, and law had any place, He obtained an undisputed Victory; and He perished at last overwhelmed, and still unsubdued by the open violence of his fierce, and unrelenting Antagonists" – But from Whitlocke We have a more minute and impressive detail of him and of his demeanor on the trial with his usual candor, He says "Never any Man acted such a part, on such a theatre with more wisdom, constancy and eloquence, with a greater reason, judgment and temper and with a better grace in all his words and actions than did this great and excellent person; and He moved the hearts of all his Auditors, (some few excepted) to remorse and pity". It is remarkable that the Historian, who expresses himself in these terms, was himself Chairman of that Committee which conducted the impeachment against this unfortunate Statesman.

Having experienced at the table of Francis Rose Drewe Esqr all the entertainment which could be derived from the originality of the character of my Host, and from his hospitable fare. I took my leave soon after six, passing in my way to Collumpton or Columbton through the rural Village of Carswell, whose fields were of the richest verdure and whose hedges were thick studded with elms: – thus, deviating from the direct road, that I might visit Priory, which as a House of some antiquity, and respectable from the Family that had had it in possession, I had a curiosity to inspect.

In the expectations however that I had formed to myself of the Mansion of the Hills and the Sydenhams, I was sadly disappointed – I found neither an extent, or magnificence of Building – it was a mere jumble of low rooms, not retaining a vestige of its having been a Religious House, which from its name might be supposed, without an arch of a circular cast and decorated with a kind of zig zag or chevron moulding might be so esteemed, which I should rather attribute to the whim of some one of the Proprietors of the Mansion than to its being a relique of the Architecture of a Norman period. Having therefore here nothing to detain me either in the Antiquarian or picturesque line, passing over a field or two I regained the public road, and soon after entered on a common called Kentisbear Moor, on the North East of which rising gently on a knoll, appeared a House of handsome structure which from a Countryman I learnt to be the place of residence of Lord Mountrath. This

Gentleman had been not unfrequently spoken of to me, as a Character remarkable for its eccentricity in which the traits were not less singular than benevolent.

Sir Charles Coote of Castle Coote in the kingdom of Ireland was created a Baron in 1621 and his Son Earl of Mountrath in 1660. The present Earl, the seventh in succession came to the title on the death of his father in 1744 – and being now a Batchelor and far advanced in years on his decease, it would become extinct. From his attachment to a female, who originated from the stock of a Farmer in this neighborhood, His Lordship had been induced to purchase a small estate, and on it to raise the neat Mansion which I had before me. Here through the medium, and I understand, instigation of this his chere Amie. He dispens'd his beneficence so as to relieve, and gladden the hearts of the poor Cottagers around him; But, as the Emperor of China (without being influenc'd by his motives of seclusion) that his Person might be held more August, He had an insuparable aversion from being seen, in so much that no one but Mrs Pratt was admitted to his presence, a curtain being drawn before the part of the room where He sat at his repasts; and if a Servant happen'd to obtrude himself, or the Coachman from his box "oculo retorto" gave a squint at his Lordship an instantaneous dismission from the service was sure to follow the offence. In his journeyings to Town, which were annually repeated He had no resting places, but what He found at his own Houses on the way; and all that He required at them; his bed, his books, and his refreshments (exclusive of the interposition of his Lady-companion) were prepared for him at his wish, as if they had been effected by the agency of invisible Beings. Superadded to this whim, possibly in a degree connected with it, He had no predilection for daylight, and therefore not unfrequently was taking his rest beyond the hour of noon, not however carrying it to the extreme of the capacious Tigellius of the Poet

> "Qui Noctes vigilabat ad ipsum
> Mane, diem totam stertebat"

With these trivial inoffensive absurdities, the aberrations of a fanciful mind from the opinions of the World and the prescribed rules of life. Yet as was also asserted of the Man, who in some shape, might be adduced as a prototype of his Lordship

> "At est bonus, ut melior Vir
> Vix alius quisquam" – *

As I skirted this Moor, which I learnt was soon to be partitioned, enclosed, and drained, I saw two low Tumuli raised from the turf of the common or at least covered with it. The views from the road, somewhat elevated above the country towards the West, were of a pleasing cast, the little river Weaver over which I soon after past by a bridge of a single Arch was seen emptying its waters into the Columb – and this latter in a larger volume, winding through pastures of the most vivid green, and flowing by the southern suburbs of the town of Columbton, whose enriched tower rose in high beauty over the watery glade.

After a ride from Grange of near six miles, passing over the River by a bridge of three arches, and ascending a short hill, I entered the Town of Columbton. Various have been the conjectures of Etymologists about the derivation of the name of the Place and consequently as to the mode of spelling it. In the book of Domesday it is written Colum – but as it has not been ascertained whether this appellation is to be referr'd to the language of the Britons, Saxons or Romans. I shall take the liberty of observing that as it is most probable the Town has taken its name from the River which flows beneath it, and the River, from its quality, which is that of swiftness, so from the assimilation of the Word Colum – to Columba, there may be no great stretch of Hypothesis in drawing it from the latter especially as in our own language the Dove is not unfrequently found to have lent its name to rivers in various parts of the Kingdom.

* 1803 at Strawberry hill obiit Earl of Mountrath aged 78 years –

View entitled 'Columb-ton',
no date given
(DRO, 564M/F17/73)

On the Buildings in the Town there is very little encomium to be pas't – the Church being the only edifice commanding a Moments attention – This however is a fabric of more than common consequence, and from whatsoever point it may be viewed arrests the notice of the Spectator. In a picturesque light, with its large Eastern window, and its high tower with ornamented pinnacles it was well seen from a leat of water, which for the use of some Mills, had been conducted through some pleasant fields and Gardens near it. The Tower, in particular, by its height, its elegance in its pinnacles, and fretted windows, and the sober tint of the Stone with which it had been built, arrested my attention; With an elevation of one hundred feet, it rose magnificent over the Church and the Houses of the Town, and was of course beautifully conspicuous throughout the whole of the wide Valley in which it was situated, and the surrounding hills. Though there are to be met with no authenticated records or documents to establish its claim to Antiquity. Yet, there are presumptive reasons for attributing it to the period of Ed. 1st. No Vestiges however of this early style of Architecture are to be discovered, arising from the circumstance of its having been beautiful in the time of Ed. 6 by John and Katherine Manning.

Attached to the Church, and constituting parts of its interior are three aisles; one of which, on the southern aspect may be remarked for its singularity. having been erected by John Lane, a rich Clothier of the Town, who in an Epitaph on his tomb is stiled "Mercator; it being the Usage in those days, (the beginning of the 16th Century, for the Manufacturer not only to go through the whole process of the Article He dealt in, but also, to export it.

The beauty of this aisle exceeds every other part of the Pile, the stone with which it is built is of a reddish hue, and is decorated on the exterior front with a course of light–coloured freestone, on which has been carved an Inscription in letters at least five inches in height, in alto relievo, memorizing the Founder and his Wife Thomasine, in addition to which on various parts of the Wall the eye is struck with a repetition of the initials of his name J. L. – so anxious was this opulent Clothier (designated in Latin by the Inscription "Lanarius, whence possibly the Etymon of his name) to hand down to posterity, that such a Person had existed as John Lane;

"Inscriptions may not unfrequently be met with on the Edifices of former days, of this kind of Sculpture, though rarely so deep and conspicuously embossed – these indeed were altogether of a pious tendency concise, modest, and of a turn to Scriptural allusions, but with a view of awakening the minds of the Readers, and fixing on them religious impressions, were offer'd to general notice, being "introduced in friezes and other decorative parts both on the exterior and interior of Antient Buildings civil and Religious – from this usage perhaps Mr Lane took a hint, and desirous of surpassing them all, by his Brobdinagian letters effectually attained the point He must have had in view of attracting attention and rewarding it with the information therein couched; Of the enrichments on the Church and Tower much may even now be spoken in praise, many Images, Escutcheons of Arms, and open fretwork still remaining; enough to awaken regret for others, which by Revolutionists and Fanatics of the 17th Century have been mutilated, or utterly defaced.

Having taken the preceding sketch of the Church and strolling further on the banks of the leat towards the eastern entrance of the Town, I had pleasure in noticing several Mills, which were set in motion by the stream and, in particular a Grist one which I thought too picturesque to be overlooked: The opposite delineation will better express its form and accompanyments than any description by the Pen, which in objects perpetually recurring to observation of a similar nature, must always be found inadequate to the task;

The Inns at this place, (notwithstanding the high road from the West passes through it, to Bath), are but of a secondary rate; at the Half Moon however, kept by a Widow, I met with courtesy and comfortable entertainment. After breakfast, the next morning I returned through the part of the Town I had entered and having repassed the bridge, turned from the Grange road to the left, following the course of the River Culm, though its waters were in no part visible from the road, from every little eminence which I ascended I was gratified with views of the most pleasing cast, such however as are often met with in the County, where the Eye ranges over a track of inclosed Meadow land, rich verdant, and dotted with groups of cattle, from whence gradually ascending Hills arise, overspread with flocks of Sheep, intermingled with fields of Corn, with farm houses and hedge-row groves.

View entitled 'Mill at Columbton', no date given (DRO, 564M/F17/79)

Having rode about three miles I skirted a small lawn in front of an antient Edifice called Bradfield, the seat of Henry Walrond Esq. on having recourse to the genealogical notices of Sir Wm Pole I find, that the family of Walrond took up their residence at this place some time in the beginning of the reign of Henry 3d, where, without intermission by the failure of male issue, they have continued to the present day. The architecture of the House now standing does not appear to be of a style more antient than the beginning of the 17th Century, though possibly as it may seem from the size and fashion of the Hall, in the renovation of a building verging to decay, while in its exterior it assumed a form correspondent to the architectural mode of the times, it might have retained a few of its antient rooms, of which the Hall might have been one: The front towards the road is of the shape following

Passing through the Entrance Gates I took a near view of the House, and observed the painted Windows in the Hall, and the Escutcheon of Arms over the door embossed in stone – around it however, in the square from a large pond, encompast by trim box hedges, by pyramids and topiary works of Yew, I could see nothing to arrest my attention for a moment, which became altogether directed to the view of the Valley, lying below towards the North, the Church tower of Willand, and the cultivated Hills beyond here seen in superior beauty, and to the best advantage.

By the most careless observer of the place impressions must be felt of regret, bordering on disgust, as He beholds on every object around him symptoms of a perverted taste of neglect and of dilapidation; thistles and other Weeds growing rampant on the lawn, and several of the attached Buildings falling into Ruin; John (said I to my Servant who had lived several years in the neighborhood) As we turned away from the Gate, "Who is this Mr Walrond? his name as belonging to an antient Family in the County is familiar to me, though I have never met the Gentleman at any of the Public meetings of the County; What sort of a Man is He, what his general Character? "Bless me Sir (replied my Old Man) I thought every Person had known the Character of Squire Walrond, my late Master Mr Drewe, was Trustee for him, but He had a world of trouble with him, for He brought going a vast sight of money in making alterations in his house; and to make the matter worse He married one of his Servant Maids. Oh dear "He wants a little of that of which I want Sir a great deal" !

Laughing much at Johns description, and ingenious simplicity, We jogged on to Uffculme which lay Eastward at the distance of two miles; In the way to which from the higher grounds several Views opened upon me of a beautiful and diversified nature. Two of these were well discriminated and in high contrast with each other – on one side, rising over a narrow vale to a considerable elevation was the far-stretched outline of Black-down singular in this its hither part by the abrupt separation of one ridge from another; not unlike the break in the Hill near Sidbury, so clearly distinguished from the heights of Haldown and called the "Gap". At the Northern end of Blackdown, where it towers lordly over the rich subjacent Country, on the very verge of the steep precipice rose a tall columnar Edifice denominated by the Country People, an Obelisc! conspicuous to the surrounding neighorhood it forcibly attracted my attention; and my curiosity of learning by whom it had been raised was soon gratified by the ready information of a venerable-looking Farmer, Who told me that "it was built by Attorney Manley of Credock a place just below" to the surprise of Us all; for we had been used to think Sir before, that Attornies knew better what to do with their money"

Just beyond this is a conical shaped Hill, separated from Black-down and very discernible to be so even at the distance of Grange, singularly remarking the Country, and ornamented with a plantation.

On the other side of the eminence on which I stood I had a most commanding view of the gently-rising hills towards the West, on one of whose acclivities the Village of Sampford Peverell most pleasingly exhibited itself embosomed in trees, but nearer in the Vale was the chief object of attraction – the verdant lawns and groves encompassing Bridwell, a Seat of Richard Hall Clarke Esq: Amidst a cultured and inclosed Country, divided into farms (chiefly arable) by intersecting hedgerows, how delightful is the appearance viewed as was this of Bridwell from a high commanding Station; of a Gentlemans House, with all those accompanyments which of late years have been attached to it by Modern Taste. In the embellished Lawn the grove, the Plantation, the rivulet and the sheet of Water we are possessed of those elegant beauties of rural Nature, of which our Forefathers knew little or nothing – surrounded by them now stands the Mansion, exhibiting to the eye a specimen of Architectural Beauty, which though now and then vitiated by the whim and caprice of those, who affect singularity in general does credit to the Artist of modern days, and evinces a taste of elegance, refinement, and comfort, which in no part of the World, beyond the shores of England, can be found so united and brought to such an admirable state of perfection! – On entering the little town of Uffculme on the left appeared a Gate introducing a Road-way from Bridwell into the street, skirted by flourishing Plantations; there was little else of beauty in the place the buildings (excepting a few which were near the Market place of a superior cast) being of a mean appearance and in general covered with thatch – contiguous stands the Church with a low tower overlooking the rich track of pasture lands through which the River Culme winds its course, here flowing with a volume of water adequate to the constant demands of a Factory which has been lately raised on its banks – I had seen one of these Buildings at Willand, from the terrace of Bradfield and indeed, there are few of our Rivers near a town in these parts unpossess'd of such Edifices, whose machinery has been applied to the manufacture of wool and cotton tho' chiefly the former; advantage being taken of the population of the Place and lucrative employment being thus dispensed to the women and Children, most of whom would have been otherwise idle, or occupied in labours of a less profitable nature.

Very soon after I had quitted Uffculme, from the road leading further up the Valley to Culmstoke, I turned on the left, ascending a hill, between high hedges richly decorated with Elm and Beech, from an open part on this Hill I had an extensive range of prospect, highly gratifying to the Eye, especially, when it rested on that part of the Valley, where the Town and Church tower of Columbstoke, having for its boundaries on the North and South high and waste Hills, lay surrounded by its Elmy groves, and evergreen pastures. A mile or two brought me to Maiden–Down, where to my regret I found the Beech trees gone, those fine old Beech trees, truly the "*patulae fagi*" of Virgil, with whom I had been acquainted for at least thirty five years. To compensate for this deprivation, I had pleasure in beholding the wild unproductive common, converted into inclosures of cultivated ground, or covered over with flourishing plantations. A great part of this Down is the property of J. Sanford Esq of Ninehead (which lies in the parish of Burlescomb) and to whom the Manor belongs – the turnpike from Columbton to Taunton passes over this high track of land, skirting on the right a lesser quantity of Common attached to the Parish of Columbstoke, yet uninclosed, and at the eastern extremity where the Hill dips into a low bottom runs a small stream which constitutes the boundary of the Counties of Devon and Somerset.

Crossing the great road in a direct line at this hither end, after a mile dropping somewhat down a declivity towards the North I came to the little Village of Burlescombe, seated with a commanding aspect on the side of a Hill, looking most beautifully down on a rich extensive Valley, which was rendered more than commonly picturesque and pleasing by its diversified Scenery of Woods, rocks of Marble, a Mansion House, the seat of J. Browne Esq and by the Priory of Canonsleigh adjoining to it, a mass of ruins overspread with ivy. The Church stands near the road approaching to the Eastern end of the Parish, where are to be seen many an antient Monument of the family of Ayshford, who had their Mansion and a considerable property here from the time of Hen. 2d to the latter end of the 17th Century, when they were succeeded by the Sanfords of Ninehead.

A mile introduced me to the Ruins of Canonsleigh. From the road passing into a meadow of rich pasturage I came at once in front of Mr Brownes House, at this time the residence of Lady [blank] . It was a structure of modern archi-

*View entitled 'South View
of Canonsleigh Abbey',
no date given
(DRO, 564M/F17/91)*

tecture, plain and simple, consisting of a Central Mansion, and on either side
a low Colonnade attached; built with the stone hewn from the neighbouring
quarries.

Contiguous as it stood to the massive Remains of a Religious House altogether of the Gothic Style, there was a discordance in this Grecian facade,
which violated all the rules of unison and taste: – It was impossible with any
degree of satisfaction to look at them both together. I therefore moved on to
the Ruin, which had one solitary Mass only to afford a specimen of whatever
grandeur it antiently possessed; this was a square Building which had
projected from the Pile, exhibiting at its several angles, strong buttresses, and
on its Western front a doorway and window with pointed arches: – over its
sides on the South and East, hung pendulous huge columns of ivy, which with
its dark green tint and the deep shade of its hollow recesses, was in charming
contrast with the grey cast of the Walls: – just behind rose a high hill, overspred with venerable trees, chiefly Beech, which from their height, and
branchy limbs appeared to have had their birth in "other times"; A garden
only intervening, from the darkened Mass of Wood, the bright Ruin, seemed
to acquire a greater degree of brilliancy, and became possess'd of that relief,
and force of contrast, which, when beheld must ever be considered as one of
the most beautiful effects arising from picturesque Scenery. Of the three
sketches which I took, the first exhibits, merely the Southern face of the
Building, backed by the Wood – the one opposite gives a view of the front
towards the West, which being taken in an oblique manner, loses the sight of
the Gothic doorway, shut out from the eye by the intervention of the projecting buttress; Here is seen a broad face of Wall, uninterrupted by any break or
fissure, as might have been expected in an Edifice which dated its origin as far
back as the twelv'th Century; and which, when happily placed, of a Ruin
becomes one of its most picturesque ornaments; all was fair and undilapi-
dated, and saving in the small pointed Window, before noticed, had nothing
but a tress or two of ivy to arrest the eye:

To much greater advantage however is this front seen, when by receding
from the Building, the Southern one, is taken into the same View – then it
forms as it were a whole! there is assumes a superior consequence, and

View entitled 'West View of Canonsleigh', no date given (DRO, 564M/F17/95)

displaying all the decorations which it possesses, its doorway window, buttresses, backed in the finest manner by the hanging wood, presents to the sight an assemblage of picturesque objects, not more gratifying to the Antiquary than to the Painter; Had this Ruin (insulated as it were, for it had no fragments of other Walls lying scattered around it) been detached from the Modern Mansion, the trim gardens, and the rich meadow of which it was encompassed, and been placed under the associated circumstances of the greater part of the Reliques of Antiquity, overhung by venerable trees, beset with briars, underwood, and huge masses of the fallen Edifice; from such a wildness and seeming desolation, it would have derived a considerable accession of Beauty, and more closely and permanently have rivetted the attention of the Admirer of Picturesque Scenery, rendered more attractive by natural and appropriate accompanyments. Having therefore taken the three sketches, I had little further to detain me, for being admitted through the Gothic doorway into the Garden, I found that the interior of the Building consisted merely of two narrow passages, through one of which a stream ran by whose rapid current, in the open space of the meadow fronting the House, an undershot Grist Mill was set in motion, thus taking advantage, as it should see, of a declivity in the ground to effect an end, which the scanty Rivulet rippling from its neighbouring source through a track of pastures nearly level would not otherwise have been able to have accomplished; Over this expanse of meadow the eye ranged upwards with delight, highly gratified with the richness of its verdure, and with the elevated ridge (on which the Church and Village of Burlescombe were high seated) shutting it in on the South East and declining in an abrupt boldness towards the Valley.

South west from the Ruin, forming an office in the farm yard I discovered the antient Gateway which originally conducted to the Abbey; now, no longer employed in the functions of its designation, but blocked up on its western side by a shed of modern date, for the reception and feeding of cattle, into whose several stalls there was admission by apertures of circular arches, excepting in a portion of somewhat greater elevation where there was a doorway, whose arch was pointed, and in unison with the windows of the Gateway. Much is it to be regretted, at least by those who are Amateurs of

View entitled 'S. West View of Canonsleigh', no date given (DRO, 564M/F17/99)

antient Architecture, that so fine a Specimen as this must have appeared to be in its perfect state, should have been, (if I may not be warranted in saying desecrated) yet so injured and defaced by the mean buildings attached to it. If, in the elevation of the Poet Thrice happy must be the Proprietor of some rural seat should He, among the happy endowments of Nature, possess an acquisition of antient Art

> *"if one superior rock*
> *"Bear on its brow the shivered fragment huge*
> *"Of some old Norman fortress;*

yet even this would be considered by him of inferior consequence and beauty to the venerable Remains of "a Fane Monastic" for He adds

View entitled 'Gateway Canonsleigh', no date given (DRO, 564M/F17/103)

194

"happier far,
"Ah then most happy, if thy vale below
Wash with the crystal coolness of its rills
Some mouldering Abbeys ivy–vested wall"

To the Proprietor of this Abbey, who had violated its solitude, and disfigured its Walls nothing of this happiness could have been known; by his grosser ideas the refinements of the Picturesque Enthusiast were not to be comprehended; and if the Domains of the One were to be sequestered from the haunts of the Vulgar and the profane where even

"if Art
"e'er dared to tread, twas with unsandal'd foot
"Printless, as if the place were holy ground"

Those of the Other were not to be considered as intruded upon if they were laid open to the eye unconscious of its beauties, or to the hand of the Mechanic, who, by his tasteless innovations would deform a structure, which if left only to the "gradual touch of Time might still have offer'd itself as an object of Antiquarian research or picturesque admiration; – So circumstanced I have little further to remark on this Gateway than that on its few remaining battlements there appeared to be an embossed sculpture consisting of letters of an antient date, too remote from the eye to be decyphered that the tints of the walls were of a brownish cast here and there dashed with red, and that from the distance this edifice was from the Ruin, (on the supposition that in its original state they were connected) an inference might be drawn of the extent and splendor of the Monastery in the day of its Patronage and prosperity – few however are the records, or documents to substantiate any such claims; We know nothing of its buildings beyond the existing Remains, exclusive of the demolition of a chapel not long ago, the loss of which is not perhaps more to be regretted, than the motives are to be reprobated as they originated (such at least is the current report) in the meanest of all sources, Avarice, the walls being of lime-stone and consequently convertible into manure to which purpose they were applied! – To this indeed we may add the income which it possessed at the period of its dissolution in the 26th of Hen. 8th; which though not to be estimated among the series of the greater Monastic Houses in the County, such as Ford, Tavistock, Buckland, Torr, Buckfast, Hartland, Newnham, Dunkeswell, was still in those days of consideration, being sec Dugdale of the amount of £202 15s 3d. – Its foundation is ascribed to the piety of Walter Clavile, (who was possess'd of the Seigniory of Burlescombe, in the time of Hen. 2d) for certain Monks who stiled themselves, Canons of the Order of St Augustine, and for whose maintenance, this rich valley of Leigh, a portion of the manor of Burlescombe was appropriated; We gather however from the Monasticon of Tanner that about the beginning of the 14th Century, possibly during the reign of Ed. 2d it received considerable annexations of lands and perhaps of Buildings from the munificence of Maud de Clare, Countess of Hereford and Gloucester, who in this period, or (as it is elsewhere reported,) in the time of Ed. 1st, had dissolved the original institution, and made the Canons of St Austin give way to an Abbess and Nuns of the same Order: the number of whom at the surrender amounted to 18.

In the 35th of Hen. 8th, the site of Canonsleigh Abbey, in exchange with the King for other lands, became the property of Sir John St Leger, whose Son sold it to the family of Culme or Columb, who at an earlier period having large possessions in the neighbourhood near the river Columb, took, as was the common usage, their denomination from thence; from them it passed into the hands of James Smith Esq, having Sir Wm Bretton kt as an intermediate Proprietor; and as I learnt from the Old Man, who had been Gardener here 36 years had been purchased by Mr Browne just at the time when He was taken into his service.

I had but just departed from the Gateway, when the road brought me in front of the extensive Marble quarries and Kilns in which the stones were calcined, of Westleigh; from a Labourer I learnt that this vast stratum of lime rock belonged to Mr Browne and to the revd Mr Walker of Tiverton, and that the sale of lime was carried on to a very considerable extent; – the property of the Stone being free and quickly reduced to a Calx, and when thus burnt, highly estimated by the Farmer for its excellent quality as a Manure; – from which circumstance, and its price, (for notwithstanding the Coal used for its burning was brought 13 miles by land-carriage from Taunton) the Proprietors were enabled to sell it at the low rate of 2s. 9d pr Hogshead consisting of 5 Winchester bushels, it was in high request and the demand for it throughout the country at times, more than could be answered.

To these rocks and Kilns the Canal is to reach, the plan of which has been long projected, and which, commencing at Topsham on the river Exe, is to pursue the track through the vallies watered by the Clyst and Columb, untill it meets the river Tone at Taunton; branching off in several directions to the Town of Tiverton and to these Quarries of West Leigh, extending in its main course over a space of 36 miles. In the intermediate country, the advantages which (not to enumerate those arising from the facilitating the intercourse of the towns and Villages in the district in the conveyance of goods, and their respective manufactures) in an especial manner must be derived to Agriculture in the melioration of the circumjacent lands by the dispersion of this manure in larger quantities, it is reasonable to conceive will amply remunerate to the Subscribers and at no distant period after its completion reimburse the sum which shall be expended in the undertaking though it shall amount to the estimate of £15,000. At Grange Mr Drewe gratified me with a sight of the map drawn out by Cary of this Canal, by which in a detail minute and apparently correct, its course was traced through all the vallies, winding among the hills, from whose rivulets in conjunction with the streams of the Clyst and Columb, it is to be fed with water; In consequence however of the depression experienced from the protraction of the War with France in the trade of the County, (on which it has been peculiarly severe) no commencement has yet been made, and as it has been with many other enterprises connected with the arts and manufactures of the kingdom it must be left to the exhilerating voice and energies of Peace, to awaken and rouse them from

View entitled 'Holcombe Court. Seat of Peter Bluett Esq.',
no date given
(DRO, 564M / F17 / 113)

the dormant state in which they have been so long and unfortunately suspended;

Winding round this mass of limestone and ascending towards the western limits of the most magnificent Wood which crested the summit, and adorned the southern side of the Hill, I reached a small track of open land, called Durdley moor, whereon was a large pond, and from which during the whole of my approach to it, I had before me full in view a very picturesque scene, formed by the Village of Holcombe Rogus, its church, and castellated mansion long a seat and residence of the Bluets; This latter I found nearly at the head of the Village street, contiguous to the Church and to the Vicarage House; a most magnificent antient Edifice, of considerable extent, and altogether such a Pile, (considering it as the Mansion of a private family) as is not to be parallel'd in the County. From the time of Hen. 3d there are Records extant to prove that it was the place of residence of a family of some consequence in the County; from which it derived the adjunct of Rogon, or Roges, which has since been corrupted into Rogus, and as Prince observes, assuredly "did not fetch its original from Rogues alias Bondsmen or from Rogus, a funeral pile" – In the Harleian MS.S is to be found *"Simon fil Rogonis tenuit Villam et Manerium de Holcomb circa principium H. III &c"* whom, of the same name (latterly with a slight alteration as afore noticed,) followed in succession eight generations; – by an Heiress it became the property of Chiseldon, and by a similar mode of transmission soon after was vested in the family of Blewet antiently Bloet, not Blort as Polwhele has copied from an error of Risdon. These, by alliances with other families of note and opulence, and by producing from their own stock several scyons of worth and eminence raised their name into high esteem among the Gentlemen of the County, during a long continued period of ten generations, and, if an inference may be allowed to be drawn from the great size of the Hall, *"la grande Sale a manger"* displayed often their Hospitality to their tenantry and neighbours. The present Hall, ornamented with carved work and painted glass is not coaeval with the tower of entrance (which perhaps is its most antient part) but was erected about the middle of the sixteenth Century, by Sir Roger Bluet Kt, as is supposed from his name being there visible! – The Proprietor of the mansion is Peter Bluett, I know not, whether of this family of Holcombe Rogus, but adopted by the late Proprietor, from Falmouth in Cornwall, and invested with the major part of the landed property which He had possessed; – Mr Polwhele passed an Encomium on this Gentm, hypothetical it is true; but suppositions are not unfrequently raised on plausible tho' fallacious foundations; and the less a Man commits himself on this score, fewer will be the impeachments levelled against his sagacity and judgment!!!

I have no encomium to pass, but from the information of Mr Drewe of Grange, that there were reports circulating that much of the fine wood behind the House was to be converted into cash and that the Mansion itself was to be let * – and from the apparent neglect of the fine old Edifice – 'quaeque Egomet Ipse vidi' – and the solitude by which it was encompast, I have to regret that not more of the estimable qualities, and hereditary principles of the antient Stock had with the Estates been transmitted to this scyon of Adoption – Within the Gateway, which with surrounding Walls inclosed a green area before the House, during the whole of the time in which I was taking the preceding View, I saw no living creature (tho I understood it was inhabited by the family) but a flock of Geese depasturing on the scanty herbage, and a number of Greyhounds basking themselves in the sun, stretched out on the low wall; By the cackling of the one, and the barking of the other, as soon as I made my entré within the gate I was at first a good deal annoyed; and in my ride afterwards, from the singularity of these two species of Animals being thus as it were associated, as I ruminated on the subject. It occurred to me that they had been in days of yore companions to each other at Rome, where the one for want of exerting that propensity given them by nature of barking (now uselessly indulged in to my annoyance) would have subjected their Masters to an extremity of danger, had not the cackling of the other atoned for the default and saved the Capitol.

Amusing myself with this lucubration, I recollected the beautiful description of the Greyhound given Us by Ovid, and having leisure on my hands shall pursue it. As so many Sportsmen in modern times have had a classical Education, and as several of them have written upon the subject of their amusement *"con amoré' – et cum eruditione –* Such as Somerville, Beckford &c it may seem strange that in the course of such discussions, no notice should have been taken of this passage. In that species of the diversion of Hunting (Hare-coursing) which in some Counties is carried on with an extraordinary degree of Emulation; perhaps there is no were to be found a description drawn with such animation and accuracy as that to which I have just alluded. It is a Simile introduced with admirable effect, and most appropriately adapted to the illustration of the Chace of Apollo after Daphné

> *"Ut Canis in vacuo Leporem cum Gallicus arvo*
> *Vidit, et Hic praedam pedibus petit, ille Salutem*
> *Alter inhaesuro similis, jam, jamque tenere*
> *Sperat, et extento stringit vestigia rostro;*
> *Alter in ambiguo est an sit deprensus, et ipsis*
> *Morsibus eripitur, tangentiaq ora relinquit,*
> *Sic Deus et Virgo est;*

which I have thus paraphrased,

> *When the swift Hare some Greyhound spies*
> *As oer the extensive plain she flies*
> *Light as the breeze He springs away*
> *Bounds o'er the space, and seeks his prey*
> *Now o'er her haunch He seems to hang*
> *And now to seize her with his fang*
> *She (all but caught) in sore affright*
> *Starts from his grasp, and speeds her flight.*
> *Thus after Daphne Phaebus sprung –*

Having dwelt a while in admiration of the beauty of the passage I am led to an enquiry after the Word *"Gallicus"* here evidently designating that species of Dog which We denominate Greyhound; and by the Annotator described as one *"Qui odore feras non investigat"*.

In the ascription of the Animal to Gaul we find an obvious deviation of the name, nor can a doubt be entertained but that the Romans collected from every nation which they subjugated every thing that they conceived to be rare and curious.

In this article of Dogs, the records of our own Island bear testimony to their requisition; the Mastiff was no where else found of such size, strength, or courage; and so highly was it prized by the Romans, that their Emperor appointed an Officer here, whose especial province was to superintend the breed, and transmit from hence to the Amphitheatre such as He might deem equal to the combats.

In like manner we may conjecture that in those days Gaul was famed for her Grey-hounds; the characteristic properties of which were swiftness, like Achilles *"swifted-footed"* [Greek] and that it pursued its prey not by smell, but by sight *"Gallice' "chasser à vue, Anglice"* Gaze-hound or, from its colour possibly, Greyhound – In as far as this Animal was a production of Gaul We have no reason to think, on such account that the Romans were inclined to entertain a predilection for it; on the contrary indeed it might be imagined, that had it not been for its peculiar quality it would for this very cause have been their detestation; since We have it sufficiently ascertained that by this people a Dog was crucified every year as a punishment, because these Animals had not warned them by barking of the arrival of the Gauls in their assault of the Capitol, thus sharing the imputation of the Guards, who instead of being on the watch, were found asleep. On this memorable occasion however, which the Romans testified their indignation against the Dog, by inflicting on him an annual and most singular punishment it should not be omitted that at the same time they demonstrated their gratitude to the Goose (who by his incessant cackling had given an alarm to Titus Manlius and saved the Capitol) by conferring on him the honours of a triumph. To this fortunate instance of the Birds sagacity Ovid has an allusion

> *"Nec servaturis vigili Capitolia voce*
> *Cederet Anseribus"*

However puerile and absurd such ceremonial Institutions may appear in these more enlightened times, on a Nation devoted to a diversity of Mythological Superstitions it may naturally be supposed that they would have an exceeding strong hold; nor perhaps is it unreasonable to conclude that (analogous in many respects to the exhibitions in modern Italy and other Roman Catholic Countries which are commonly conducted with great public pomp and decoration) they might thus subserve a political use, and by occupying the minds of the populace with amusing pageantries abstract them from considerations of a more serious nature. That this show, displaying the ignominy of the Dog (whether Gallicus or not we have no records) and the triumph of the Goose must have wonderfully attracted the gaze and attention of a Roman mob, there can be little doubt! – the following passage from Rosinus will demonstrate with what solemnity and splendor it was annually celebrated, *"Illud etiam non omiserim, moris fuisse apud Romanos ut quotannis certo die solenni in pompâ gestaretur "Canis in crucem actus" et Anser splendidé admodum in lecticâ, et veste stragula pretiosa sedens; ob eam causam, quod illi in obsidione Capitolii Gallis, irruptionem in arcem tentantibus, Romanos clangore et strepitu excitassent, canibus interim somno indulgentibus"*, I have now only one further remark to add, and that is in regard to the Epicurism or Gluttony of the Romans which, in this point seems even to have mastered their superstition; for, surely, if the Goose by its good services had deserved thus well, like the Ibis of the Egyptians, it should have been held in reverence and as an encouragement to other Geese *"ne quid detrimenti in futurum capiat Respublica"* their persons should have been held inviolable and with their honours they should at least have shared security; This however we find, so far from being the case that at their tables a Goose, (or rather a Gander, for that only is white) was considered inter delicias and especially its liver after it had been well crammed with luscious figs:

> *"Pinguibus et ficis pastum jecur Anseris albi"*
> *Hor. lib Sat 2d*

From this Lusorium of the Dogs and Geese, whom I left at their several occupations, I return to the Mansion merely to observe, that its walls are formed from the marble Quarries with which this Parish also abounds, and that in the front towards the West, the same injudicious alteration in the form of the windows has taken place, tis may be remarked of the Principal one in the sketch the Gothic style having been converted to the Grecian, and the antient Mullion modernized to the trim sash!! In the Church as might be expected, are to be found a number of Monuments in honour of the family of Bluett, many of them of considerable beauty and magnificence, and one in particular of white marble of John Bluett Esq and his Wife Elizth Daughter of Sir Jn Portman Bart, whose effigies are in a recumbent posture, surrounded by eight daughters kneeling.

The Road winding round the House, ascended immediately a steepish Hill giving me a view of the Garden which it skirted and of the noble hanging wood, that defended it from the Northern blasts; Notwithstanding however the contiguity of this Road to a Gentlemans place of residence, and to Lime rocks, the chippings of whose stones must necessarily afford abundant materials for its repair, it was so rugged and full of ruts as to render it, in addition to the steepness of its acclivity extremely incommodious to the Traveller; – this hill being mastered, I reached Hockworthy, and near the Church I found a small Village, and Court-Hall the Manor House, the property of Charles Webster Esq, now occupied by a Gentleman of the name of Foy and commanding, as it stands high, a prospect of a pleasant cultivated Country; the expectations which I had formed of the whole of this track of land were those of barrenness and want of culture, but it gave me pleasure to find it of a very different cast, instead of the roads commonly passing over bleak and wild wastes, without trees, or habitations, it was surrounded by inclosures well-cultivated, beautified by rich Woods, frequently seen cresting the hills which rose from the interjacent vallies, and exhibiting a display of blended population in the recurrence of Farm-houses, Villages, and the Mansions of Gentlemen. From the elevated ground behind Hockworthy I had however rather a less pleasing view of a Country, which forming the North Eastern boundary of the Parish touched upon that of Ash-brittle in the County of Somerset, and I had moreover the dissatisfaction of travelling over roads, even more rough than those which I had already traversed.

Having advanced a mile or two, it was my intention to have deviated a little from the direct road to Bampton, that I might visit Huntsham, the seat of Mr Troyte, but from a misapprehension of some vague notices which I collected from a countryman, I overshot the way, and came into some fields, rising behind the House, from hence however little but the roof was visible, staying therefore awhile to gaze upon a rich, and finely-wooded Valley, similar to those I had lately passed, watered by the Loman. Here a scanty stream and deriving its source from the higher grounds of the Parish. From the family of Bears or Bere's as the name is now spelt, who have their residence in the adjoining parish of Morebath, Huntsham passed by purchase into that of Lucas, and by the same mode of conveyance became the property of the present Possessor Wm Troyte Esq. a hardy old Gentleman, of plain manners and powerful exertion, being one of the most animated Hunters in the County, of the antient school of his relation and Compeer Sir Thos Acland Grandfather of the present Baronet (and well assimilated to the nature of the Country and the name of his seat, which as Etymologists tell Us, imports "the Huntsmans Home". Getting by means of a sporting gate) which was to be found in every field into a common (, by a gentle descent I cut athwart it to a road traversing

View entitled 'Bampton Bridge',
no date given
(DRO, 564M/F17/129)

its bottom, as well as the bogginess of the ground) decorated with the silvery tufts of the Cana, would permit, which I was glad to find was infinitely more smooth than those I had lately passed, being composed of Schist, which for a short space intervenes between the marble strata of Westleigh and Bampton; The ridge on which I now travelled offer'd to my view, a scenery, which though apparently well-cultivated, had yet bold features, pleasingly diversified by an intermixture of hill and valley – from this, a steep rugged descent introduced me to the town of Bampton, which had too many picturesque accompanyments to allow of my leaving it for the evening.

After a latish dinner of between five and six o clock, the Evening being fine, I strolled from the Inn, to reconnoitre the Castle scenery which I had briefly noticed in the year 1796, and at my leisure to explore the vast marble quarries and other picturesque points which lay upon the River, of these the three sketches here introduced will exhibit a most pleasing specimen: – To the Mount, rising from the meadows near a House of Lucas Esq on the eastern quarter of the Town I first directed my steps. When beheld from a distance, it is seen to advantage, so as to ascertain the precise form, which on a near approach, crowded as it is in many of its parts with plantations, cannot well be determined – this being conical, stamps instantly on the mind an impression of its being the Keep of a Norman Castle, and though from its vast magnitude no idea can be entertained of its being altogether artificial yet there is no improbability in conceiving that the upper parts of the Hill, naturally rising to a point, may have been made to assume by the hand of Art that shape which the Soldier of the day, whether Saxon or Norman, according to the usage of his country deemed best calculated for defence and Security. Beyond the period of the former of these Nations we have nothing but conjecture for the occupation of this Hill, at least in a military view plausible however is the supposition that it may have been a place of residence of the Romans – their Tormolus was doubtless not very remote, either at Molland, or as I have elsewhere hazarded an opinion near the junction of the Taw with the Mole; to which station and to Artavia (if Artavia be Hertland) a Via from Somersetshire through Bampton might have led; – If it be true, that there were warm springs here, as it has been asserted, and as it is said, there even now are at Morebath

View entitled 'Mill at Bampton', no date given
(DRO, 564M / F17 / 133)

in the immediate vicinity, (which place, and Bampton or Bathampton Bathermton in their denominations may be considered as corroborating the fact) there is additional reason for the belief, that the Romans had a residence here – for it is a matter of certainty that this People, on the subjugation of the Country formed settlement wherever they found medicinal waters, or *"warm springs"* [Greek]. Bathing was one of their chief luxuries, and we know of no spot West of this Aquae Solis, that could have contributed to the supply of this gratification, but this town on the Batham.

Of the place being a possession of the Saxons We have somewhat more than Hypothesis to depend on, for by the Saxon Chronicle, we learn that in the year 614 the Danmonians were here defeated by these Northern Invaders, in a most desperate battle in which their loss amounted to 2046 men; Hence then We may not unfairly conclude, that a place so teneable even from natural circumstances, would receive additional strength and become a bulwark against the sudden incursion of a warlike and irritated People; from them it would necessarily devolve as a fortress to the Normans for there is the utmost reason to believe, that the defensible stations, of the Romans, were taken advantage of by every succeeding People whose military tactics (as far at least as they had regard to the point of local protection and security) were grounded nearly on the same principles; the modes of attack and defence depending in a great measure upon the nature of their weapons, particularly the missile ones, which in most cases, were common to the Nations in those ages opposed to each other: –

As I ascended the Hill on the quarter towards the Town, I had but few difficulties to surmount, the acclivity being far less steep than on the S. E. side, which, perhaps from the want of power to convert it to other uses, had been covered with plantations – by a green-sod way making a rising circuit of the Mount I advanced two thirds of the ascent, where I found a fosse of considerable depth – and soon after, at but little distance from the summit I crossed another, both of which were of such magnitude as at a remote point of view to mark the sides of the Hill, as may be observed in the succeeding sketch; On the Area above, vestiges of the antient Castle were still to be seen in portions of Walls yet standing and in vast masses of mines which cumbered the ground, in the midst of these, obscured by long grass, and by bushes I discovered a pit which had water in it, probably the Well, I know not of what depth, but considerable enough I should conceive to be dangerous to the cattle which pastured on the Hill, as there was no sort of fence around it, higher than this was the Keep, which without doubt was artificial and had been formed of the Stratum of the Country, which was here altogether Schist: this in its antient day of Strength must have been impregnable; it was now crested with firs and, remarkable by its elevation and conical figure, exhibited itself to the circumjacent Country in a marked and very picturesque manner. The views from this summit (as far as they were not intercepted by the trees) were varied and pleasing in most points; on the opposite side of the River Batham the prospect indeed was chiefly of a Hill over which were spread innumerous mounds like tumuli or entrenchments, being the waste or deads taken from the Strata in which a calcareous stone had been bedded; the features here of the Country were rather too rude and wild to be agreable, and would be a deformity to the picturesque Eye, were they not now and then intermingled with underwood – on the aspect towards the Town the assemblage of objects was more pleasing. The Church and its open green with the range of Houses descending from it to the Valley through which winded the River, the green meadows which surrounded Castle grove (a seat below the Mount, belonging to Mr Lucas) and these all enclosed by Orchards and Elm hedge rows contributed a Scenery of no common beauty.

From the castellated Mount I past into the verdant pastures watered by the River: on the banks of which I had a charming view of the Bridge and the high Hills beyond forming an inexhaustible mass of Marble hewn into quarries and decorated partially with coppice; To these passing the River by the mean of an old tree which had fallen across it, – the prototype of artificial bridges, I bent my way attracted in part by an overshot Grist Mill whose accompanyments

*View entitled 'Bampton',
no date given
(DRO, 564M/F17/139)*

were of a very rural and picturesque cast. Among these Quarries I seated myself, in admiration of the beautiful Scenery by which I was surrounded. Behind me rose a high Hill, which for several centuries had been operated upon by the industry of Man, insomuch, that for a very considerable extent, instead of a slope descending to the river it now exhibited in some parts a facade, smooth, abrupt and perpendicular; and in others, masses prominent from the plane superficies, upon which a profusion of underwood, willow, hazle and oak grew luxuriantly, and by their checquering tints and shades contributed to enhance the picturesque appearance of the Rock, which had been converted into a Quarry – There were two strata, Limestone and schist, which latter was superincumbent, and not unfrequently incorporated, or intermingled with all other, different however in their worth, the Limestone which had been dug from the Hill, having undergone calcination had been dispersed, as manure over the surrounding Country, but the Schist, unprofitable in its quality, had been wheeled away into vast mounds, or lain down in a terrace, dipping steep towards the meadows over which the eye ranged with delight, taking in the Town, the Castle and the green pastures through which the Batham rolling itself as a Serpent had worked its way in a singularly circuitous course through the rich and yielding strata: it was the Land as it were and the river of the Poet,

> – *"Rura, quae Liris quietâ
> Mordet aqua", taciturnus Amnis!* –

At the Kilns just by I fell into conversation with an Old Labourer in the Quarries; from whom I learnt that the price of Lime at this place was 3s–10d. thirteen pence more pr Hogshead than that at Westleigh, to which my remark He assigned the following reasons, that Here labour was somewhat dearer; that there was greater difficulty in coming at the Stone, embedded as it was in the schistose rock, which formed what He termed "deads" and were all of them to be wheeled away; and moreover that the Culm or stone coal used in the burning was brought from Watchet, a distance of 20 miles. – The Sun had now declined far towards the West *"majoresq cadunt de montibus Umbrae".* – I therefore moved away from this enchanting Scene, returning to the Bridge, and from thence to the Green that lay before the Church, which though a Pile of some consequence I regretted to see in a state of neglect the Edifice itself in its exterior apparently dilapidated and its seats ruinous; –

Sleeping at the little Inn, where the civility of the People gave a recommendation to entertainment which without such a zest would have been but very moderate; the next morning half past seven I quitted Bampton, taking the road towards Dulverton, and after three miles, descending a long hill to Exebridge, was again gratified with the singularly beautiful Scenery which in my last Tour to these parts was so much a subject of my admiration. It consisted of two long and narrow Vallies running parallel to each other, the Hill which separated them and rose beyond, being covered with old oak-woods, that on the left ornamented with Pixton, the finely-situated Mansion of Lady Harriet Acland; the other on the right with Barham the seat of Mr Lucas, which appeared less distinct as being at a remoter distance in a line beyond Dulverton.

About a mile from the Bridge, being now in the County of Somerset, I turned from the road on the left to the Village of Brushford which lay a short way off to the North in a Valley surrounded by most pleasing rural accompanyments – my visit here was directed solely to the Rev'd Robt Savage, Curate of the place, who with his Sisters had his residence in a Cottage contiguous to the Church.

With them I took my breakfast and at the usual hour accompanied them to the sacred Edifice, where I heard the duties of the day gone through in a most serious and exemplary manner, and had very high satisfaction in observing how well affected the Minister and his Parishioners seemed to be with each other; – Both the Morning and afternoon Service were attended by a numerous, and well-behaved Audience, who appeared to cooperate with their Clergyman in the best performance of their religious offices; exhibiting altogether a well regulated whole, edifying in the highest degree and gratifying beyond what in general I had been accustomed to experience – in short, I was very soon enabled to remark that very different from some of his Bretheren. He was occupied conscientiously in the discharge of his Holy function, so as to have it in his power to say "*Omnis in Hoc sum!*" and most satisfactory must be his feelings, when on reviewing his "labours of love" He shall find them attended by the desired success; – when instead of a small congregation, He sees himself surrounded by the whole of his Parishioners, and instead of half a dozen communicants He shall administer to more than the number thrice told; –

After the whole Service of the day had been thus (not merely as I may say *ex officio*, but *cum amore*") performed, having taken my dinner, viewed the fine oak which in lieu of the more sombrous Yew, overspread much of the Southern side of the Churchyard, and examined the only Monument which was in the Chancel recording the deaths of three Rectors in the following rather remarkably successive series of the Grandfather in 1700, the Son in 1740, and the grandson in 1770 with the short though simple and pathetic notice of the surviving friend who erected the mural tablet

"*flere, et meminisse relictum est*"

I took leave of my friends and about six in the Evening set out on my ride homewards for Tiverton. Under the escort of a Son of the Farmer who rented the glebe and beneath whose roof my Friends had taken up their residence I proceeded on an intricate and rugged road to Oakford bridge, passing other Lime kilns, much of the Country having calcarious strata, but these being of a more indurated nature, were not so easily reduced to a calx, and the Coals also being brought from Minehead, a distance nearly of 20 miles the Lime could not be afforded to the public at a lower rate than 6s pr Hogshead; Still however I was pleased to observe that the surrounding Country was in a fair state of cultivation, that the fields were kept clean and neat, and that their produce of grass and corn was strong and verdant. On the descent of a steep and stoney lane I had a catch of the River Exe – of a long line of Valley watered by it, of

the bridge of Oakford crossing it, and of hills rising high above its banks, richly covered with woods of Oak, but it was merely a catch, the lane being too precipitous and rugged to admit of a long gaze, unaccompanied by apprehension! – I had now passed the boundary of the County of Somerset, and entering Devon soon reached the bridge of which I was in quest – Picturesque in a high degree from its planks, and wooden rails which were supported by five piers of stone masonry it had little as a Bridge to recommend it, and considering it as a public and frequented pass of communication between the Parishes of Oakford and Bampton over a wide and rapid River, it was both insecure and disgraceful to the County; With the Scenery however every Admirer of rural beauties must be delighted and after as long a stay, as the ride I had before me would admit, I pas't away from it at last with reluctance;

From the Village of Oakford to which, having lost my guide, I had been erroneously directed I retraced my steps about half a mile, and having fortunately procured another Conductor, by a narrow road, quick rising and falling, having in a deep glen cross'd a simple bridge, which in the vernacular language of the Country was called "a clam, after three miles I approached near to the Village and Church of Studely; – The elevation of lands here is beyond any in the neighboring Parishes and, on the authority of Risdon I learn that a stream deriving its source from near the summit of one of its hills with little difficulty might have its current directed either towards the Northern or Southern coast of the County; On the acclivities of the Hills verging on the river I had a view of Woods stretching onwards to a remote distance; they were chiefly those which I had in a former tour pass'd through, from Cove bridge to Duvale in my way to Bampton, and were the property of Mr Brickdale, whose seat of residence was at Monkton near Taunton; a repetition of the same grand scenery, with a quick interchange of hill and glen, continued with little variation for two miles, untill I came near unto a Hamlet in the parish of Washfield where the Views became more mild, and the features of the country softened; Here from the last eminence, high seated over woods I stopt awhile and renewed the pleasure which about three years ago I had experienced when, on a tour towards Dulverton I had visited the rich and

View entitled 'Oakford bridge', no date given (DRO, 564M/F17/147)

romantic Scenes of the maeandering Exe from Tiverton to Cove bridge on its Eastern bank.

Many of these scenes with whose picturesque beauty I was then struck were again recognised by me with reiterated delight – those Eastern banks, and hills however, in a comparative view with these over which I had now travelled, were of a scale more diminutive, and of features less bold; of consequence the prospects from them to the Western Hills and Woods must necessarily be superior – there were moreover on that side of the River more numerous objects of picturesque beauty, such as cottages and mills, all of which could we got at with the greatest facility, as the country was more level and the road generally good. At the spot where I was now resting, all the inequalities and difficulties of the Way were over, and as I gradually made my descent from the Eminence, I was able to trace at the foot of it a road which appeared to lead very near the River towards Cove-bridge (which I afterwards understood was so in fact) – This must undoubtedly be highly beautiful, and had I been aware of it, it would certainly have been an object with me to have directed my course from Stoodley to Cove-bridge that I might have been gratified with the views on this hither bank of the river which must necessarily have been of a more picturesque cast; and I should conceive that a ride from Tiverton to Cove bridge on the Eastern bank and a return on the Western – a circuit of about 10 or 12 miles, must be superior in rural and picturesque beauty to any other in the Country.

Having reached the Valley of Washfield or at least the low grounds through which the Exe pursued its course I was gratified with the sight of several most magnificent Oaks standing contiguous to the road, and having parted with my rustic Guide I soon after reached the gate which led me into the grounds of Worth, and passing through a grove of noble trees, at a sharp angle the road brought me in front of the House which looked towards the town of Tiverton from which it was distant about a mile; The family of Worth, or de la Worthe, was seated here in the time of Henry 3d, and it still remains in the possession of a Gentleman of the same name; the old Mansion having become dilapidated it was taken down and rebuilt by the present Owner about 7 years ago on the same site; the rooms appeared to be very large, two of which seemed to occupy the whole of a considerable front – but the fabric being without stucco, and raised with a squared stone of a reddish tint did neither carry with it an appearance of magnificence, or of picturesque beauty; the Situation, perhaps a little too low, had however a good deal to recommend it for the lawn was agreeably expanded, skirted by trees of a good growth, and opened through their trunks to the rapid clear River, which flowed near, and was its boundary towards the East. On a road, winding by the fall of the River which had been lately formed through some fields, I pass'd on to regain that from which I had deviated on entering the grounds and soon after entered on the turnpike which led from Southmolton. On my approach to the town of Tiverton I was much gratified with the appearance of the suburbs, which had received considerable improvement since the year 1796 when I was last here and, from the surrounding green fields and gardens in which were a varied collection of Scarecrows, had an air of gaiety and cheerfulness; By the bye, in regard to these, straw stuft images, there can be little doubt but that they are derived to Us from a Roman usage; In those times indeed it appears that they were more formidable than they are now seen to be, for we are told by Horace that they were accoutred for a contest not only with depredating Birds but with Robbers of the Human species. The following is the description He has given Us of their God Priapus –

> "Deus inde Ego – furum aviumq
> Maxima formido; nam fures, Dextra coercet;
> Ast importunas volueres in vertice arundo
> Terret fixa, vetatq novis considere in hortis"

In this pleasant Town, when I last saw it deformed and dilapidated by fire, but which had since risen, like the Phaenix of old comparison, more beautiful from

its ashes I slept, and after breakfast the next morning pursued my ride. Instead of passing the Bridge over the Exe, on my approach to it, I turned to the left, and immediately after cross'd the Loman which here united its stream to the nobler River; a bad road led me into the grounds of Collypriest, the seat of Mr Winslow, who had lately assumed the name of Philips; – traversing the lower part of the lawn, which was intersected by a most miserable road leading to the Farm, I quitted it at the bottom by crossing a light elegant wooden bridge which spann'd the River by a single Arch, and reconducted me to the public road, near this was the turnpike gate, where a number of Carts and Horses were assembled, half of which having brought lime from the kilns of Bampton and Westleigh, were here exchanged for others which had come from the country beyond Thorverton and Crediton; and the bags and carts were to be re exchanged on the next trip, by which means the trouble of shifting the load was avoided;

Not far from hence I past a neat mansion lately erected by a Mr Dennis of Tiverton on an eminence above the road, commanding a fine reach of the river, and of the House and grounds of Mr Philips which rose in high beauty over the rich flat of meadow, intermingling cultured fields, and grazing pastures with Woods of considerable extent.

I had heard that sanguine expectations had sometime ago been formed of the probable success of Coal being found on the acclivity near the House; and in consequence of appearances which seemed to warrant such expectations Mr Dennis, unwilling to become the sole Adventurer procured subscriptions among his friends at Tiverton; these however had been exhausted; and tho' strata had been discovered which indicated coal, yet the spirit of enterprize had evaporated, and all active operations had ceased. Such a discovery would be of incalculable importance to a town like Tiverton, engaged in the manufacture of various sorts of woollen cloth which required abundance of fuel, and this exclusive of wood drawn from the neighborhood, not to be procured nearer than Exeter or Topsham, a distance of 15 and 18 miles. That the County possesses coal cannot well be doubted from the symptoms discovered here and at Cleave near Exeter; at Tavistock indeed a culm or stone coal has been

View entitled 'Collypriest', no date given (DRO, 564M/F17/157)

found in considerable quantities; but times of War, and public expence are inimical to researches of this nature, and the discovery, if at all made, in all probability will be left to a more productive and tranquillised period. From hence I had moved on but a short way when my Ears were assaulted, I may not say, by a "concord of sweet sounds" and I found, on my approach to some of these Lime Carriers that they were "waking the echo of the Woods by joining in a favorite ditty" – Tho' the twang of the strain, especially the closing part, was monotonous and harsh to me, yet to these rustic Choristers it was doubtless delightful; and, at the worst, tended to deceive the length and weari-someness of the way, for they had probably often experienced the truth of the Poets assertion

"*Cantantes licet usque (minus via laedet) examus*"

It is an axiom indeed, which few people have not verified, that by singing or the social intercourse of conversation, the toil of a journey, or the fatigue of labour, or even the solicitudes of the mind are most materially alleviated;

"*minuentur atrae carmine curae*" says the Poet, and the Philosopher, actuated by the same sentiment, tho' in a higher degree, enhances the delights of oral inter-communication, and feelingly expatiates on the effects produced by it, in the increase of Pleasure arising from the view of any object of beauty – Such have been the opinions of many acute investigations of the nature and impulses of the Human mind, and, as Cicero has recorded were those, in particular of Archytas the Philosopher of Tarentum who said "*si quis in Caelum ascendisset, naturamq mundi et pulchritudinem siderum perspexisset, insuavem illam admira-tionem ei fore quae jucundissima fuisset, si aliquem cui narraret, habuisset.*"

After a space of three miles, on the descent of an eminence a most beautiful view opened upon my eye of the river, and the Woods, and bridge of Bickleigh, the picturesque association of these – cottages interspersed with the green pastures and hedges thickly studded with trees, and a foreground bold and impressive, could not fail of having peculiar attractions and of claiming a page in my sketch book.

On crossing this Bridge I entered the Parish of Bickleigh, of the derivation of whose name Etymologists entertain different opinions – some deriving the primary part, which indeed is the only one in doubt from Bûch a Cow, and others from the Beech tree; after the ascent of a little Hill I past the Parsonage House, which is contiguous to the Church, in which are Monuments of the Carews, who, by the marriage of Thomas brother of Sir Wm Carew of Haccombe with the Heiress of Humphry Courtenay became possessors of Bickleigh Court, seated on the opposite bank of the River, and as I have

View entitled 'Bickleigh bridge', no date given
(DRO, 564M/F17/163)

View entitled 'Bickleigh Court',
no date given
(DRO, 564M/F17/167)

noticed in a former volume had their residence there – of this family was that eccentric character Bampfylde Moore Carew, who was baptized in the Church in the year 1690, and after a life past in every species of low humour and imposture, obnoxious to the laws of the land, and disgraceful to his family was here buried in the year 1758 – From the road a little further on, this antient Pile of Bickleigh Court was seen to vast advantage, frowning with its ivied walls over the River which ran hastily by, and richly embosomed in its Woods.

Much of this very beautiful Scenery I enjoyed for several miles, and as arable inclosures with little variety rose high on the left, the whole of the attraction lay in the pastures the river, and the woodlands beyond – and such was the natural arrangement of these picturesque ingredients, which indeed had hitherto been the accompanyments of the road, as to entitle it to the claim which it is known to possess, of being one of the most delightful Vallies in the County.

The Village of Silverton through which I now pass'd consisting merely of low and mean buildings, had nothing to detain me, though it may be noticed, en passant that in consequence of the size of the Parish and the fertile lands with which it abounds it is reputed to be one of the richest Benefices in the County. Instead of pursuing the direct road to Killerton which I had in view by Combsatchfield, I continued on the public one to Exeter, and rising from the level tract on which I had hitherto journeyed, I soon found myself on the summit of an eminence from whence I had my last catch of the delicious Valley of the Exe, whose lower windings from the bridge of Thorverton around the Hamlets of Upex and Netherex I had now the additional pleasure of discriminating – between the hedge row Elms of a farm of mine at the latter place. I caught the silver glimm'ring of its waters, from whence, having soon after received the River Columb, it passed away from my sight by burying itself amidst the Hills and Woods of Stoke and Bransford Speke.

On my approach to the Village of Rewe, turning quick on the left for Columb-John, by a pound for stray Cattle I entered a lane which as I had been apprized, soon became watery – Pent up between hedges and lying on a level

with the banks of the Columb the overflowings here found no outlet, so that I found it little otherwise than riding through a still River.

The continuance for more than a quarter of a mile staggered me somewhat as to its being the road to which I had been directed, no possibility however of escaping into the adjacent fields having occurr'd, I persisted in my route onwards, and though as John Gilpin of facetious note, my pace being less hurrisome, I did not "throw the Wash about" as He did at Edmonton still however by the unintermitting splashing my boots soon became nearly wetted through. Passing through a grove of Oaks, I reached the banks of the River, and as I observed the track of wheels on the opposite side I pushed my Horse into the water and tho the current was rapid, yet as at this season it was not deep, I got through without difficulty.

Soon after appeared a Gate-way, having an Arch of a semicircular cast, which by the Remains of a Building connected with it appears to have been a lodge appertaining in former times to a Mansion of the Aclands which was probably seated on the banks of the River Columb distant from hence in a strait line across the glade about a furlong. In the stile of architecture of this little Edifice which originally consisted of a room or two, the inconsistency of having three arches all of them differing from one another in their curve obtruded itself at once on my notice; – there being nothing to detain me here I proceeded across the green to a structure which on my approach I found to be a Chapel; In the cursory observation which I made I could discover no vestige

of the Mansion, which was erected at the close of the 16th Century by Sir John Acland Knight (according to the report of Sir Wm Pole) "on a former foundation begun by a Courtenay Earl of Devon; Prince In his Worthies" observes that, this Gentleman Who was Knighted by James 1st "of blessed memory" in the year 1603 "brought, builded and added to his name that pleasant seat of Cullome John, lying in the parish of Broad-clyst. "It is a large Pile, nobly situate on an advanced Ground just over the River Culme – in which Mansion the worthy Knight erected a very fair Chapel, and endowed it with five and twenty pounds a year for ever, for the encouragement of a Chaplain to preach and read prayers in it every Sabbath day" – If Prince was well advised that the Chapel formed a portion of the Mansion, We shall have to wonder that there are no other Remains that this Edifice, unless they were removed by the Grandfather of the present Baronet when He made alterations in the seat of Killerton, and this as a consecrated Building with an unalienable endowment was left untouched. Looking through a Window I perceived a large pew forming the whole of the Chancel appropriated probably to the Acland family, and nearly equal in size to the remainder of the Building.

Here I saw also, a desk or low Pulpit and a surplice which evinced that though there was not at this time an Acland a Residentiary at Killerton, Yet that the Chapel was still applied to sacred Uses. Situated on the verge of the River, it exhibited its Western end with its bell turret, in a most pleasing and picturesque stile, contiguous to its walls of inclosure was a wooden bridge for the accommodation of the foot passenger of the simplest and most rural cast, and this being overhung with old Alders produced an effect of no common attraction; Somewhat higher up the stream rose a Mill, perhaps an antient appendage to the family seat, but to which I found I had not time to make a visit. Ere I pass away from Columb John it may not be amiss to introduce a word or two respecting the derivation of its name. In the annals of Risdon and Sir Wm Pole it is thus reported "Columb-John" (anciently written Culm) taketh his name of the river Colum which runneth adjoyninge unto it on the west, and of the owners thereof John de Culme ye Son of John" the last John was livinge anno dni 1233 which was the 17th of King Henry 3d" – passing through the hands of Clifford, St Aubyn, Prideaux, Courtenay, Bamfield, Basset and Rowswell it became the possession of Sir John Acland by purchase as I have already noticed in 1603" but it appears from the Annalists, that the assumption of the latter part of its name, was referable only to the earliest period of which there is any record, the John thus noticed, not being known by a Patronymick, but by local circumstances – his place of residence on the banks of the Columb (thus stiling himself "De Columb or Culme", and discriminating that place of residence from other families of Pyne, David, Sachville &c by the annexation of his Christian name, John, to which it has continued an adjunct to the present day. But, from Mr Polwhele we procure derivations of another cast, for after He has told Us, that some "adopting the common spelling of the River Culme, derive this word from the Cornish Cylm rapid, which agrees with the general velocity of the current" adds "but I conceive that Columb is the right spelling; and that the compound word indeed of Columb John is no other than a corruption of Columba Jon – the sacra Columba, or) as exprest in the Chaldaic Jöna"

Was I to controvert this Etymology, which seems to flow from the same fount from whence the "Start" point near Salcombe was deduced from the Phaenician Goddess "Astarté", I should perhaps ask, where might be the connexion between a simple Parish in the County of Devon unmarked by fame, and unconsecrated by a Saint, and an isle of the Hebrides, the memorable Residence of the sainted Columba "that illustrious Island (in the words of the moralizing and emphatic Dr Johnson) which was once the luminary of the Caledonian Regions, whence Savage clans, and roving Barbarians derived the benefits of knowledge and the blessings of Religion"

In this instance the name of the Saint, in consequence of the fame which had attached to him from this holy character, became annexed to the island; but Here was a Mansion, as was the case with several others, seated on the River Columb, which with a view of distinguishing itself, from them assumed, as they had done in the instances of David, Pyne, and Sachville (the Christian or Sirnames of the several families to which they belonged) the font appellation which was prevalent in the family, of John, and this being joined with the River that derived its name from its rapidity, in the language of Mr Polwheles own province if he pleases "*Cylm*", or, if it may be deem'd more apposite, in that of the Romans Columba, or the Dove, (an appellation not unfrequently given to Rivers, whose current, as the flight of the bird is swift) formed, (as may be conceived by those who have no Favorite Hypothesis to support) the compound title which it now bears of "Columb John".

With this digression I pass away from this antient seat of the Aclands to their more modern one of Killerton but a little removed from the Bath public road, and placed on a gradually sloping acclivity, which at the back of the Mansion rose more steep, assuming the shape of a vast cone, whose sides were cloathed with indigenous woods, of old growth, and whose summit was graced with a crest of firs – the Building was of simple Architecture, finely brought forward to the view by the dark shade of the grove behind, but was an object of less attraction than the woodclad conical Hill which arrested the eye of the Traveller and was a point of consequence in the perspective to all the surrounding seats and country.

The Plutonist has fixed upon this cone, amongst others in the neighborhood to support his Volcanic Hypothesis, symptoms of which He authoritatively affirms are to be met with in all the circumjacent Country, for most of the red strata which prevail in the environs of Exeter, and of the Quarries especially of reddish grit, which have a porous appearance and a flat unctuous kind of matter somewhat like soot, often found in interstices of the stone, are attributed to this origin; There can be no doubt, but that masses resembling Lava are to be met with perpetually in the parts of the County around Exeter, and it is certain that many stones collected from fields, some of which I saw in the road near Silverton broken in pieces by the Sledge, had very much the appearance of having been in the fire, looking like the scoriae of iron from a Smith's forge, but, it has been observed that a stone found in Derbyshire by the Geologist Monsr de Fond and called Trapp, has similar properties and exhibits, when it has been long exposed to the air appearances of the same porosity; the small particles of steatites and calcareous matter which were embodied in it, having been acted on by the atmospherical air and undergone a perfect decomposition. If it be not Volcanic then, of this nature possibly, may be the stone of the Thorverton Quarries, and that (I know not whence taken) which was used in the original structure of the Castle at Exeter, of whose singular appearance the Gateway and Walls exhibit at present curious specimens. There is another Hill of a similar form pointed out, as of like nature in the Parish of Exminster or Alphington – a conspicuous knoll of a conical shape, which not long ago belonged to Mr Coxe of Peamore and is now become conspicuous by a crest of firs which He planted on it. This in its figure is perhaps more striking than that at Killerton, as it is bare and naked on the whole of its sides, which are in common cultivation. A strong objection to the hypothesis in regard to these hills, is, that the Cone runs into an apex, terminating precisely in a point. If we see nothing but the spiraculum, may we not put the question, "where is the Crater? how came it to be filled in such a continuous manner, as to form one uninterrupted inclined plane from its summit to the base? We are told indeed that the area of the yard of the Castle at Exeter, was a Crater, and that another is still to be found in the Parish of Holcombe near the road which leads to Moretonhampstead, but as the whole Hill is overgrown with brushwood and old trees, the Crater can be obvious to no one who does not enter on a premeditated and laborious research;

The seat of Killerton has been several times rebuilt having for Centuries been a possession of Families of consequence; on the old foundation We are told that a handsome House was raised by Ed^d Drewe Serjeant at law in the time of Queen Elizabeth, and again we learn that within the space of half a Century, passing by sale from the Drewes to the Aclands it was either rebuilt or underwent great alterations. By the Grandfather of the present Sir Thomas Acland the present Edifice as I have noticed, was erected, whose chief place of residence was at Holnicot near Exmoor on the Northern coast of Somerset, more antiently the seat of Steynings who married a Martyn of my House of Oxton, and Here this Sir Thos, during the season of hunting the forest Deer, kept open House, and by his liberal hospitalities, and courteous manners so ingratiated himself with the principal Gentlemen of the Counties of Devon and Somerset that during his life time, and since his decease I have never heard his name mentioned without the highest respect.

Having now entered on the turnpike road I pursued my way for a mile on it towards Exeter when reaching an old Gate with two pillars decorated by large stone balls, I turned through it to the left and passing near a mile on an inclosed lane came to a few Houses surrounding a small church which constituted the Village of Poltimore; contiguous to which (having rode through a thick grove appeared the seat of the Bampfyldes: I found it to be an Edifice of modern date, consisting of a handsome front with two small projecting wings, which detracted very much from the degree of Elegance that the Mansion would otherwise have possess'd; I have not a word to say in regard to the grounds or Park, which lies in front, extended into an unvarying flat & having few, if any circumstances of local or adventitious beauty to recommend it.

The Estate and Manor of Poltymore became the possession of a Bampfylde in the time of Edward the 1st according to the Harleian MS which thus reports *"Simon de Monteacuto per cartam datam 26 Ed. 1st dedit manerium de Poltymore Willielmo Pontington Canonico in Ecclesia Cathedrali de Exon et cuidam Johanni de Baunfield"* "whom (says Sir Wm Pole) the Canon had brought up for He styleth him Alumpnus" since which period they have continued in the same family – "de Baunfield having been converted into Bampfylde – and it is now the Property, tho not the residence of Sir Charles Warwick Bamfylde of whom (whatever other merit He may possess) I fear it cannot truly be said, as was predicated of his Ancestor Sir Copplestone in the middle of the 17th Century that "He was the honour of his time and of his Country"

I was now in quest of Watton which had been a Seat of Sir John Elwill, and wore (I was told) marks of Antiquity; to gain this I was directed to the Broad Clyst road, which having entered through a gateway similar to that on the Cullompton road, I pursued as far as to a stragling part of the Village of Pin

View entitled 'Polslo Priory', no date given
(DRO, 564M / F17 / 189)

View entitled 'Polslo Priory',
no date given
(DRO, 564M/F17/191)

and then deviating to the right, after a mile of bad lane I found that I had made a considerable circuit and on reaching the place, discovered nothing to compensate my trouble and badness of the road. The House was of brick, having as I understood the Elwell Arms on a escutcheon over the chief door of entrance, and above, the date of its erection 1679 – the Estate (about £300 a year) is a possession of Mrs Freemantle, the Daughter and Heiress of Sir Jn Elwell.

Thence, about a mile brought me to Polslo, lying in a flat, watered by a small stream, and surrounded by Orchards and gardens. This was a Religious House founded by William Brewer Bishop of the Diocese about the beginning of the 13th Century, and liberally endowed for the reception of Nuns – to the honour of St Catherine of the Benedictine order – its valuation at the dissolution according to Dugdale was £164.8s.11d, but as Speed reports £170.2s.3d. When a surrender was made of these religious establishments in the time of Henry 8th this became a possession of Sir Arthur Champernowne of Modbury who exchanged it with "one Ailworth of London (as Prince has it) for the more noble seat of Dartington. It afterwards pass'd through the family of Izacke into that of the Parkers of Saltram, and it is now the property of Montague Parker of Whiteway. The Remains of the Priory are but few, the Buildings having received the alterations of successive periods. It still however has the garb of an antient Mansion, and, as may be collected from the preceding sketches exhibits itself in a view somewhat picturesque. Scarcely a mile from hence brought me to the suburbs of Exeter, where at a bivia of the Cullompton and Broadclyst roads forming the angular point stands a Building of old date for the reception of Paupers of a peculiar institution.

INDEX

This index includes the introduction to this work. Whereas Swete's original journals contain idiosyncratic spellings, especially of placenames, the modern placename is used in the index where appropriate.

SUBSCRIBERS

Ann Adams, Zeal Monachorum, Devon

Dr N. W. Alcock, Leamington Spa, Warwickshire

Gwyneth M. Andrew, Chudleigh, South Devon

Mr and Mrs R. J. Annett, Askerswell, Dorset

Eileen and Michael Arnold, Wembury, Devon

The Countess of Arran, Castle Hill, N. Devon

Jeffrey L. Attwood, Stoke Gabriel, Totnes, Devon

Mr D. J. Barr, Brixham, Devon

Mrs M. V. Barratt, Chudleigh, Devon

M. J. Beaver, Whitchurch, Devon

Heather W. Bebbington

Dr Roger B. Beck, Tavistock, Devon

Charles Beckerleg, formerly of Tavistock, Devon

Trevor Beer, Barnstaple, Devon

Caroline F. Belam, The Strole, Ludgate, West
    Buckfastleigh, Devon

Roger K. Bendell, Topsham, Exeter, Devon

Stephen Benson, Heasley Mill, Devon

Brian and Lorraine Bewsher, Buckfastleigh, Devon

Dr S. Bhanji, Topsham, Devon

J. A. R. Bickford, Kirk Ella, E. Yorks

Mr and Mrs Ken Biggs, Camerton Court, Nr Bath

Sheila Bird, Falmouth, Cornwall

Margaret Bird, Sticklepath, Okehampton, Devon

Marilyn Bishop BA, Newton Abbot, Devon

Allan Bissett, Roborough, Winkleigh, Devon

Mr E. Blank, Bishopsteignton, Devon

Stuart and Shirley Blaylock, Cullompton, Devon

Miss B. Bolt, Exeter, Devon

C. H. Bolton, Kilmington, Axminster, Devon

John R. E. Borron, Near Sawrey, Ambleside, Cumbria

John Boulden, Plympton, Devon

Ingeborg C. R. Bowen, Dawlish, Devon

Jane C. Bowring, Tedburn St Mary, Devon

Dr J. Braven, Yelverton, Devon

Mrs Joan Breach, Widdicombe, Kingsbridge, Devon

Collin W. Brewer, Egloshayle, Wadebridge, Cornwall

Mrs Kath Brewer, Torquay, Devon

Mr and Mrs Mark Bridges, Silverton, Devon

Mr Rhys Brough, Plymouth, Devon

Mr and Mrs Andrew Brownsword, Waddeton Court,
    Devon

John Brushfield, Bath

Art and Claire D. Brussel-Leslie, Hatherleigh, Devon

T. C. Bryant, Llwyngwril, Wales

Martin Burdick, Shaldon, Devon

Peter Burdick, Topsham, Devon

K. J. Burrow, Bideford, Devon

Jeremy Butler, Torquay, Devon

J. Cadoux-Hudson, Little Wolleigh, Bovey Tracey,
    Devon

Sir David Calcutt Q.C., Porlock, Somerset

Mrs Christine N. Caldwell, Exeter, Devon

Christopher A. J. Cann, Coleford, Crediton, Devon

C. A. and H. E. Cardale, Staverton, Totnes, Devon

The Right Reverend R. F. Cartwright, Exeter, Devon

Nicholas Casley, Peverell, Plymouth, Devon

Mrs Penny Castle, Galmpton, Devon

R. E. Channing AFM., Northam, Devon

Roger and Paula Chapple, Barnstaple, Devon

Mumtaz and Alan Cheshire, Winkleigh, Devon

Sarah Child, Rackenford, Devon

Donald Church, Pluckley, Kent

Jason Clark and Marianne Bos-Clark, Tavistock,
    Devon

Mrs Mary Clarke, Doccombe, Devon

Mrs Yvonne Cleave, Exeter, Devon

Mrs Marion Clinch, South Zeal, Okehampton, Devon

Mr R. Coakley, Exeter, Devon

Miss E. A. Coakley, Exeter, Devon

Joy M. Cook, Cheltenham, Glos.

Mr William J. Cork, Uffculme, Devon

H. Cornish-Bowden, Avonwick, Devon

Royal Institution of Cornwall Courtney Library

Michael G. Cousins, Brentwood, Essex

G. E. Cruwys, Tiverton, Devon

Dartmoor National Park Authority

Francis Davey, Topsham, Devon

Edward R. Day, Chudleigh, Devon

Count Charles de Salis, Yarlington, Somerset

Mr and Mrs B. E. de St Paer-Gotch, St Pinnock, Cornwall

Gordon Denley, Barnstaple, Devon

Devon and Exeter Institution Library

Charles Doble, Ashbrittle, Somerset

Pamela L. Donne, Broadwood-Kelly, Devon

Miss E. M. Drydale, Torquay, Devon

John C. Easterling, Hayling Island, Hants.

Martin Ebdon, Bath

C. E. G. Eden Esq., Culver, Exeter, Devon

Dr John Edgcumbe, Exmouth, Devon

P. D. Egan, Exeter, Devon

John Elliot, Bournemouth, Dorset

Mr Neville Enderson, Coleford, Crediton, Devon

Audrey Erskine, Exeter, Devon

Joy Etherington, Torpoint, Cornwall

Geraldine Evans, Hennock, Devon

Elizabeth Ewings, South Milton, Kingsbridge, Devon

John Faircloth, Oxton House, Devon

Mrs Niki Faircloth, Twickenham, Middlesex

Keith and Judith Farmer, Cornwood, Devon

Peter Faulkner, Exeter, Devon

Nigel Faulks, Mariansleigh, South Molton, Devon

Mr John F. Finlay, Exeter, Devon

Miriam Fitter, Dolton, Devon

Dr. R. P. Flower-Smith, Llanveynoe, Herefordshire

Miss Brenda J. Ford, Exeter, Devon

Peter E. B. Ford, Loxbeare, Devon

Ian M. Forrest, Lamerton, Devon

Mr and Mrs W. Foster, Tavistock, Devon

Harold Fox, Leicester

Dr Mary Freeman, Tavistock, Devon

Dr Terry Friedman,

M. L. Friend, Bridgwater, Somerset

C. R. Fry M.Sc., MIEE., Crowthorne, Berks.

Sarah Fulford, Exeter, Devon

J. Galpin, Exeter, Devon

Michael T. Giles, Elham, Kent

Rhoda M. Gill, Turnchapel, Plymouth, Devon

A. K. Gordon, Tiverton Castle, Tiverton, Devon

Margaret Gould, Dunster, Somerset

Russell Green, Upton Leigh, Torquay, Devon

Vincent Lovell Macnamara Green, Torquay, Devon

Dr Tom and Mrs Elisabeth Greeves

Dr John H. L. Griffin, Culmstock, Devon

D. M. Griffiths, Exeter, Devon

Michael W. Grist, Llantwit Major, Glamorgan

Barbara Groves, Penryn, Cornwall

Trevor J. Haddleton

Mr P. Hamilton Leggett BSc., Tavistock, Devon

Jennifer Hanson, Upton Pyne, Devon

N. T. Hardyman, Dawlish, Devon

M. J. Harris, Exminster, Devon

Susan Harvey, St Andrews, Bristol

Jonathan and Susan Hassell

Jonathan M. Hawes, Enfield, Middlesex

Mrs Brenda Heath, Torquay, Devon

Miss L. E. Henley, Bradninch, Devon

Paul W. R. Hewson, Newton Abbot, Devon

Derek E. Hexter, Newton Abbot, Devon

Brian Hicks, Cookham, Berkshire

Mrs Ann Hildred, Woodbury, Devon

Peter Hirst, Dartmeet, Devon

Janet Hiscocks, Bristol

Hon. James Holland-Hibbert, London

Patrick L. Horrell, Plymouth, Devon

Lorraine R. Howes, Torquay, Devon

Priscilla Hull, Budleigh Salterton, Devon

Christopher P. Humphries, Launceston, Cornwall

Andrew Hunt, Bristol

W. L. Hutton, Guernsey, Channel Islands

The Irvine Family, Haccombe, Devon

James Jackman, Danbury, Essex

Andrew R. Janes, Taunton, Somerset

Elizabeth Jarrold, Dartmouth, Devon

Janet and Stephen Jenkins, Dunsford, Devon

John Loveys Jervoise, Sampford Courtenay, Devon

Mr and Mrs John Kekwick, Liverpool

Ruth Kidson, Nigeria

Colin C. Kilvington, Plymouth, Devon

James Savery King, Tampa, Florida USA

Celia M. King, Exeter, Devon

Susan M. King, Totnes, Devon

Susan Kitch, Torquay, Devon

Sir Frank Kitson, Yelverton, Devon

Alan Knowles, Brixham, Devon

J. M. Laithwaite, Seaton, Devon

Barbara Larah, Barnstaple, Devon

Dr and Mrs M. Laver, Budleigh Salterton, Devon

Brian Le Messurier, Exeter, Devon

Rosemary Leach, Trobridge House, Crediton, Devon

Andrew Robert Leadbetter, Topsham, Devon

Keith Leadbitter, Crafthole, Cornwall

Mr and Mrs Ian Lear, Urchfont, Wiltshire

Miss J. Lee, Tavistock, Devon

David C. Lee, Exmouth, Devon

Dr K. W. Leech, Moretonhampstead, Devon

Leverton and Sons Ltd, Camden, London

Yvonne Lewes, Exeter, Devon

John Light and Lesley Taylor, East Putford, Nr
    Holsworthy, Devon

John Locke, Oxton, Devon

Jonathan Lovie, Rugby, Warwickshire

Mr J. S. Lowry, Exton, Exeter, Devon

The Hon. Mrs Anthony Luard, Barnstaple, Devon

Melvyn R. Luckham-Down, Chislehurst, Kent

Paul Luscombe, Solihull, West Midlands

Norah Luxton, Newton Abbot, Devon

Mrs P. Mallet-Harris, Curry Mallet, Somerset

Dr and Mrs Rupert Manley, St Ives, Cornwall

Dr and Mrs Gerald Manley, Southerton, Ottery St
    Mary, Devon

Sheila A. Manning, Brighton, Sussex

P. G. Marchant, Heavitree, Exeter, Devon

Douglas Marsh, Chagford, Devon

N. A. Maxwell-Lawford, Honiton, Devon

Miss E. H. Maycock, Exmouth, Devon

Mr M. P. McElheron, Kingskerswell, Devon

N. D. McMorran, Exeter, Devon

Miss E. A. A. Meaden, Exmouth, Devon

Dr Roger Meyrick, Peter Tavy, Devon

Doreen Mole, Plymouth, Devon

Patrick and Lesley Mole, Newton Abbot, Devon

David Morgan, Bath, Somerset

Quentin and Helen Morgan Edwards, Glebe House,
    Sampford Courtenay, Devon

Gilbert E. Morris, Hereford

Dr S. A. Mucklejohn, Wigston Magna, Leicestershire

Edward Murch, Dousland, Devon

National Trust, Devon

Jack Neale, Truro, Cornwall

S. C. Needham, Widecombe-in-the-Moor, Devon

T. H. C. Noon, Cadeleigh, Tiverton, Devon

Barry J. Northcott, Launceston, Cornwall

Jennifer Norton, Exmouth, Devon

Dr John Ogle, Broomfield, Somerset

Mary Osborn, Yelverton, Devon

John A. M. Overholt, London

Mr and Mrs K. Owen, Tavistock, Devon

Sir John Palmer

Margaret Parkinson, Woodbury, Devon

Graham J. H. Parnell, Silverton, Devon

Mrs R. I. Payton, Exeter, Devon

Bruce R. Peeke, Sidmouth, Devon

Domini Pepper J. P., Exeter, Devon

John W. Perkins, Babbacombe, Torquay, Devon

Angela C. R. Perkins, Sandford, Devon

Professor John Perrin, Devon

Roger Perry, Zeal Monachorum, Devon

The Revd Dr and Mrs Douglas E. Pett, Truro,
    Cornwall

Mrs Jean Phillips, Exeter, Devon

I. C. Picornell, Ivybridge, Devon

David and Gail Pirkis, Manaton, Devon

Miss R. Pitts, Exeter, Devon

Lady Pond, Topsham, Devon

Clive N. Ponsford, Bath

John Antony Pook, Teignmouth, Devon

Mrs G. S. Pope

Frank E. Potter, Exeter, Devon

Mrs P. Preller, Bude, Cornwall

Miss U. A. Pridham, Plymouth, Devon

Audrey Prizeman, Plymouth, Devon

Anthony Pugh-Thomas, Somerset

Graham C. Pyke, Appledore, Bideford, Devon

Bill Ransom, Ilsington, Devon

Adrian Reed, Uffculme, Devon

Terence A. Rhodes, North Pool, Devon

Brian and Elizabeth Rice, Horsham, West Sussex

James Richards, Abbotskerswell, Devon

Yvonne Roberton, Berrydown Manor, Gidleigh, Devon

John C. de V. Roberts, Littlehampton, West Sussex

George H. Robertson-Owen, Ilsington, Devon

Mr and Mrs Rolfe, Tamerton Foliot, Plymouth, Devon

Colin Hugh Roulstone, Torquay, Devon

Kenneth Rowe, Exeter, Devon

P. A. Rowe, Yelverton, Devon

B. G. and V. O. Sanders, Exeter, Devon

Mrs Jenny Sanders, Tavistock, Devon

Kristin Saunders, Totnes, Devon

Mrs Muriel Sawtell, Winchcombe, Glos.

Anne Scarratt, Kingston, Kingsbridge, Devon

Gill Selley, Woodbury, Devon

Paul Shannon, Exmouth, Devon

Mrs Yolande Shrubb, Ashley Court, Nr Tiverton, Devon

Claire E. Siddall, Newton Abbot, Devon

Margaret Simpson, Worthing, W. Sussex

Roger Slape, Bovey Tracey, Devon

Michael and Lesley Sleeman, Oxton

Dorothy Ann Smerdon, Liskeard, Cornwall

Robert (Budge) Smith, Salcombe, Devon

Marjorie F. Snetzler, Barcott, Buckland Brewer, Devon

Mr R. C. H. Soans, Ashprington, Devon

Anne South, Totnes, Devon

Dr J. C. Speller, Tavistock, Devon

J. A. Spooner, Gt. Rissington, Cheltenham, Glos.

Dr M. M. Stenton, London

Dr A. J. Stenton, France

D. I. Stirk, Barnstaple, North Devon

Shirley Stirling, Exhall, Warwickshire

Michael Stone, Buckland Monachorum, Devon

Richard Stone, London

Mrs Dorothy E. Stone, Exeter, Devon

F. Sturdy Dowler, Denbury, Devon

Peter G. Swete, Cornish Hall End, Essex

G. N. Sworder, Dunkeswell, Devon

Mrs B. Tacchi, Lynch, Allerford, Somerset

Michael J. Tamlyn, Topsham, Exeter, Devon

Mrs P. Theobald, Haslemere, Surrey

D. L. B. Thomas, Exeter, Devon

Neil C. Thomas, London

Commander N. B. Thomas, Cornwood, Ivybridge, Devon

Mary C. Thompson, Tavistock, Devon

Dr M. G. Thorne, Ringmore, Shaldon, Devon

Graham Thorne, Maldon, Essex

Anthony Timms, Axminster, Devon

John Tremlett, Bickham, Exeter, Devon

Andrew J. Trussler, South Zeal, Devon

Miss M. Tucker, Uffculme, Devon

William H. Tuckett, Buckland Monachorum, Devon

Michael W. Tyler, Morchard Bishop, Devon

Mr J. P. Vasey, Totnes, Devon

Mrs M. Verniquet, East Allington, Devon

Dr. Denys J. Voaden, College Park, Md, USA

Kenneth J. Wakeling, Clayhidon, Devon

National Museums and Galleries of Wales, Library

John F. W. Walling, Newton Abbot, Devon

Mr Thomas John Wallis, St Austell, Cornwall

Mr J. and Mrs A. J. Watts, Millaton House, Bridestowe, Devon

Arthur H. Way, Seaton, Devon

Alan E. Webb, Dulverton, Somerset

Mr C. J. Webb, Winchester, Hampshire

Mr and Mrs F. W. West, Dawlish, Devon

Richard Wheeler, Silverton, Devon

Mr P. D. Whitcombe, Brent Tor, Devon

Patricia E. White, Exeter, Devon

Mrs Edna L. White, St Marychurch, Torquay, Devon

Canon Sir C. W. Wigram, Headington, Oxford

John Bruce Wilkie, Plymouth, Devon

Freda Wilkinson, Poundsgate, Devon

A. F. J. Williams, Exmouth, Devon

Brenda Williams, Paignton, Devon

Dick Wills, Narracombe Farm, Ilsington, Devon

Anthony D. Wood, Liskeard, Cornwall

F. W. Woodward, Ivybridge, Devon

Chris Woodwark, Farnham Common

J. H. G. Woollcombe, Hemerdon, Plympton, Devon

Robin and Pamela Wootton, Exeter, Devon

Peter Wright, Bovey Tracey, Devon

Nigel Wright, Eggesford, Chulmleigh, Devon

Chris Wurtzburg, Bovey Tracey, Devon

Prof and Mrs P. A. H. Wyatt, Sidmouth, Devon

Kathie M. Yeo, Exeter, Devon

Peter Yeo, Corfe Mullen, Dorset

Peter Yolland, Bromley, Kent